The Satir Model
Family Therapy and Beyond

The Satir Model

Model

Family Therapy and Beyond

Virginia Satir

John Banmen • Jane Gerber

Maria Gomori

SCIENCE AND BEHAVIOR BOOKS, INC.
Palo Alto, California

Printed in the United States of America

Library of Congress Card Number 89-060194

ISBN 0-8314-0078-1

Dustjacket and interior design by
Gary LaRochelle/Flea Ranch Graphics
Interior art by Chris Jensen/The Last Word, Menlo Park,
CA, *and* Barry Ives, St. Helena, CA
Editing by Rain Blockley
Production editing by Jim Nageotte
Typesetting by TLC Graphics
Printing by Haddon Craftsmen

Dedicated
To the memory of Virginia Satir
1916-1988
Our teacher, colleague, and friend.

Contents

Preface

I am delighted that this book is being written at this time. I have enjoyed being with John, Jane, and Maria both in writing this book and in working with them all these years, especially since the Process Community International Summer Institutes started in 1981. I consider all three of them my close friends, my colleagues, and my advisors.

My hope is that this book will fill a major place in the hearts and minds of many of my former students, therapists of all kinds and orientations, and professionals interested in the development of the human potential.

After working over fifty years in the field, I still hold high hopes and great enthusiasm for the ability of the human spirit to make this world a better place to live. I hope many of you will join me in making this dream a reality in our own lifetime.

Virginia Satir
March 1988

Introduction

This book is the result of our many years of working and learning together with Virginia Satir. We three all knew Virginia since 1970, or earlier. We were amazed, impressed, challenged, and most of all inspired when we met her. None of us could get enough of watching her work with families. We followed her to the many places in the world where she gave workshops, frequently four weeks long. We studied with her in many settings and various cultures, including Mexico, Israel, Germany, Aruba, France, Canada, and most frequently the United States. Most of Virginia's earlier teachings were through demonstrations *with* the participants. This approach gave us numerous opportunities to experience the powerful impact of her interventions as well as her dynamic personhood.

In 1981 Virginia began an International Summer Institute, also called the Process Community. All three of us have been involved with the Summer Institute since its inception. Since 1982 we have worked together as a faculty triad on staff. (The institute is managed by the Avanta Network, which Virginia founded in 1977.) We three have also extended our joint training workshops to include Hong Kong, Venezuela, Canada, and the United States. Our training programs are expanding to other areas of the world, including Taiwan and China, as this book goes to press.

Virginia's work began much earlier. Her first book, *Conjoint Family Therapy* (1964), became a major success and had a strong impact on the whole field of psychotherapy. Instead of attacking the existing profession, the book provided a major alternative for dealing with individuals and families. With the help of this book, Virginia Satir became a world leader in a field dominated by men.

Not only did she focus on helping individuals and families, she became very interested and active in developing ways of shifting the critical mass of various systems from negativity to positive and growth-directed patterns. Out of her research and experimentation, she began to see that most of the ways that we had been looking at people were irrelevant. Putting new ideas together as with a jigsaw puzzle, she began her growth model and started developing her own therapeutic tools.

She believed that there is nobody in the world, no matter what the conditions are on the outside, who cannot change. Over and over she saw the high prices people paid for doing the best they could. These prices were often disease, lack of intimacy, guilt, lack of achievement, and lack of joy. She knew people could ask for more in life than just putting up, or just surviving. At the Evolution of Psychotherapy Conference in Arizona in 1985, Virginia Satir said: "I see the universe in process. We are in the process of becoming more fully human. We are at the beginning of something new, not at the end."

She believed that human beings can fulfill what they were meant to fulfill; that they can use themselves more positively, more effectively; and that they can have more choices for greater freedom and power. This, in effect, motivated her to go to all corners of the world bringing hope, new perspectives, and new approaches to family therapy and to becoming more fully human.

This book, a presentation of that model of human growth, focuses on Satir's belief system, her innovative approaches to change, and the growth vehicles she developed and modified over the years. It is not about pathology but human dignity, strength, and the manifestation of a higher state of consciousness.

The book is divided into twelve chapters. The first conveys Satir's growth model in juxtaposition with the more commonly held hierarchical model of perceiving the world. It states the major tenets of her approach to therapy and some of her concepts about the internal process of each human being. The core is the self ("I am"), and the major processes involve self-esteem and congruence. This chapter also lists Satir's major therapeutic beliefs.

The second chapter introduces the primary triad, which refers to the relationships in which we learn our first lessons about being human. The third chapter covers the whole continuum from surviving at a basic level to becoming more fully human—or self-actualized, in Abraham Maslow's terms. This includes the coping stances, Satir's best-known aspects of demonstrating how we cope. The stances of blaming, placating, acting superreasonable, and acting irrelevant are physical, emotional, and verbal manifestations of low self-esteem.

Chapter 4 covers congruence, one of the major tenets of the Satir model. It also suggests the importance of the therapist being congruent during the practice of therapy.

The fifth chapter focuses on the process of change. One of its major stages, called chaos, is essential to helping individuals and families move from a dysfunctional status quo to a healthy, functional status quo. The role and use of resistance within the change process is discussed, as is the role of the therapist.

Chapter 6 is devoted to what Satir called the Ingredients of an Interaction. Here we look in detail at various levels of what happens internally during an interchange and learn how to track this process. This is the theoretical basis for intervening at each level to help people become more responsible and congruent. The internal process also shows how external behavior, which might seem strange or inappropriate, actually is consistent with one's level of self-esteem, expectations and perceptions. Several short illustrations demonstrate the steps of the Ingredients of an Interaction.

The seventh chapter deals with how to transform dysfunctional internal processes and coping behaviors into alternatives that are more present-focused, responsible, and congruent. Special attention goes to the whole area of emotions and feelings, and to Satir's approach to dealing with anger, hurt, and fear.

Chapter 8 deals with the Parts Party, Satir's vehicle for integrating the self. Even though this vehicle is well known to students of the Satir model, its purpose and the components of its process are delineated and explored in considerable detail here for the first time.

Chapter 9 describes another well-known vehicle called Family Reconstruction: a three-generational therapeutic intervention designed to transform a person's dysfunctional past learnings and present copings into positive resources, choices, and growth.

Chapters 10 and 11 discuss in briefer form many of the other vehicles or tools that Virginia Satir evolved or applied to her model. These include the use of metaphors, sculpting, the self mandala, transforming rules, and making contact. These other tools are relevant in the change process. Chapter 11 also gives an example of how to apply the Satir model in individual therapy.

The last chapter discusses organizations, resources, and directions for continuing evolution now that Virginia Satir is no longer physically in our midst.

John Banmen
Jane Gerber
Maria Gomori
Summer 1991

1

Perceiving the World

Within any model of therapy are basic assumptions about people. For a long time, models had a very limited view of human beings: they were either right or wrong. Social systems were based on a dominant/submissive power differential, and people were treated with inequality. Most early therapies were based on the idea that people were either good or bad, or that they were sick or healthy. This is an oversimplification; nevertheless, how people perceived the world determined how they designed therapeutic interventions.

Over the last fifty years, Virginia Satir developed her family therapy model from many hours of observing clients, testing her hypotheses, and creating interventions. Her approach reflected her observations of the world, namely, that people have internal resources and choices, and that they can change.

Satir saw her first family for conjoint therapy (in which the therapist sees all members in the same sessions) in 1951. Initially, she treated a young woman who had been labeled schizophrenic. After about six months of therapy, things were turning out rather well. Then Satir received a call from the client's mother saying she would sue Satir for alienation of affection.

Instead of listening to the mother's words literally, Satir chose to hear the plea in her voice. Satir asked the woman to come with her daughter to the next session. When that happened, though, the relationship between the daughter and Satir fell apart. The young woman reverted to square one in her therapeutic process.

As Satir continued working with these two, a new therapeutic relationship gradually formed among mother, daughter, and therapist. It occurred to Satir to invite the family's father/husband to participate. But as he became part of the sessions, the therapeutic progress that had been established fell apart again.

At this point, Satir realized she was on to something.

She asked if anyone else existed in the family. When the remaining son/brother, described as the "Golden Boy," came into the therapy sessions and revealed his powerful place in the family, Satir saw more clearly the disempowered role the daughter held and how she attempted to survive in this family system.

That early experience and similar subsequent ones gave Satir a sense of the dynamics and power of the family process. Therapy obviously involved more than treating just the identified patient. Satir developed and tried out ideas about how to intervene at the systems level, meaning she could bring about change in the entire family (or system) by improving the way its members communicated with each other.

This helped individual family members as well as the whole family system to move from a dysfunctional status quo to a more open, flexible, and satisfying interrelationship.

It also gave her a strong beginning in the use of sculpting, in which she had clients portray postures that physically emphasized the messages they were communicating. Sculpting externalizes our internal process of coping. These physical postures bring to awareness covert messages that are often out of the client's consciousness.

Clients thus gain a bodily awareness of feelings and perceptions that they may otherwise deny or project.

For example, Satir had envisioned the Golden Boy standing on a chair, with his parents in a worshipping position toward him, leaving no room for their daughter. By having the family act out this scene, Satir got them to recognize the feelings that they often denied or projected. That recognition also allowed them to consider changing their interactions.

Satir presented these and other ideas in her first book, *Conjoint Family Therapy* (1964). Following the publication of this classic work, the therapeutic world made a major shift toward a systems approach to helping families. Satir's book was a radical departure from that era's psychoanalytic approach, which strongly advocated seeing individual family members separately and not discussing clients with other therapists.

Because she was an innovative, independent thinker and scientist, Satir reached outside the existing therapeutic practices and helped develop two new concepts related to helping people grow and be healthy. The first concept moved away from the old Aristotelian, linear, singular cause-and-effect approach and toward the systems thinking of Alfred Korzybski, Ludwig Von Bertalanffy, and, later, Gregory Bateson. The second concept was based on the positive existentialism of Sören Kierkegaard, Martin Buber, and Johann Heidegger. It held that human beings were manifestations of positive life energy, and that this energy could transform people's dysfunctional coping into high levels of self-care within the context of high self-esteem.

Conjoint Family Therapy incorporated other elements that Satir had found missing in the existing therapeutic professions of psychiatry, social work, and psychology. She discussed the role that love plays in the therapeutic process; differences between what people intend and what they do or say; and why such differences exist so frequently. She also emphasized that everybody needs his or her own space, big or small, and needs something that validates the self. Above all, Satir found that people needed to have a high level of self-esteem to live and function successfully.

In her search to help people, she came across some unique answers that became the basis of her conjoint family therapy model. Ultimately, she developed it into a comprehensive growth model for all human beings.

In her early practice, she often saw people with whom nobody else wanted to work. She also treated clients who had not moved beyond their predicaments despite many hours of other therapy. She worked in state hospitals as well as with people who were "pulled out of the gutter," as she put it. In short, it was important to her to work with people for whom it appeared, to all intents and purposes, there was no hope.

Looking back later, she believed being a woman and not a psychiatrist gave her the opportunity to develop her ideas with minimal professional interference. Even though she was extremely effective with her clients, she practiced a long time before she wrote about what she was doing. She said she could not have articulated at that time the theoretical context of her work. People who were interested in her approach learned from her by spending a month at a time watching and participating in her process of change.

What she was doing was helping people find what she called their wisdom box—their sense of worth, hope, acceptance of self, empowerment, and ability to be responsible and make choices. She also focused on clients' sense of uniqueness; she suggested looking in the mirror each morning and saying three times: "The world is a better place because I am here." She helped people find their resources and their ability to make choices based on their own high levels of self-esteem. Continually demonstrating acceptance and understanding instead of judging, she encouraged them to look with appreciation at all their inner parts, using them to grow and become more fully human.

After Satir had seen thousands of people all over the Western world, working more and more with entire families, she identified several universal patterns of communication and coping (explored in detail in later chapters). She also found universal yearnings that help people change toward higher self-esteem and wholeness.

As she continued defining her system of therapy, her conviction grew that anyone in the world, regardless of any external condition or circumstance, can change on the inside. The price people pay for not changing often includes disease, guilt, and a lack of intimacy, productivity, and joy. She knew people could ask for more in life than tolerating pain or merely surviving. She believed human beings could fulfill what they were meant to fulfill and that they could use themselves more effectively and with more choices. Paralleling the vision of Abraham Maslow and Carl Rogers, Virginia Satir advocated a faith in human beings and their ability to manage and grow from an inner sense of strength, motivation, and reality.

How can we see all of our own possibilities and choices? To see the whole picture, we need to be in a place that offers that perspective. It is like being in the control tower at an airport: we need to be able to see the relationships among people, as opposed to being on the ground and involved in their interaction.

Gaining perspective has to do with the distance between up and down, inside and outside. The air traffic controller's job is to give information that allows airplanes to maneuver safely. The controller tells pilots where they are in relation to other planes. Similarly, a therapist working with a family may be aware of something family members are not aware of themselves. For example, you may see a tear in someone's eye and ask, "Did any of you notice that tear?" Then you might follow up with, "I wonder how you feel about that." Conveying such information and concern typifies your control-tower position.

Wholeness always entails more than people can see of themselves. Wholeness includes all that is present, manifest or not. Often, aspects that are not obvious can be brought into awareness with the help of an outsider, the therapist. This awareness benefits our coping. For instance, we cannot see the bones in our fingers, but we move our fingers with the knowledge and awareness of those bones. Wholeness is the outcome of our own investigations about things that are present in us, whether or not we can see them.

For the therapist, it is important to look at clients and issues from all angles: from underneath, from the top, from all sides, from close by, and from afar. These perspectives help us see the whole. We can vary their sequence, but we need to include them all.

UNIVERSAL ASPECTS OF PERCEIVING THE WORLD

Out of Satir's research and experimentation came her model of growth. She described people's ways of perceiving the world as belonging to either the hierarchical model or the growth model. How we see the world can be assessed from four aspects: how we define a relationship, how we define a person, how we explain an event, and what attitudes we have toward change. These four phenomena are universal and characterize all people and their relationships with one another.

Satir often said that if she understood how people understood these phenomena, how they lived them, and how they communicated about them, she could understand practically everything about those individuals. The ensuing sections examine how the hierarchical model and the growth model look at these four phenomena.

Defining a Relationship

In the hierarchical model, relationships exist in only one variety: somebody is on top, and somebody is on the bottom. It is a dominant/submissive arrangement, sometimes called the threat-and-reward model. This type of relationship has been considered normal for centuries. Often, the only question is: "Is it malevolent or benevolent?" Dominant/submissive relationships fall along a continuum from having uncaring tyrants to having kind ones, and from unhappy victims to compliant ones.

Hierarchical relationships are often described in terms of roles: father–child, boss–worker, priest–parishioner, teacher–student. Usually these roles imply a form of superiority, whether well-intentioned or not. Whoever is in the submissive or "down" position is vulnerable and could be called "little," "poor," "minority," and so on. The people on top think and act as if they were "better than" or "bigger than." Simply put, every such relationship entails an either/or comparison. Regardless of the specific roles and their status, these pairings are all based on the dominant/submissive model.

Feelings that arise within hierarchical relationships include emptiness, anger, fear, and helplessness. The accompanying body language includes postures of placating, blaming, being super-reasonable, and coping irrelevantly. Such stances tell us about the psychic wounds hidden below the surface.

It is therefore important to distinguish between a person's role in a relationship and the definition of that person. For example, sometimes on first meeting, someone asks us, "Who are you?" We might give a response such as, "I'm an artist," or "I'm a doctor." To make the distinction between our roles and ourselves as people, we might then ask ourselves, "Am I doing that now?" To sharpen this distinction, we can practice expressing roles as verbs: "I am a teacher" thus becomes "I am teaching."

Without such distinctions, we risk overlooking each person's unique and special existence. We represent ourselves to ourselves and to the world through our labels; the trade-off is that these labels take our attention away from our identity. In a family, for instance, the adult male and female have the labels husband and wife. Once they have children, they add father and mother to their roles. These definitions tend to obscure personhood, though, and place the emphasis on the roles instead. Role becomes identity, and individuality gets lost. People then manifest themselves through their roles, sometimes negating their own thoughts and interests.

Most relationships in our Western culture have been and still are based on dominance and submission. In therapy, by tradition, the therapist is often considered healthy, sane, and good; the client is deemed unhealthy, insane, or bad. How we perceive this or any other relationship determines how we behave; unfortunately, according to Satir, most of us are raised to handle our reality, self-worth, and communication by placating, blaming, or being super-reasonable or irrelevant.

Satir believed the biggest obstacle to personal, interpersonal, and international peace was that people do not know how to perceive and accept their equality of value. Our existing differences usually serve as an unspoken rationale for accepting the dominant/submissive power differential in our relationships. Satir hoped to promote equality and to consolidate it between therapist and client. Her premise was that we all have—but do not always use—the capacity to be whole. When we finally get in touch with this capacity, we are embracing the idea that we are beautiful and capable manifestations of life.

Regardless of age, skin color, gender, or health, all humans are of equal value. The hierarchical model of relationships denies this principle and treats people as better or worse. In the Satir growth model, the thrust is toward parity: person equals person.

Defining a Person

Let us look at how the two models define a person. For those who use relationships so that they can dominate somebody, a person is one who conforms and obeys. Conformity pervades the hierarchical model, in which people often think, "I am too fat/thin/stupid," and feel they should be something else.

Whenever we feel we are too much of one thing and should be something other than what we are, we deny our personhood. We are measuring ourselves by something external; if it does not fit, we do not fit. For the most part, this is like having to fit into a box, to conform and obey. Satir used the metaphor of the procrustean bed, a medieval torture instrument. Whenever someone deviated from the dominant point of view, that person was sent for "rehabilitation." This particular method entailed making someone fit the mold, quite literally, by cutting off his or her head, legs, or other body parts. One usually did not survive this "treatment," but one always ended up fitting the mold.

People still grow up facing many external expectations and comparisons. Standards and judgments exist at the personal, political, and family levels. In general, they demand that we be something other than what we are. Many of us hear frequent and persistent messages that something is wrong with us, we do not fit according to some authority, and therefore in all likelihood somebody else fits better. Our consequent conforming and obeying have a major crippling effect on our sense of self.

When we judge ourselves in terms of conforming and obeying, we often feel anxious. We may think we cannot do anything right. Nevertheless, many of us spend great energy to correct what is "wrong." In extreme situations, when people are being pushed to do and be something else, they might just give up and start feeling depressed. By accepting the view that our value comes from outside ourselves, we will try to conform for a long time, hoping to be accepted for our obedience.

The tyranny of this push to conform is so strong that most people start early in life to live according to others' expectations. We bypass—and finally ignore—our own selves. Even though the tyranny hardly ever produces total conformity, we usually feel awful, discount or devalue our feelings, and gradually lose our identity. We compare ourselves to others and say, "If I can be like so-and-so, I will be all right."

To set aside the expectations of others, without rebellion, and find ourselves is a major task. Yet even to start noticing that nobody is exactly like us helps increase our self-acceptance. Then, when somebody calls it to our attention that we are different, we can comfortably respond, "Thank you for noticing."

In the hierarchical model, one's definition of oneself depends on other people's rules. Satir found this very limiting. When she helped people unleash their inner resources and define themselves from an inner source of strength, she discovered most of them were eager and able to do so. This process became part of her growth-model concept of becoming more fully human.

Satir defined people as being equal in value. Each person is unique in his or her combination of human samenesses and differentnesses. No two people have the same fingerprints, yet we are so alike that a surgeon can operate on any human being and find the same relationships among that person's internal organs.

Satir's view included a spiritual base for all human beings. Whatever race, gender, or nationality, we each began as an egg and a sperm that came together and activated us as individual beings. She hoped the time would arrive when people would overcome prejudice, especially looking down on others. This view of equality is still in its infancy but is much more prevalent and influential today than it was only a few decades ago.

Explaining an Event

In the dominant/submissive model, which relies on conforming and obedience, events are explained in a linear mode. That is, only one right way exists, and only one cause for any effect. Within this one-right-way frame of thinking, people accept the external expectation that there is only one right way to look at reality. They turn to each other for that one answer to any question or the one solution to any problem.

Of course, even if we try, we do not find the only right way. Somebody else usually comes along and provides a better method. Yet, even knowing this, people often expect us to behave as though we too believe in their one and only right way.

One consequence is that we often act as though we do not see what we see, do not hear what we hear, and do not feel what we feel. In an effort to preserve somebody's ego, we behave as though what is false is true. That is often hard to do, and it gives us another reason to feel uncertain. We work hard to find the single-variable answer to our question or problem. The hierarchical model perpetuates that kind of expectation and limitation. Sadly, we persist with the hope that people will consider us good and lovable.

In her growth model, Satir defined an event as the relationship between a set of essential variables contributing to a joint outcome. Rather than looking for a single cause, in other words, we need to recognize and acknowledge the interactional relationship between and among events. We also need to consider the context in which these events occur.

From this perspective, event A is the outcome of events B, C, D, and E. Various things happen and are somehow related in an interactive way; they are not caused linearly (B alone does not cause A). Furthermore, events occur in relation to their history, location, and point in time. For example, when a father taps his foot, his wife cries, and their child yells, what is happening? Is anyone to blame? How are these three events connected?

Instead of judging people's actions, reactions, and interactions, we can start to explore not only surface activities but also events beyond the obvious. To explain an occurrence requires understanding what goes on inside of people, their internal processes. Events do not happen without being connected to something else, either internal or external, and usually both.

We can thus look at behavior as an outcome of inter-relationships among our internal and external worlds. We can then look at those relationships and see what is present but not necessarily obvious. One familiar example in a family involves two young boys having dinner with their parents. Andrew suddenly hits Bob in a consider-able state of annoyance. The parents send Andrew to his room without his meal. What is present but not readily apparent is that Bob had been kicking Andrew under the table for some time.

To help change any system of interacting people and events, one needs to search for such connections without judgment or blame.

Attitudes Toward Change

This is the fourth aspect of how we perceive the world. People who work on a dominant/submissive basis, who insist on obedience, and who look for one right answer consider change undesirable. Maintaining the status quo means people cannot move forward or grow, of course, but keeping the current order intact is a way of feeling safe. Therefore, any new possibilities must be rejected. Thoughts such as "You don't know what you will get into," "Don't rock the boat," and "You might fail" are common in this model and reinforce the existing state of affairs.

Many people in the world still feel moving beyond their secure status quo means risking death. This attitude toward change can be one of the greatest hindrances to personal growth and effective therapy. In this frame of mind, people sometimes prefer a familiar dysfunction to an unknown improvement or comfort.

In Satir's growth model, change is essential and inevitable. When people perceive their equality of value and are conscious of their uniqueness and sameness, they accept and welcome change. Of course, they may have some fear about the unknown, but taking risks is part of their willingness to experiment. Security and trust are based on confidence, not familiarity. If they try something new, they can tell whether it fits for them. And, once they are open to change, new choices and possibilities become available.

The growth model provides choices and encourages taking risks. Love is a stable component of the model, which means people feel free to express their feelings and differences.

The chart on the next two pages summarizes the four aspects of seeing the world as they occur in the hierarchical model and the growth model.

SATIR'S GROWTH MODEL

Until relatively recently, very little was talked about in terms of perceiving the world psychologically. Maslow began sharing his views in the mid-1940s; Rogers concurrently developed a similar thread of exploration into our internal processes and self-focused growth.

Meanwhile, the Second World War helped open the door for alternative treatment. Workers were in great demand, and many people in therapy wanted to work full-time. Formal psychoanalysis came to be considered too slow in this regard. New views and methods were encouraged and accepted.

Ways of Perceiving the World

DEFINITION OF A RELATIONSHIP (How we perceive a pair)	
Hierarchical Model	**Growth Model**
People are of unequal value.	People are of equal value.
People dominate or submit to each other.	Relationships are between equals in value.
Roles and status are confused and blurred with identity.	Roles and status are distinct from identity.
Roles imply superiority and power, or minority status and powerlessness.	Roles imply a function in a specific relationship at a particular time.
The hierarchical view implies superiority and submissiveness.	Equality is manifested in: equality of persons, connection, interest and acceptance of samenesses and differences.
People have power over each other but feel isolation, fear, anger, resentment, isolation, and distrust.	People feel love, ownership of self, respect of others, freedom of expression, and validation.

DEFINING A PERSON	
Hierarchical Model	**Growth Model**
People need to conform and obey "shoulds" for physical and emotional survival and acceptance.	Each person is unique and can define him- or herself from an inner source of strength and validation.
People are born with the potential to be evil.	People have an inborn spiritual base and sacredness, and they manifest a universal life force.
People are expected to think, feel, and act like each other, and to live up to external norms by competing, judging, comforting, and imitating.	Combining and respecting samenesses and differences, people delight in discovering themselves and others by cooperating, observing, and sharing.
People devalue or deny their feelings and differences.	People articulate their feelings and accept their differences.

14

Ways of Perceiving the World

DEFINING AN EVENT

Hierarchical Model	Growth Model
A causes B in a linear, cause-and-effect fashion.	Any event is the outcome of many variables and events. $A = B + C + D \ldots$ etc.
Only one right way exists to do something, and the dominant person knows what it is.	Many ways usually exist, and we can use our own criteria to choose an approach.
People deny their own experiences so as to accept the voice of authority.	People look beyond the obvious event to understand its context and its many contributing factors.
Thinking such as "That's the way it is" and "It's black and white" generates manipulation and shuts down originality and discovery.	Circular thinking and a systems approach (action-reaction-interaction) generate relevance, discovery, information, order, and connection.

ATTITUDES TOWARD CHANGE

Hierarchical Model	Growth Model
Security requires maintaining the status quo.	Security grows out of confidence in the process of change and growth.
People view change as undesirable and abnormal. They therefore reject and resist it.	People view change as ongoing, essential, and inevitable. They therefore welcome and expect it.
The familiar is more valued than the comfortable, even if the price is painful.	People view discomfort or pain as a signal for change.
People fear the unknown.	People take risks and opportunities to move into the unknown.
People judge changes as being right or wrong.	People delight in discovering new choices and resources.
People feel fear and anxiety when they face the prospect of change.	People feel excitement, connectedness, and love when they encounter the prospect of change.

Other changes took place as well. Minority groups, women, and people in colonial situations voiced their need to be heard, to have their value acknowledged, and to have their equality accepted. Many sacred cows were finally challenged, and many dominant/submissive beliefs and practices were revamped. In that search for equality and justice, people began perceiving the world differently.

Satir was an early champion of equality and value, both in personal relationships and in therapy. Her growth model is based on the human ability to change, expand, and manifest that growth. Along with love, discovery of and the freedom to express one's feelings and differences are major components of the model.

SATIR'S THERAPEUTIC BELIEFS

Before we look at the primary triad, we want to state some of the more common beliefs and principles of the Satir model.

1. Change is possible. Even if external change is limited, internal change is possible.

2. Parents do the best they can at any given time.

3. We all have the internal resources we need to cope successfully and to grow.

4. We have choices, especially in terms of responding to stress instead of reacting to situations.

5. Therapy needs to focus on health and possibilities instead of pathology.

6. Hope is a significant component or ingredient for change.

7. People connect on the basis of being similar and grow on the basis of being different.

8. A major goal of therapy is to become our own choice makers.

9. We are all manifestations of the same life force.

10. Most people choose familiarity over comfort, especially during times of stress.

11. The problem is not the problem; coping is the problem.

12. Feelings belong to us. We all have them.

13. People are basically good. To connect with and validate their own self-worth, they need to find their own inner treasure.

14. Parents often repeat the familiar patterns from their growing up times, even if the patterns are dysfunctional.

15. We cannot change past events, only the effects they have on us.

16. Appreciating and accepting the past increases our ability to manage our present.

17. One goal in moving toward wholeness is to accept our parental figures as people and meet them at their level of personhood rather than only in their roles.

18. Coping is the manifestation of our level of self-worth. The higher our self-worth, the more wholesome our coping.

19. Human processes are universal and therefore occur in different settings, cultures, and circumstances.

20. Process is the avenue of change. Content forms the context in which change can take place.

21. Congruence and high self-esteem are major goals in the Satir model.

22. Healthy human relationships are built on equality of value.

These are the major beliefs underlying the Satir model. Throughout the book these principles are discussed in greater detail and applied to the therapeutic process. Readers are encouraged to assess their own beliefs, especially in terms of how change takes place in counseling and family therapy.

2

The Primary Triad

The way we perceive the world first takes shape in our family. We come into this world as part of an original, or primary, triad: mother, father, and child. This is the first in a series of systems of which we will become a part. The family system is also perhaps the most influential of all systems. Within it, the child becomes both agent and manifestation of change.

Our basic nature as humans is a combination of samenesses and differences, just as our conception entails the union of a man and a woman, an egg and a sperm. We are all part of the same life force, according to Satir, and we activate rather than create life. She believed people have an internal drive to become more fully human. This intrinsically positive energy, also called the life force, exerts wholesome pulls and pushes on us—physically, emotionally, and spiritually—throughout life.

Stemming from this idea of a universal life force is the premise that we all come into a world with intrinsic and equal worth. So the question of self-worth is not whether we have it, but how we manifest it. Self-worth is always inside us, struggling to be recognized, acknowledged, and validated.

Satir began her theory of human growth with the moment of conception, which she saw as a characteristically dynamic balance of constancy and change. At birth, we are in an alpha state, the natural state of the brain's right hemisphere. We are open to all stimuli through all our senses. This means we are vulnerable to our environment, with little protection. What we take in may be chaos, pieces that do not fit together, as well as nurturing experiences. Within the context of the primary triad, we need nurturing beyond the physical requirements of survival to be able to grow into more fully functioning, conscious human beings.

Over the next nine months, the foundation is laid for what our bodies can expect. Our learning is body learning. We learn from our caretakers by their breath, their touch, and their movements more than their words. Conversely, they guess about our needs and disposition by our grunts, our cries, and our movements. Out of this panoramic collection of experiences and interactions—all of which we store—we make images of ourselves.

How the family evolves and accommodates the continuing growth and change of each of its members may be as beautiful as a symphony in harmony with life. Or it may be a desperate struggle, immutably sculpted in pain and self-survival, that develops into a dysfunctional family system.

By age three, we develop speech to a degree that may affect how we perceive and interact with the world. We may discount a lot of our earlier learnings. Imagine a little boy, for example, who sees his mother cry frequently. Making sense of this nonverbally, he might feel it is his fault. Once he develops speech, he may discover that his mother's tears do not relate to him but to some external event instead.

Often, however, our experiences as toddlers confirm what our bodies have sensed all along. Sometimes life continues replaying what we learned in earlier years. In the beginning, everything we learn comes from outside ourselves. It affects our genetic endowment, which also establishes our physiology, some of our predispositions, and some of our uniqueness.

Initially, our affirmation also comes from outside ourselves. Our parents teach us what they know about this world, validating and not validating some of the thousand things going on around us. This is when we learn what we can expect from others, how to deal with others, what to expect from ourselves, and what others expect from us. We soon develop some mastery of our environment, making life safer and more pleasant.

Thus begins our coping with vulnerability. How we learn to cope depends in large part on the two people who activated us and became our parents. What preparation did they have to become partners and parents?

- How old was each one when they first laid eyes on each other?

- Having met, what connected them?

- What voiced or unvoiced hopes and dreams did they expect each other to fulfill?

- What family rules (shoulds, oughts, dos, and don'ts) had each of them learned?

A common interest may have brought them together. Satir said we come together on the basis of sameness and grow by discovering and respecting our differences. This respect and growth are not automatic, though; disappointment often colors what actually happens in terms of the initial hopes between people. Unrealized dreams can initiate internal and external dialogues of self-doubt, blame, conflict, and sometimes violence. Or people may make believe that their dreams are no longer necessary, that they have made their beds and now are going to lie in them.

Children are often their parents' next step toward the fulfillment they haven't found with each other. We may use our spouses and children as another playground for trying to complete our incomplete lives. Often we have disowned our own dreams, and we look to our children to achieve them instead. Our desires thus become part of how our children perceive and cope with the world. This is just life completing itself in a projected manner.

As caretakers, parents also teach their rules for behavior. Within the primary triad, children learn the family rules about safety, about their bodies, their lovability, and their ability to love. Parents expect and frequently say what and how their children should be, showing them approval for certain acts and punishing them for others. The children's identities are the outcome of this three-person learning situation. Their self-worth and their unique essence develop rather early.

So the infant whose survival depended on others becomes the child whose identity depends on others. From their newborn state of being open to everything, children soon learn to avoid potentially painful situations, including disapproval. Eventually they use family rules as a yardstick to measure their worth; if they follow the rules, they feel more likely to receive love and esteem. Toward this end, they cultivate and crimp various aspects of their unique essence as human beings.

Children want their parents' approval, and parents want their children to be safe and successful. Naturally, what parents teach their children is not all there is to be learned; it is simply the best they know how to do. Hundreds of things are usually going on at one time, so parents give selective attention—positively or negatively—to what they consider important for the child to learn. The child later takes these learnings from this primary triad, this first social unit, and repeats them with other people in other situations until he or she learns to manage or cope differently.

Like a child who doesn't learn to value reading, for example, the child who doesn't learn self-worth faces severe obstacles. Low self-esteem impairs our ability to learn, to work, and to relate to others. Without the sense that we are of intrinsic value, we do not have enough confidence to try new things, pursue goals, or reveal ourselves to any meaningful degree.

Again, it is not a matter of whether we have worth, but of what condition our self-worth is in. Behind every defensive posture and incongruent response, each of us has a self-worth that always makes the same request: "I just want to be loved." All our relationships—in families, with friends and lovers, in business, and so on—are based on love and trust. When an event raises the question of whether that love and trust really exist, we activate our survival responses. Underneath the question of survival are usually the beliefs that others are in charge of our lives, that we could not cope without them, and that they define us.

We can thus look at survival in terms of context, self, and other:

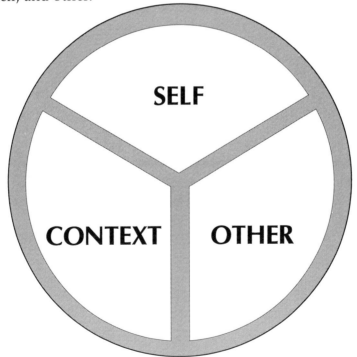

Similarly, we often think and feel another person is in charge of our self-esteem and defines our self-worth. When we accept ourselves, though, we accept that we are each persons of worth. This does not mean thinking we are perfect or that all our actions are magnificent. They are not. Becoming more fully human does not involve equating people with their actions. The task is to help people come to a new space for themselves so that their actions represent their radiance rather than their survival needs. It means instead of saying, "Oh, how stupid I am. How could I have done such a thing?" we can say, "Well, let me take a look at myself. Maybe I can learn something from what happened."

From this level of self-acceptance, we can connect with other persons. It doesn't mean we like everything anyone else does or that everyone adores what we do. Rather, we can comment about ourselves in relation to the other person and our mutual situation. We can describe how we feel rather than how we judge ourselves or others. When that happens, trust is high and many new choices are possible.

Otherwise, we might consider this example. A husband arrives home from work for dinner, which his wife has taken a lot of effort to prepare. As he carves the roast, he says: "This meat is tough!" She runs into the bedroom and cries.

This shows how his comments about the meat triggered her low self-esteem. She interpreted his comment as a statement about her worth, whereas someone with high self-esteem could have separated her sense of worth from the condition of the beef.

Satir spoke about worth well in one of her posters*:

---

*Reprinted by permission of (and available in poster form from) Celestial Arts Publishing, Millbrae, CA.

I Am Me

In all the world there is no one else exactly like me.

Everything that comes out of me is authentically mine because I alone chose it.

I own everything about me—my body, my feelings, my mouth, my voice;

All my actions, whether they be to others or to myself. I own my fantasies, my dreams, my hopes, my fears.

I own all my triumphs and successes, all my failures and mistakes.

Because I own all of me, I can become intimately acquainted with me.

By so doing, I can love me and be friendly with me in all my parts.

I know there are aspects about myself that puzzle me, and other aspects that I do not know.

But as long as I am friendly and loving to myself, I can encourage me

And hopefully look for solutions to the puzzles and for ways to find out more about me.

However I look and sound, whatever I say and do, and whatever I think and feel at a given moment in time is authentically me.

Later, if some parts of how I looked, sounded, thought, and felt turn out

To be unfitting, I can discard that which is unfitting, keep the rest,

And invent something new for that which I discarded.

I can see, hear, feel, think, say, and do.

I have the tools to survive, to be close to others, to be

Productive, and to make sense and order out of the world of people

And things outside of me.

I own me, and therefore I can engineer me.

I am me and I am okay.

REBUILDING SELF-ESTEEM

Whenever we see a client, our questions and interventions are based on our perception of the client's learnings. The primary triad is therefore a major construct in therapy using the Satir model. Past experiences can contaminate the present; how we learn to survive in our families doesn't always serve us well as adults in other systems. Good therapy thus entails examining the multigenerational learning of dysfunctional patterns, viewing them from a different (present-day) perspective, and transforming them. Much of Satir's work focused on updating people's experiences and freeing them from limiting or dysfunctional coping patterns acquired during childhood.

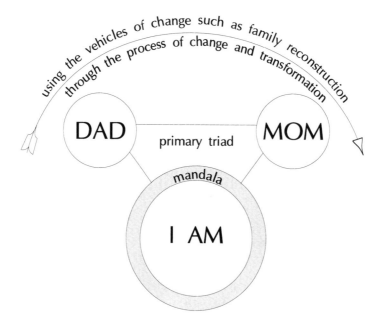

The therapist, as the foreign element, is the basic change agent for the family system. As such, his or her use of self becomes paramount in the Satir model. The therapist who manifests high self-esteem lights the way for clients seeking functional coping. Accepting the uniqueness of each individual, the Satir therapist can also be effective with each new client by recognizing human samenesses and by making meanings that enhance that client's sense of self.

One approach that Satir stressed is the add-on concept of change. Much of the transformation from dysfunctional to functional being involves adding on to what we already are or know. This concept usually is important at the early stages of therapy and is especially significant in terms of the client's perceptions.

To rebuild high self-esteem, we need to move the person through the process of change and transformation. Process is the avenue of change. Its numerous levels include everything from simple one-two-three sequences to looking carefully at what and how something happened, and changing perceptions, expectations, and feelings. Awareness and appreciation of the transformation process was at the hub of Satir's whole approach.

Satir maintained that change—especially internal change—is possible for everyone, regardless of age or other circumstances. This belief is very important in terms of helping people who are stuck and do not feel any hope. Positive change often centers on their expectations, perceptions, and feelings.

If I hold on to an expectation that no longer is possible, such as wishing my father had played with me when I was small, I keep myself focused on the past. This does not promote my growth or fulfillment.

By letting go of that particular expectation, I can move my yearning into a present-day context and find ways to satisfy it. The same is true of anger or hurt: we can work through these feelings by looking at our underlying expectations and updating them.

Change is also possible externally, that is, in how we react to external events. This is not to say that once we have a particular feeling, we deny it. We may wish we didn't have a certain feeling ("Oh, how petty of me!"), but pushing it aside does not remove it.

Examining our external responses means acknowledging our reactions without concern for whether we find them good or bad. Even distasteful ones are of value: they are part of our inner resources. When we respect all our feelings, we can make heartfelt choices about how to handle them.

LOW SELF-ESTEEM	HIGH SELF-ESTEEM
I want to be loved.	I am loved by self and others.
Coping stances: incongruent:	Coping stance: congruence:
I'll do anything [placating]	I do what fits
I'll make you feel guilty [blaming]	I respect our differences
I'll detach from reality [be super-reasonable]	I include you and me
I'll deny reality [be irrelevant]	I accept the context
Rigid Judgmental	Validated Empowered Confident
Reactive	Responsive
Motivated by family rules and "shoulds"	Aware of choices and responsibility
Externally defined	Accepting of self and others
Defensive	Trusting
	Honest
Suppress feelings	Accepting of feelings, wholeness, and humanness
Stay with the familiar	Willing to risk the unfamiliar
Past-focused; wants to maintain the status quo	Present-focused Willing to change

In other words, we have choices of reacting, coping, and being. How we choose to cope often relates to our level of self-esteem. With low self-esteem, we tend to think some "cause" determines our reaction. We believe that events make us angry when, in fact, our choices of reacting range from extremely dysfunctional behavior to optimally functional behavior and a very positive, growth-oriented state of mind. Causes do not determine our reactions. We can take charge of the meanings we make of ourselves, others, and our context. We can also take charge of our feelings and our feelings about those feelings. This capacity enables us to make the major shift from being victims of circumstances, others, or ourselves, to being empowered and taking personal, emotional responsibility. We can use our internal resources to move our lifestyles from the survival level to better coping and, finally, to healthier functioning.

So how is it that we do not always live as well as we might? Satir believed we prefer the familiar and so function on automatic pilot in much of our internal and external life. We need to be aware of any automatic pattern before we can change it.

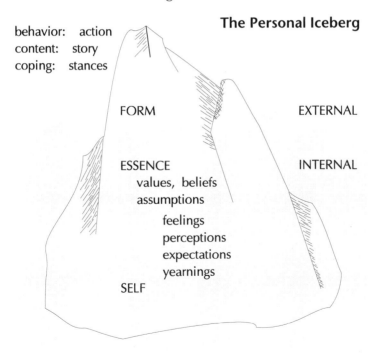

The Personal Iceberg

behavior: action
content: story
coping: stances

FORM

EXTERNAL

ESSENCE
 values, beliefs
 assumptions

INTERNAL

  feelings
  perceptions
  expectations
  yearnings

SELF

Most of us have experienced difficulty when we try to change even a simple habit. Out-of-awareness, automatic patterns are even harder to change. They are the relatively small external protrusions that indicate the unseen mass of our beliefs and attitudes about the world.

Satir looked at people's choices from the inside out: their earlier experiences of the world had inspired inner rules for survival, and they were now acting accordingly. Unfortunately, this principle of the Satir model escaped many observers who focused instead on Virginia's hallmark sculpting, or demonstrations of external movement and change. Actively involving clients or volunteers from her lecture audiences, she would arrange them in postures to depict some situation and then invite them to continue interacting within assigned roles. She had countless scenarios to show different patterns, and the effect was often unforgettable: participants and audiences both were profoundly moved toward recognizing and reclaiming valuable aspects of themselves.

Satir's demonstrations started with the dramatic and basically helped individuals tap their noncognitive yearnings. Knowing that cognitive change is not enough to transform our deeper patterns of coping, she made wide use of the experiential mode. Direct experience was more than a technique for her. It had changed the course of her initial practice, served as the base for her models of therapy and human growth, and inspired most components of her theory.

The next chapter looks more closely at how people manifest their survival coping, how Satir pictured these patterns as internal and external stances, and how we can revamp our old patterns to achieve congruence.

3

The Survival Stances

The four survival stances mentioned in the previous chapter originate from a state of low self-esteem and imbalance, in which people give their power to someone or something else. People adopt survival stances to protect their self-worth against verbal and nonverbal, perceived and presumed threats.

Newborns enter the world in a state of equilibrium with the potential for growth. We cry when we feel pain, and we withdraw from things we dislike. As infants, we experiment with various behaviors to get our basic needs met. For example, smiling might get us attention and affection; crying may get us food. Before long, we learn what gains us approval and disapproval.

Most of us define ourselves before we talk. We receive information through sound, sight, touch, movement, and people's tone of voice. We then infer meaning and messages about ourselves, and we begin using this kind of communication with our families and others to develop a sense of our worth.

Communication can be defined as how people convey information, make meaning with one another, and respond—internally and externally. How we communicate is the key to discerning our external and internal processes, how we handle reality, and how we value ourselves.

Internally, we interpret what we see and hear as best we can, despite not having all available information at our disposal. Often, what we interpret bears little relation to what is actually occurring, for the people who are affecting us do not necessarily communicate clearly. The meaning we interpret as infants, children, and adults, for that matter, may not be what the speakers intend to convey. As a result, we may feel any number of emotions that, with repetition, come to restrict our self-worth.

For example, let's say my father loses his job when I am an infant. My parents are worried, and they seem to change their attitude toward me. Things are not the same. I get less attention, less affection. Based on my perceptions, I conclude that either they do not love me any more, or I have done something terrible.

After we develop speech, we are even more affected by messages from people around us. Any communication contains two messages: the verbal and the affective, or nonverbal. Someone who makes a verbal statement also automatically expresses some message with facial changes, gestures, skin tone fluctuations, tone of voice, and rate of breathing. These nonverbal expressions reflect people's internal states.

When people's verbal messages conflict with their nonverbal ones, we call it incongruent communication. Questions of believability arise in our minds and impel us to choose between the two messages. For example, if someone says, "Now, my dear friends, I'm going to talk about joy" and uses a saturnine tone, we hear a verbal message that contradicts the affective one. Diagrammatically, the words go in one direction and the affect goes in another:

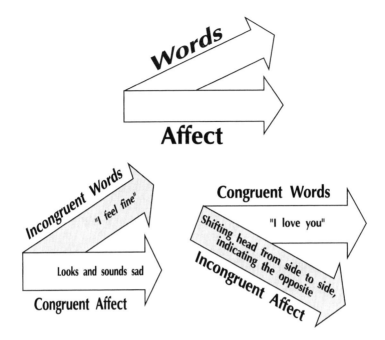

Which is the true message? Or what is the meaning of the discrepancy? To form a response, we need to know or guess.

Frequently we receive contradictory messages when we ask people how they feel. "I'm just fine," they say in a depressed tone. Such incongruencies are common, and as toddlers we absorb both messages. We also absorb the spoken and unspoken family rules that govern communication.

The child who is beginning to talk often precipitates a crucial time in the family. In families characterized by mixed messages, this child's early communication reflects incongruencies and gaps in learning. In any family, what the child expresses obviously reflects what the child has learned within the context of the family. So parents and others may respond with amusement, mortification, delight, or embarrassment as they provide the child with either more information or rules about communication. Examples of rules include:

- "In our family, we don't speak of our private things outside the home."
- "We don't criticize our mother."
- "We don't ask people for things if we think they don't have anything to give us."
- "We do not show love, except when someone does something to deserve it."

We learn rules about what we can see and hear, what we should feel, and what we can comment on or ask questions about. We also learn rules about change. These rules have life-and-death significance for us as children and therefore are compelling. For a little child, not following the rules might result in fearing the loss of being loved, fearing abandonment, or—in the extreme—fearing his or her own imminent death.

When we follow family rules that endanger our self-worth, we often develop physiological symptoms of illness. Our symptoms are desperate compromises that preserve self-worth—in some small measure—and also preserve the rules.

So we learn from family rules and from other people's double-level communication, and we protect ourselves to survive. We find adults speaking to us with contradictory words and body messages, and we may feel a negative response; but we learn that to survive, we have to please others. When we feel angry, we may think, "I cannot let myself show it because of our family rule ('Nice people are not angry'). I should be nice." We therefore say, "I feel fine." Like icebergs, we show only parts of ourselves. Much of us lies below the surface.

We also show only parts of what we know. Like computers, our brains insist on categorizing and explaining all events, experiences, and ideas. To make sense of our experiences, we sort and code every piece of information we encounter. This stored information often surfaces with or without apparent reason, but most of it is overridden by the "shoulds," "should nots," or "why nots" from family rules.

As children, we also imitate our parents' patterns of communicating. Sometimes we copy a placating parent, sometimes a blaming one. If both parents blame or placate, we may get their attention by being irrelevant. Society later reinforces these behavior patterns because people confuse placating with niceness, blaming with assertiveness, super-reasonableness with objectivity, and irrelevance with spontaneity.

If we operate from the survival stances, we are trying to gain acceptance while hiding our desperate need to feel connected with others. Human beings are essentially gregarious. The survival stances dictate that we must not let others know this need for affinity, however. Subconsciously, we believe we will die without their acceptance.

Our coping process results from how we feel about ourselves. If anything raises the question of our survival, we immediately feel defensive. In any relationship, for example, if something leads us to question whether mutual love and trust really exist, our survival responses automatically come into play. These rest on beliefs that others are in charge of our lives, that we cannot continue living without these people, and that their opinions and feelings always define us and our worth correctly.

To demonstrate (in an exaggerated way) people's internal feelings of self-worth, Satir developed the concept of communication stances. As noted, four are survival stances: placating, blaming, being super-reasonable, and being irrelevant. The fifth is being congruent.

PLACATING

Placating is one of the four major ways we respond when we feel our survival is threatened. When we placate, we disregard our own feelings of worth, hand our power to someone else, and say yes to everything. Satir represented this with the following diagram, in which the person who placates honors the other person and the context of their interaction but does not honor his or her own true feelings.

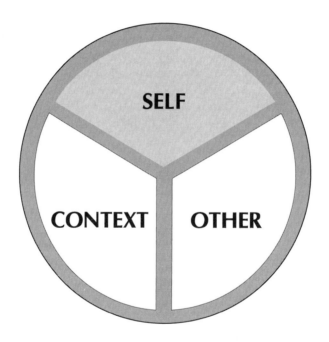

Placating masquerades as pleasing, a highly acceptable act in most cultures and families. However, placating differs from a congruent attempt to please. We placate at the expense of self-worth. Placating denies our self-respect and gives people the message that we are not important.

When we placate, we have interior monologues such as:

- "I don't count. I'm not lovable."
- "I should always be nice to people."
- "I should never make anybody mad."
- "I shouldn't invade anybody."
- "It's all my fault."

When we placate, we are nice to others even when we do not feel nice. We often hide our clenched teeth and lie very convincingly. Another characteristic is rushing to rectify any kind of trouble. When people look as if they are in the least bit of pain, we placate by giving our time, money, and even our lives to alleviate the trouble. We act as if our sole purpose is to resolve their problems.

In addition, we insist on taking the blame for things that go wrong. We take responsibility even if we have to go to exaggerated lengths to find evidence of our errors, such as "I am to blame for your pain because I had the wrong mother. If I had grown up with a different mother, you'd be better off." We try to appease with the following phrases: "Oh, I'm sorry. I didn't mean it." We wish to please in a way that makes everyone else feel satisfied.

In a typical placating stance, we kneel, extend one hand upward in supplication, and clamp the other hand firmly over our heart. This gesture exemplifies that "I want to do everything for you, and if you see me protecting my heart, maybe you won't kill me."

When we placate, our physical position or body language often looks like this:

Or we may be down on our knees with one hand on the ground for support while the second hand wards off an impending blow. Sometimes our second hand is cupped around our neck, making it ambiguous as to whether we are asking for something or protecting ourselves.

In any of these positions, we open our mouths, gasping, as if waiting for crumbs to fall in from others. We speak in high, whiny voices. We may arch our backs unnaturally in an attempt to relieve the overall discomfort and strain of these stances. Breathing is characteristically shallow. Maintaining any of these highly vulnerable positions requires enormous energy and engenders extreme anxiety.

The point of enacting these admittedly exaggerated poses is to recognize our own placating and our responses to people who placate us. We can also consider how our placating evokes predictable reactions from others. The most common incongruent response is to want to abuse and destroy the placater. Some people feel contempt, others feel like vomiting. People who placate often seem infantile and dependent, provoking reactions such as, "Get off your ass and don't be such a sniveling idiot."

We cannot placate effectively with people who are congruent. Each survival stance, for that matter, requires the support of another person who is also communicating incongruently. People who placate essentially say to their partners, "I put you in charge of me." People who most often accept this omnipotent role take the blaming stance, the complementary survival stance. Abdicating our power and relying on others and other things for self-definition are insecure and incomplete ways to feel that "I count." When our placating succeeds in pleasing one person, we feel adequate only until someone else becomes displeased.

Placating means handling stress by telling ourselves, "The way to keep myself alive and keep peace is to say yes no matter what I feel." This attitude causes us to repress our anger and manifest physical disorders instead. If we placate constantly, we often suffer gastrointestinal problems, especially ulcers, diarrhea, constipation, and vomiting. Taken to extremes, placating can lead to self-sacrifice, self-annihilation, and suicide as an expression of total worthlessness.

Therapists who placate usually experience problems. After spending eight or more hours a day placating clients, they may feel drained. In an attempt to alleviate their exhausted feelings, they often placate even more, using their off hours to return telephone calls from other clients. Placating therapists sometimes develop dependent relationships with clients that last many years. The suicide rate among therapists who placate routinely is probably disproportionately high. Placating accounts for much of the burnout among helping professionals.

To summarize Satir's observations and findings from over fifty years of experience with people and working with the survival or coping stances, we present the following chart about placating.

The Placating Response

WORDS	AFFECT	BEHAVIOR
Agreement:	**Begging:**	**Dependent Martyr:**
"It's all my fault."	"I'm helpless."	"Too good" conduct
"I'm nothing without you."	Pleading expressions and voice	Apologizing, excusing
		Whining and begging
"I'm just here to make you happy."	Weak body position	Giving in
INNER EXPERIENCE	**PSYCHOLOGICAL EFFECTS**	**PHYSIOLOGICAL EFFECTS**
"I feel like a nothing."	Neurotic	Distressed digestive tract
"I'm worthless."	Depressed	Stomach disorders, nausea, etc.
	Suicidal	Diabetes
		Migraines
		Constipation

COUNTS "SELF" OUT:

Resource: caring, sensitivity

BLAMING

Blaming is diametrically opposed to placating. The blaming stance is an incongruent way of reflecting society's rule that we should stand up for ourselves and not accept excuses, inconvenience, or abuse from anyone. We must not be "weak."

To protect ourselves, we harass and accuse other people or circumstances. To blame is to discount others, counting only the self and the context:

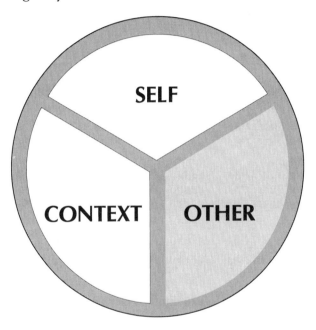

When we blame, we are often described as hostile, tyrannical, nagging, or violent. Instead of prostrating ourselves in the placating stance, we vociferously express the following attitude: "I'll beat the goddamn hell out of you! If it weren't for you, we wouldn't be in this mess." Continually finding fault, we also tend to refuse requests and disagree with suggestions whenever we get the chance.

Characteristically explosive, those of us who blame routinely also often sever intimate ties with others. We spend a lot of time in self-inflicted ostracism. When we become aware of our loneliness, we often cry profusely and claim that if it weren't for everyone else, we would be all right. We cry when we are alone, for we do not admit our vulnerability; we believe on a deep level that we will die if we disclose our low self-esteem.

Symptomatic extremes stemming from the blaming stance include rape, wife- and husband-battering, and other forms of assault. In blaming, we decide that the only way we succeed in life is to fight our way through.

The blaming stance looks like this:

To capture blaming in a physical sculpture, we stand with our back straight and point a fully outstretched finger at someone. To help scare people, we put one foot out; to balance, we put the other hand on our hip. We raise or furrow our brow, and we tighten our facial muscles. Our poor backs suffer terribly, but we can't avoid it if we try to survive in such a dysfunctional way.

Blaming activates fear in others. Adolescents frequently choose this stance because it gives them a feeling of domination, especially in families that prize orderliness and quiet. Others of us blame because we believe we can experience life fully only if we have periodic outbursts of hostility. And some therapists operate as "blamers" because their training frequently focused on finding fault.

Yet if a person operates from a source of strength and challenges people who blame, they topple easily. Although people who blame have a gut sensation that they are in charge when they blame, this feeling is illusionary. Adrenalin pumps into their bloodstream quickly, causing feelings of excitement. It also enters the blood more quickly than the oxygen they breathe. If this condition persists, people who blame get into a blind rage and become oblivious to the rest of the world. Carried to extremes, blaming results in paranoia and homicide.

Another physiological response characteristic of blaming is rapid and shallow breathing. In this stance, the breath is very thin; people draw it in skimpily to accommodate their vigorous shouting. Their muscles and tissues starve and therefore become increasingly tight. Chronic stiffness is symptomatic of blaming. Because people who blame constantly fight tensions, their voices are hard and strident.

The aim of some therapists, especially those popular in the sixties, has been to get people to express hostility—an act in which people who blame participate easily. Hearing their voices rise and feeling the adrenalin rush when they vent their anger gives them an initial sense of power. They feel alive. Yet treatment that stops at this level is insufficient; it fails to help people cope with their feelings. The Satir model goes beyond just venting feelings, as we will see in the next chapter.

Meanwhile, we all act and speak the way we do as a means of survival. Harsh blaming, for instance, indicates a plea for help. Even if it is no longer necessary or helpful, any coping technique is worthy of respect for having helped us survive. It represents our self-worth and will to live. Nevertheless, one of the hardest tasks therapists encounter is helping people go beyond these survival stances.

The Blaming Response

WORDS	AFFECT	BEHAVIOR
Disagreement: "You never do anything right." "What's the matter with you?" "It's all your fault!"	**Blaming:** "I'm the boss around here." Powerful body position Tightness	**Attacking:** Judging Dictating Finding fault
INNER EXPERIENCE	**PSYCHOLOGICAL EFFECTS**	**PHYSIOLOGICAL EFFECTS**
Isolated: "I'm lonely and unsuccessful."	Paranoid Delinquent Homicidal	Muscle tension and back trouble Circulation problems and high blood pressure Arthritis Constipation Asthma
	COUNTS "OTHER" OUT: S C O Resource: assertive	

BEING SUPER-REASONABLE

The super-reasonable pattern of communicating discounts the self or the other person. Being overly reasonable means functioning with respect to context only, most frequently at the level of data and logic.

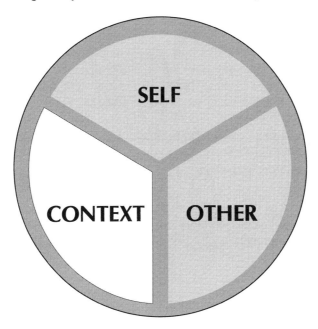

To illustrate the super-reasonable stance, we stand stiffly erect and immobile, with both arms at our sides or folded symmetrically in front of us. We soon feel severe back pain from standing too rigidly. Our feet are perfectly together. Held very straight, our faces appear expressionless. When people speak to us, we pontificate at length, seemingly wise and stately.

The outstanding characteristic of this stance is being inhumanly objective. When we act this way, we do not allow ourselves or others to focus on feelings. This reflects society's rule that maturity means not moving, looking, touching, or feeling emotions.

It's also often mistaken for intelligence. As super-reasonable communicators, we speak and think as impeccably as possible, using complicated jargon, minute details, and lengthy descriptions. We derive pleasure from being academic chauvinists, never perturbed if our listeners fail to understand. We handle conflict by citing research or data to support our view. We want to prove we are always right.

In an effort to be truly objective, we rephrase whatever anyone else says—"I'm cold today," for example—and put it into a sentence that obviates human responsibility or involvement—such as, "It is cold today, yes!" Again, this moves the focus away from feelings and onto the context.

When we are super-reasonable, we withdraw from others and suffer loneliness. People see us as rigid, principled, boring, or obsessive. In extreme cases, being super-reasonable means withdrawing from society or going into catatonic states.

Physiologically, being super-reasonable restricts our glandular secretions. Satir often said, "Breast milk, semen, sweat, tears, and mucus are not created freely when we are super-reasonable . . . . The juices are drying out." When we are being super-reasonable, we also breathe steadily and guardedly to sustain a dry, monotonous voice, as if we had a very short supply of air and had to make it last as long as possible.

Some professions are known for having super-reasonable practitioners. If our families have encouraged our super-reasonable attitudes, we become even more computerlike when we take up such a profession. A significant number of us, especially in our middle-age years, are attached to our field of work because we feel at home with its unspoken rules that let us manifest our super-reasonable qualities. However, we seldom feel internally comfortable; we are not allowed to comment freely on any of our dilemmas.

Therapists are frequently tempted to use this survival stance with clients. Behaving super-reasonably often means therapists are preoccupied with the information they have to offer clients. They do so at the expense of contributing to any therapeutic insights or changes.

The Super-Reasonable Response

WORDS	AFFECT	BEHAVIOR
Extreme objectivity:	**Rigid, aloof:**	**Authoritarian:**
References to rules and the "right" things	"One must be cool, calm, and collected— at all costs."	Rigid, principled conduct
Abstract words and long explanations: "Everything is academic."	Stiff body position	Rationalized acts
	Superior expression, if any	Manipulative
"One must be intelligent."		Compulsive

INNER EXPERIENCE	PSYCHOLOGICAL EFFECTS	PHYSIOLOGICAL EFFECTS
"I feel vulnerable and isolated."	Obsessive-compulsive	Drying-up illnesses involving mucus, lymph nodes, other secretions
"I can't show any feelings."	Sociopathic	
	Withdrawn socially	Cancer
	Catatonic	Mononucleosis
		Heart attacks
		Backaches

COUNTS OUT "SELF" AND "OTHER":

Resource: Intellect

BEING IRRELEVANT

The fourth survival stance is being irrelevant, commonly confused with being amusing or clownish. The irrelevant pattern is the antithesis of the super-reasonable one. It makes super-reasonable people appear silent and stable by contrast.

When people are irrelevant, they move continually. This is an attempt to distract people's attention from the issues under discussion. They keep changing their ideas and want to do myriad activities simultaneously.

The self, the other person, and the context of their interaction do not matter to such people when they are being irrelevant.

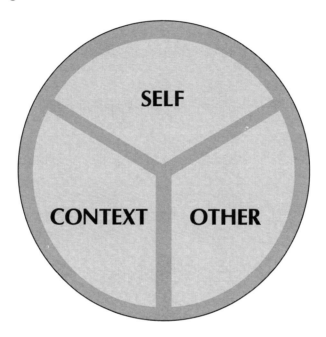

Society labels people who are being irrelevant as spontaneous and cheerful. People often enjoy their presence because they break any mood of despair. For this reason, many people who were hyperactive children or school clowns did not receive help; they were considered entertaining. Today, their irrelevant behavior is often erratic and seems purposeless. As long as they can direct attention away from topics that carry any degree of stress, they believe they will survive.

They cannot keep themselves focused on a subject. When people ask them how they are, for example, they may talk about the high cost of living, the weather, or the latest football standings. They will also be physically inattentive, continuously moving some part of their bodies, whistling, singing, blinking, tousling someone's hair, or otherwise fidgeting.

One physical sculpture of irrelevant communication looks like this:

This person looks very askew. In a hunched yet standing posture, both her knees are facing in and both arms and hands are facing up and out. Her head is cocked severely to one side, both eyes bulging. Her mouth is gaping and twisted, and many parts of her face are twitching.

To maintain any equilibrium in this extreme state of imbalance, people who are being irrelevant need to keep moving. Their posture and motions are often inappropriate, hyperactive, and purposeless.

The Irrelevant Response

WORDS	AFFECT	BEHAVIOR
Extraneous: Make no sense, not to the point Constantly "leave the field" verbally	**Confusing:** "I'm not really here." Features in constant motion Angular and loose body position	**Distracting:** Inappropriate conduct Hyperactive Interrupting
INNER EXPERIENCE	**PSYCHOLOGICAL EFFECTS**	**PHYSIOLOGICAL EFFECTS**
"Nobody cares." "There's no place for me." Out of balance To interrupt to be noticed	Confused Inappropriate Psychotic	Distressed central nervous system Stomach disorders, nausea, etc. Diabetes Migraines Constipation

COUNTS OUT "SELF," "OTHER," AND "CONTEXT":

Resource: fun, spontaneous, creative

According to Satir, habitually irrelevant communicators suffer from disorders of the central nervous system. They breathe irregularly, increasing their tendencies toward erratic responses. They have a distinct feeling of imbalance. All this induces dizziness and trembling. Extreme psychological manifestations include psychosis and hebephrenia.

SWITCHING STANCES

To get relief from being in one type of survival attitude, people often switch stances. None of these postures is in balance for health. To get relief from placating, we can start blaming. We may later turn from blaming to being super-reasonable. To show this in the physical sculpture, we could then slowly turn our toes inward and try to balance while we move everything else. If we can move enough of ourselves, we can keep ourselves from toppling over. This demonstrates being irrelevant.

Most of us can't stand the same stances all the time. In different situations, we might use different coping styles. If we are threatened too much, for instance, we could flip our lids and become even louder than our partner. When we see that person down, we might say, "Oh my God! What did I do!" We may get down and try to comfort him or her. But when we do that, we may become disgusted with such weakness and revert to blaming again, starting a new cycle in our pattern.

We usually use one stance more frequently than others when we interact under stress. For instance, perhaps we placate when our fathers are blaming us for something. As far as we are concerned, the stress point in our relationship with our parents is one-up and one-down, and this is how it has always been. We have always felt put down by them, and they have always towered above us.

Most of us are locked into these patterns in a deep way. Most people do not stay in one classic stance all the time. Enough change occurs, inside or outside, to activate another coping method. The salient point is that we are confined to some form of placating, blaming, being super-reasonable, or being irrelevant unless we learn how to be congruent.

HOW SURVIVAL
STANCES DEVELOP

All communication stances contain seeds of wholeness. Placating harbors the seed of caring; blaming, the seed of assertiveness; being super-reasonable, the seed of intelligence; and being irrelevant, the seed of creativity and flexibility. We need to make clear distinctions between our external behavior and our internal yearnings. When our basic yearning to love and be loved is threatened, we may placate, blame, be super-reasonable, or be irrelevant to maintain a relationship.

The first relationship any of us ever strove to maintain was with our parents or caretakers. If they had not kept us warm and well fed, we would have died. As children, we soon learned that our survival depended on doing everything we were told. Our survival responses were conditioned in the context of this relationship.

As adults, many of us still carry those same survival responses. Our early learnings were extremely strong. If the threat-and-reward model was the only communication we learned, as it was in many cases, we had no way of coming into our own power as we grew up. If our parents acted on our needs in a delayed fashion, we may have concluded that they did not care for us—a conclusion that may have been erroneous, but one we have maintained for years.

Parents have good intentions, and they do the best they can based on what they have learned. Many of these learnings follow from generation to generation to generation. Therefore, the Satir model uses a three-generational perspective. She was among the early pioneers in this respect, and her vehicles for change address more than the dysfunctional aspects of what a client learned from his or her parents. Satir's model also looks at what those parents learned from the grandparents. Therapists can thus help clients appreciate their childhood learnings and use them as resources instead of judgments against themselves and their families.

Satir believed children want to change their parents' survival behavior and usually fail. Children usually feel they know what would make their parents happier, and they frequently act to make their views come true. This is often expressed in a judgmental manner, but actually it is intended to be helpful and caring.

As adults, many of these children choose marriage partners with the same behaviors and again attempt to get that partner to change. When we fail with our spouse, we try to accomplish the changes with our children. Repeatedly we fail to transform others, and we may accuse them: "You betrayed me. I thought you said you loved me." This shows we have tried to make the other person responsible for our own expectations. The price we pay is that we define ourselves by the other person's behavior, which ultimately diminishes our own self-esteem.

Neither our current family nor our parents are at fault for failing us. Rather, we need to acknowledge them as human beings with shortcomings. We all have shortcomings of one type or another. If we blame our parents rather than accepting them as people, we will continue to react to threatening situations with dysfunctional coping patterns.

Using Our Senses

Part of pleasing our parents and disregarding our own needs involved denying our senses. We were not supposed to cherish our senses and use them creatively. Most of us still follow an injunction against this: against feeling our skin, looking at things we are not "supposed" to look at, and talking about subjects we are not "supposed" to discuss.

But human beings do not operate in isolation. We respond to varieties of stimuli. A feeling and a thought accompany every body response, forming a cycle of physical, emotional, and intellectual information. This cycle may start with our skin, which has millions of pores. These pores have two capacities: they receive and they put forth. Every hole in our bodies—nose, eyes, ears, and so on—operates in the same way. Without holes, our nervous system could not function: nothing would enter or leave our bodies.

"Senses" are another name for our holes. The ear holes hear, the nose holes smell, and the mouth hole tastes. Our senses are feeling stations of physical, emotional, and intellectual stimulation. One of the best reasons for breast-feeding a baby, aside from nutritional aspects, is this fullness of stimulation. The child feels pleasure and makes an intimate connection with an adult.

Our senses play an important role in our survival. We receive with our senses, experience with our nervous systems, and translate information with our brains. Our senses, nervous systems, and brains rule our bodies like a three-headed driver. We hope these three cooperate—knowing, accepting, and valuing one another's existence. Satir used an image of a fountain to illustrate their integration: sights, sounds, smells, taste, and thoughts that enter the brain flow to the center, mingling harmoniously and being freely available to come out of the mouth as a report of what exists in the nervous system. An integrated person reports uninhibitedly what he or she sees, hears, thinks, and feels. If we are not integrated, we ignore or deny various senses, turning them off. We can legitimately tune out specific senses if we choose. We endanger ourselves only if we lose control over choosing.

Childhood Misunderstandings

Our nervous systems carry physical, emotional, and intellectual information throughout our bodies. The branches and parts of this carrier system interrelate closely. For instance, if one area hurts, the entire nervous system becomes aware of the pain and takes steps to balance the situation. Our nervous system channels this information constantly.

This differs from interpersonal communication, which is not always received or transmitted so accurately. Children and parents often misinterpret messages they receive. Their respective survival patterns often prevent the messages from being received as intended. As children, we may have often misinterpreted our parents' messages, especially if these communications sounded like orders without any explanations. We may have heard, "Pull down your pants," for example, instead of, "What I want to find out is whether you've got measles, so will you pull down your pants and let me see?"

To make people aware of exactly what we want, we need to share our pictures with them. Any shorthand form of communication works only if both parties share a common meaning or understanding. Otherwise, when we are confused about messages we are receiving, we begin to believe we are losing control or that we are stupid. This usually raises questions of our survival, which brings on one of our patterns for coping.

One way we may handle this kind of strain is to prove we are right. We all tend to select experiences from our lives to validate our beliefs. We usually have a thousand experiences to justify ourselves; we each have filters that notice only those things that fit our ideas about our worlds and ourselves.

These ideas begin developing early. Although most of us are between eighteen months and two years of age when we learn to talk, we learn a great deal before we reach the age of two. Our parents may communicate with us in words, but we interpret their messages from their touch and tone, their hands and their voices.

These main channels of our young learning—touch and tone of voice—can also be channels of dysfunctional learning. Adults do not often think of this. We register their words before we are able to speak; later, we put words and sensory experiences together. By the time we reach adulthood, words enter our consciousness via the left brain, and we forget that infants depend on tone and touch. A father's strong hands or a mother's anxious words may register with the baby as threatening and unloving; the parents are not necessarily aware of or intending these nonverbal messages.

Childhood Helplessness

Unless our parents teach us, we do not develop effective ways of dealing with threats. Usually, when we are adults, we continue to use the same ways of coping that we learned as children. Whatever we decided was a threat to us at an early age will prompt us to react the same way as adults. Different situations threaten different people and therefore trigger different coping behavior.

Children develop feelings of helplessness according to how their parents treat them. Adults often imagine that if infants cannot speak, they also cannot see, hear, or think. As mentioned, children have learned a great deal about people by the time they are able to talk. They also learn from their physical position in life. Looking straight ahead and standing close to adults, children first see the knees of their elders. As they grow, their eye level comes into line with adults' genitals, bellies, and then breasts. During much of this time, children have to look up to see the faces of their parents. This reinforces the one-down position reflected in the dominant-submissive model.

During therapy, many people describe their parents in inaccurate ways because their images were formed

from—and have not been updated since—the limited perspectives they had as children.

Learning to Judge

Faced with adult insensitivities to their senses of need,
pleasure, and curiosity, children often feel overwhelmed
and powerless. Their options include resisting these power

threats or succumbing to them. Again, no one necessarily intends to harm us in this way. Nonetheless, children learn blaming and judging from their parents. Adults frequently point their fingers close to children's noses, admonishing them and trying to teach them what their bad behavior meant. Pointing fingers indicate how desperate the parents were for the children to behave differently.

Usually children do not hear the lesson, but they do learn what being blamed feels like. They learn to such a degree that they begin to sense blame even when they are not being criticized. Dysfunctional ways of coping with this blaming include dodging the finger or ignoring it.

Another example of children feeling powerless is head patting. Some people cannot tolerate having their heads patted today because of their experiences as children. The head is a very vulnerable spot, and some adults pat children there too hard, without being in touch with how it feels. For the child, being patted on the head may seem like a put-down rather than affection or approval.

Mixed Messages

Even though we may feel powerless, we still receive messages that urge us to be effective in the sense of duty, obedience, achievement, and responsibility. These are heavy loads for children who do not have any sense of personal power. Given such contradictory messages, we develop frustrating ideas about ourselves. Old learnings taught by loving but unaware adults reinforce split expectations of ourselves.

To communicate congruently, our loving has to flow from a sense of respecting people's self-worth. If parents decide to be centers of their children's lives, giving up everything to be with them, the outcome can be emotional suffocation. Children who are closed in and given routinely mixed messages have to struggle to say, "I love you, Mommy, Daddy." For them, surrounded by incongruent communication, loving and intimacy have become equated with falseness. This context also results in low self-worth.

HOW SURVIVAL STANCES PROTECT US

Most of our communications are efforts to protect ourselves. We learn these communications before school age through interactions and interpretations that nobody ever intended to happen. These are survival communications, based on not knowing any other ways to survive. Many people tell us that to say how they feel makes them vulnerable. Unfortunately, not being able to show their feelings also exposes them to possible ill health.

The human body always tries to stay in balance. The question is whether anything suffers in the process. A fat person and a thin person on a teeter-totter can balance it; the fat one moves toward the middle, and the skinny one moves toward the end. As they teeter, the fat one moves up and down relatively little, and the skinny one goes way up and way down. It is a precarious tradeoff.

Survival stances are likewise a precarious balance between self-expression and self-repression. Self-expression moves us toward the healthy goal of wholeness. Our rules and beliefs—our "shoulds" and "should nots"—can counteract this by limiting what we allow ourselves to sense and to say.

One of these limits is that we sometimes see and hear what "should" exist instead of what does. We also restrict ourselves from reaching out for what we want, taking risks on our own behalf, and saying what we think we should say rather than what we feel and think. To feel what we feel is freedom; to feel what we "ought" is compulsion.

"I can't feel what I feel" is also the basic restriction, the one that underlies all our limits on and rules about sensing and expressing ourselves. This is where self-condemnation starts. And it can start in the crib. Later, it shows up in the four survival stances, all of which communicate another self-damning message: "I can't be my own decision-maker."

Satir's "Five Freedoms" express the opportunities and possibilities of using our resources positively and our choices creatively:

The Five Freedoms

The freedom to see and hear what is here, instead of what should be, was, or will be

The freedom to say what you feel and think, instead of what you should

The freedom to feel what you feel, instead of what you ought

The freedom to ask for what you want, instead of always waiting for permission

The freedom to take risks on your own behalf, instead of choosing to be only "secure" and not rocking the boat

Communication is the tip of an iceberg that is supported by the past—a terribly convincing, automatic, and habitual past. We need to help people become aware of areas in which they put themselves on automatic pilot a long time ago. Taking risks on their own behalf may constitute freedom, but people often feel more sure and secure in the unfreedom of looking to others for direction or decisions. Stress prompts most people to go into their survival stances without a second thought.

At some point, we may want to find some other way to feel comfortable. Drugs, alcohol, illness, and being institutionalized are dysfunctional ways of coping. They are efforts to get some kind of relief and attention. Many of us turn toward these or similar external gratifications to meet our unmet needs and expectations.

Magical thinking and escape fantasies are other ways we meet needs. We can think of how good it would be to get away from our families, our jobs, or our communities: "If I could find another person, life would be better"; or "If I could go to another situation, life would be better. There must be a place where life can be better."

Runaway teens do more than fantasize. Many of them are running away to get something else, and they don't always know what it is. Many husbands and wives also escape each other: they spend a long time at work and as little time as possible together. Their work becomes a way of leaving.

People who have trouble coping usually have difficulties arising from a lack of self-worth. The problems that people outline as their sources of frustration are usually not the major issues. Rather, coping is the main difficulty.

Satir saw family members' symptoms as efforts to grow and an alarm signal that says, "I can't live." Another way to express this survival cry is: "I can't feel like a valued, loving person."

Along these lines, therapists often see very angry, very punitive fathers who come in with their adolescent sons. The sons are equally punitive and vengeful. We would do well to think about these people's respective feelings of disappointment, distance, vulnerability, and not being loved. Instead of tackling the revenge issues, we can look for ways to help them get in touch with their feelings and begin to make bridges between them at that level. It doesn't happen quickly, but we need to focus our attention in areas that help build self-esteem by looking at each person's intent rather than reactive behavior.

Chapter 5 examines this and other aspects of transforming our survival stances into congruent communication patterns. Meanwhile, the next chapter discusses congruence in detail.

4

Congruence

The previous chapter discussed the four survival stances. These are manifestations of coping with low self-esteem. This chapter discusses the "fifth stance," *congruence*. It is actually not another stance, but another choice of becoming more fully human, as well as a state of wholeness. Much of the rest of the book describes Satir's tools and vehicles to achieve this sense of being and becoming.

Congruence is one of the main constructs in the Satir model. It is a state of being and a way of communicating with ourselves and others. High self-esteem and congruence are two of the main indicators of more fully functioning human beings. Congruence is characterized by:

- An appreciation of the uniqueness of self
- A free flow of personal and interpersonal energy
- The claiming of personhood
- A willingness to trust oneself and others
- A willingness to take risks and to be vulnerable
- The use of one's inner and outer resources
- An openness to intimacy

- The freedom to be oneself and to accept others
- A love of oneself and others
- Flexibility and openness to change

Satir presented congruence with the following diagram, in which self, other, and context are all honored.

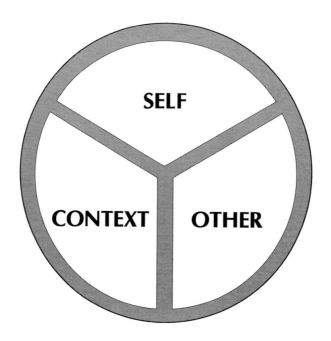

When we decide to respond congruently, it is not because we want to win, to control another person or a situation, to defend ourselves, or to ignore other people. Choosing congruence means choosing to be ourselves, to relate to and contact others, and to connect with people directly. We wish to respond from a position of caring for ourselves, for other people, and with an awareness of the present context. It does not mean being happy and without any problems, or being polite regardless of the situation.

LEVELS OF CONGRUENCE

Through our training programs around the world, we have realized that congruence has three levels. Satir's work in the 1950s concentrated on what we are calling Level 1; in the 1960s, she began emphasizing Level 2; and in the 1980s, she spent more and more time conceptualizing and working with Level 3 issues. The following diagram illustrates these levels.

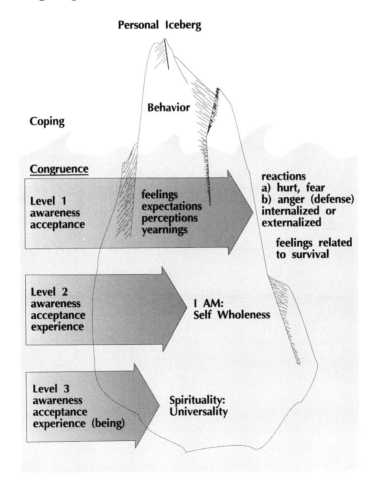

Personal Iceberg

Behavior

Coping

Congruence

Level 1
awareness
acceptance

feelings
expectations
perceptions
yearnings

reactions
a) hurt, fear
b) anger (defense)
internalized or
externalized

feelings related
to survival

Level 2
awareness
acceptance
experience

I AM:
Self Wholeness

Level 3
awareness
acceptance
experience (being)

Spirituality:
Universality

When we experience Level 1, we are aware of our feelings and can acknowledge and accept them. They belong to us. We willingly deal with them, without denial or projection. We are in a state of honesty with our feelings in a nonreactive way. We know they are like double-edged swords: we can use them to bring us more pain or more joy, and we can share them freely with others if we choose.

The Satir model makes a major contribution to the therapeutic field by showing how to help clients become more congruent at Level 1. People can learn to manage their feelings in a wholesome way as well as to enjoy the many positive feelings that are part of our humanness.

The second level of congruence affects our lives more dramatically. Level 2 is the state of wholeness, inner centeredness. It focuses on the deeper, inner self. People at this level manifest high self-esteem in harmonious and energetic ways. They are at peace with themselves, with others, and in relation to their context.

CONGRUENCE

Level 1: Feelings	Awareness	High self-esteem
	Acknowledgment	
	Ownership	
	Management	
	Enjoyment	
Level 2: The Self ("I am")	Centeredness	High self-esteem
	Wholeness	
	Harmony	
Level 3: Life-Force	Universality	High self-esteem
	Spirituality	

Level 3 moves into the realm of spirituality and universality. In her later years, Satir found greater and greater significance in these aspects of becoming more fully human. *The New Peoplemaking*, published just before her death, devotes a chapter to the importance of spiritual exploration. Among other facets, she encourages our awareness of a *universal life force* that creates, supports, and promotes growth in human and other natural forms.

CONGRUENT COMMUNICATION

In addition to a state of being, congruence is also a way of conveying information. In communicating, we have at least three choices:

- Using incongruent words and congruent affect

- Using congruent words and incongruent affect

- Using congruent words and congruent affect

Affect includes voice characteristics, facial expressions, body gestures, body posture, tonus, skin color, and breathing. Satir found and frequently stated that nonverbal communication provides more than half the information in most interactions. Over the years, Satir stressed the importance of nonverbal aspects of therapy and encouraged therapists to pay special attention to their own affects as well as that of their clients. It was important to her that therapists who used the Satir model be congruent and be aware of their own incongruencies.

As soon as videotapes became available, Satir pioneered using them to help people become aware of their verbal and nonverbal discrepancies. For example, a smiling face accompanied by a high degree of anxiety exposes the person's lack of awareness of his or her mixed message. Seeing this on tape is a dynamic way of gaining self-awareness about incongruence.

Another way to understand congruence or its absence is to imagine verbal and nonverbal messages going in various directions. *Directional communication* can be illustrated as follows:

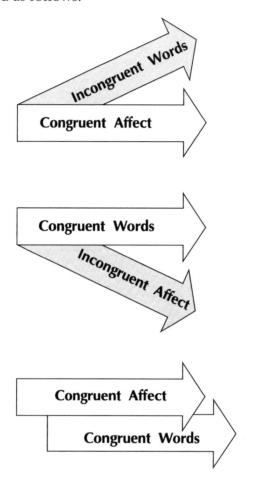

When the words go in one direction and the affect in another, we have a *double message*. The communication is manifested in an incongruent way. For example, if somebody says, "I feel wonderful," and his head shakes "No," the internal process might be: "My body tells me I don't feel wonderful, but at this time I should say I do."

Body responses usually carry a message in the present. Words might carry a message of the past, often based on family rules. Both messages might be accurate but may be coming from two different places, and possibly from two different times. They may therefore seem incongruent.

Words come from the left hemisphere of the human brain and are associated with our survival rules, defenses, and "should" injunctions. People with low self-esteem often use their old survival rules even when they understand that those rules no longer serve them well. For many, the rule is not to say how they feel. Therefore they often say, "I feel fine" when they actually feel miserable.

Verbal expression is part of our awareness and can indicate past, present, or future. Affect, on the other hand, always reflects the present. Our nonverbal expressions come from the right hemisphere, connecting us with our feelings and senses as we experience each moment. Discrepancies thus arise between verbal and nonverbal levels of communication. Both levels indicate sincere but incomplete messages. Placating, blaming, and being irrelevant or super-reasonable are attempts to cope with ourselves, others, and context in our effort to survive. We try to express ourselves fully, yet we end up conveying a contradiction.

This is also true of the sunbather who beams with enjoyment while talking about how terrible life is. The smiling originates from the immediate right-brain message about comfort from the sunshine. The verbalized subject matter relates to a painful experience in the past.

One goal in therapy is to help people become aware of their conflicting messages so they can begin the journey toward congruence. The same goal is present in the growth process. Incongruent messages represent some form of denial, projection, or ignoring. Incongruent behavior expresses our need to survive when our self is at stake in a relationship. It indicates our lack of awareness, not our intentions.

Our bodies provide us with the signals that help us become aware of our messages. If we say we feel fine when our bodies feel tight, we communicate a double message. It is wise to pay attention to the tightness, which indicates an imbalance. This imbalance could come from our family's rule that we should always be nice, even if someone has just stepped on our toe or we have just bumped our head.

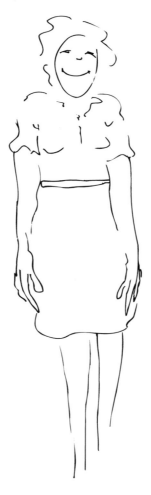

When both words and affect go in the same direction, as illustrated previously, both levels of the message express the same meaning. For example, if a woman says, "I am happy" and her voice sounds content, and her body movements, skin color, eyes, and other nonverbal expressions support her words, she is communicating in a congruent way. Similarly, when she says she feels disappointed, her voice sounds sad, and her body movements, skin color, eyes, and other nonverbal expressions support her words, she is also communicating in a congruent way.

To respond congruently is a choice. It is not another rule or a way to control the situation. Choice at a conscious level is based on awareness, acknowledgment, and acceptance of self, other, and context, and of being in charge of self. Communicating with others, we find the message intended is often not the message received; this arises because of discrepancies between our words and our affect. The accompanying chart summarizes the congruent response.

The Congruent Response

WORDS	AFFECT	BEHAVIOR
Real: Words match the body position, the voice tone, and the inner feelings. Words show an awareness of feelings.	**Consistent with words:** Expressions flow	Alive Creative Unique Competent
INNER EXPERIENCE	**PSYCHOLOGICAL EFFECTS**	**PHYSIOLOGICAL EFFECTS**
Harmony Balance High self-worth	Healthy	Good health
	COUNT SELF, OTHER, AND CONTEXT:  Resource: Relatedness, contact, high self-esteem	

To assess the gap between a person's current coping patterns and congruence, we can consider the following eight points. Satir said an individual manifests congruence when he or she:

1. Replies to questions directly rather than first asking, "Why do you want to know?"

2. Shows some sexual vitality

3. Names specific desires without giving a long rationale

4. Says yes or no honestly (makes honest choices)

5. "Puts on a detective hat" to look at comments, ideas, acts, and situations instead of passing judgment first

6. Takes risks on his or her own behalf, even before settling all fears

7. Still asks questions about life, is open to new possibilities, and doesn't pretend to have all the answers in advance for every new situation

8. Listens to his or her intuition or "wisdom box" for new possibilities, choices, and resolutions, and includes these in any decision-making situation

WORKING TOWARD CONGRUENCE

Helping a client build congruence is not a problem-solving approach in which the focus is on content and the implication and expectation are that the therapist will help solve the client's problem. Rather, it is a process-oriented approach that focuses on what the client wants to learn and change. This reflects Satir's growth model of the world and its acceptance of people as they are. It helps them gain access to their inner resources and their choices.

In this process, acknowledging and accepting how a client feels is often the beginning of hope for that person. That hope helps the client move into the unknown venture of therapeutic change. In therapy, if a person shows a discrepancy between words and feelings, the task is to explore what keeps the verbal and nonverbal messages from being congruent, and then to resolve the difference. In the Satir model, congruence is not a matter of choosing one message over the other.

Rather, Satir saw incongruent communicators' perceptions as being out of harmony with the self. To build congruence, we need to change our interpretations and then reconfirm our self-esteem at the level of self ("I am"). We need to teach ourselves and our clients to breathe regularly, to center ourselves by going inside for some self-validation, and to stay in the present by accepting our context, the other person, and ourselves.

Otherwise, when we *react* to a situation, our feelings and inner interpretations usually reflect past experiences. Whatever hurt, fear, and anger we have stored within may be triggered by our current encounters. Early learnings, history, feelings, and coping patterns are all sorted, coded, and recorded in our neurophysiology. When we feel punched in the stomach by a word, a sensation, a sound, a picture, a taste, or a smell, we usually react to it with our old ways of coping.

Instead, as Satir showed, we need to keep our self-worth intact when we feel threatened. As children we learned the concept of cause and effect, and that person A's behavior causes or justifies person B's reaction. The Satir perspective suggests we have choices about how to behave and how to respond, and that we are responsible for our choices.

Congruence is based on an awareness of what is going on within: our thoughts, feelings, body messages, and the meanings we ascribe to our experiences. We learned to be incongruent to survive; to learn congruence requires reevaluating and hearing ourselves anew, being able to gauge our self-worth at any moment, and moving from the submissive/dominant model to Satir's growth model.

Recalling Satir's add-on theory, we can now look at congruence in terms of the four survival stances. For instance, to someone in the placating stance adding the resource of self-care moves the person to congruent caring about self and others. Similarly, if someone in the blaming stance adds an acknowledgment of the other person, congruence and assertiveness can be achieved.

When someone in the super-reasonable stance adds an acknowledgment of the self and others, his or her intellectual resourcefulness helps manifest congruence. With the irrelevant stance, all the aspects—self, other, and context—need to be accepted and integrated. The person can then achieve congruence through the use of creativity, fun, and appropriate humor.

To illustrate the congruent "stance," people can stand on their own feet, with their own self support. The body manifests balance, harmony, fluidity, and vibrancy. Congruence is a form of open communication, a state of strength, and a state of being.

Our bodies need practice with this. We all have had thousands of experiences to date. Based on these experiences, most of our actions have become automatic. As we begin to listen to ourselves again, we begin examining our automatic patterns. Reading and thinking about this are usually not enough. Practicing is important. As we give ourselves the chance to see and hear again with awareness, we can find all our old pictures, all our old ways of coping, and all our old familiar feelings.

WORKING TOWARD CONGRUENT COMMUNICATION

Often we find in others the unfinished business of our own internal processes. Especially in long-term relationships, we often hope our partners will change their incongruent ways of being so we can feel better. Actually, we are hoping the other person will change because that might save us from dealing with our own dysfunctional coping styles.

Fortunately, we can develop conscious, congruent ways of being, even in response to someone who is communicating incongruently. Our usual tendency is to react to that person; nonetheless, we also have the choice of responding congruently. This often seems hard in practice, but it's possible. Again, what the other person says does not define us unless we allow it to.

When we are congruent, emotional triggers lose their power, and we cease being victims of our past. Once we acknowledge and accept our experiences, past and present, we are no longer on automatic pilot, living by rules and assuming dysfunctional stances that stem from other times in our lives. Nor do we studiously attempt to ignore, deny, or rename those past experiences.

To help people communicate congruently, Satir developed some pointers:

1. To be aware of self, other, and context.

2. To give their full attention when they relate to others.

3. To be aware of their body messages. Satir conceptualized and enacted the survival stances, for instance, so that people could recognize and become aware of their bodies and their body messages.

4. To be aware of their defenses and their family rules.

These steps are shown in the accompanying figure.

1. Focus on Self
   a. Attend to body signals
   b. Breathe to become calm
   c. Confirm self-worth
   d. Become centered and aware

2. Make Contact
   a. See and hear
   b. Attend to body signals
   c. Show respect
   d. Accept and trust

3. Change within the context
   a. Change "the problem" to coping
   b. Deal with feelings
   c. Reframe expectations and perceptions
   d. Increase choices and possibilities

4. Transform and integrate new status quo with Self, Other, and Context, and with levels of experience

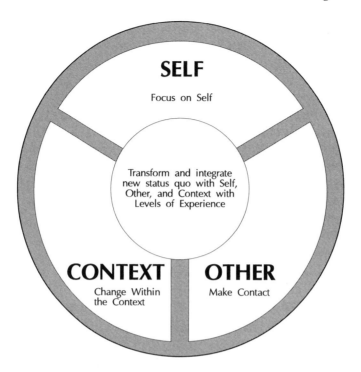

Working at Level 1

The first level of congruence focuses primarily on being in touch with our feelings, accepting them, acknowledging them to others, and dealing with them. So if a client feels angry or hurt, or both, encourage him to acknowledge and accept his feelings and then act in terms of them. He might say, "I'm angry, and therefore I need some time before discussing this issue."

When my anger relates to an external event, I have choices about what to do with my feelings. I might need to check my old family rules to see what messages I still follow. For example, my old rule might be: "I should not be angry." If I can be congruent with myself, I will acknowledge and own my anger, and be in charge rather than allow it to dictate my actions.

We often use events to define ourselves. For example, Mr. Jones went to visit his buddy the other day. As soon as he arrived, his buddy's other friends left. Mr. Jones immediately decided they did not like him; he was unworthy of their staying to visit with him.

This perception was based on his interpretation of their behavior. Later he discovered they were late leaving for the airport. Meanwhile, though, he had used their departure to define himself negatively.

The therapist working at first-level congruence helps Mr. Jones acknowledge, accept, and share his feelings. With the new information available, he can feel differently about himself and others.

Working at Level 2

At the second level of congruence, people often need to change their perceptions and then reconfirm their self-esteem. This brings their perceptions, interpretations, and Self into harmony. They can then express themselves congruently at Level 2.

The same process of change is necessary with regard to expectations. Otherwise, we might use an unmet expectation to define ourselves. For example, when we expect to be accepted but feel unworthy, rejected, or discounted, we need to work on our perceptions and expectations. To do so, we need to change our perceptions and let go of our expectations of Self and Other. This builds congruence at the level of Self. Having our self-expectations in harmony with our sense of self helps establish the confidence, empowerment, and self-esteem we need.

Our basic focus at Level 1 was to listen to our feelings and body messages, and to acknowledge and own them. At Level 2, the focus is to change perceptions and let go of unfulfilled expectations we have projected on others. This keeps us and our communication in harmony with our inner experiences.

Working at Level 3

At the third level of congruence, we move into harmony with our spiritual essence, or what Satir called the universal life force. In her later meditations, she expressed this third level of congruence by the following:

> *Also remember that being in the universe, we have access to the energy from the center of the earth, which brings us our groundedness; and from the heavens, which brings us our intuition. These are there for us to use at any time. We are already part of it. Our job is to know it and access it. When we do, we create that third energy, which allows us to move out to those on the outside who are ready. Not those who we desire should be ready—only those who are.**

In talking about third-level congruence, Satir also said:

> *When I can be in touch with another person's spiritual energy, and he or she with mine, there is a change in the state of consciousness. We each have the whole world within us, and we each have special functions. We are not attached to one another but connected by the spaces between us. We are part of one universal whole. I am part of the whole and also the whole. Birth and death are transformational processes. I keep on knowing more and more about the deeper layers of the universe without having to give up any of my other awarenesses. Life talks with life.*

Third-level congruence reflects Satir's overall philosophy, which recognizes the inner life force of human beings. When we connect at our universal essence, we have the ability to achieve a new universal consciousness and world peace, to which Satir was devoted. This book's subtitle, *Family Therapy and Beyond*, therefore alludes to this third level of congruence.

---

*From the book *Meditations of Virginia Satir*, edited by Anne and John Banmen (Palo alto, CA: Science and Behavior Books, 1991).

THE CONGRUENT THERAPIST

Satir encouraged therapists to make contact with their clients on this same basis of equality in value as human beings. This implies empowerment for both, and it bolsters each person's sense of inner strength.

Also stressing the importance of modeling congruence—which maximizes clients' opportunities to grow—Satir identified these main steps in congruent communication:

1. Be aware and accept that you have choices about how you respond.

2. Be in touch on all levels (expectations, perceptions, and feelings) with what is going on within you in the present.

3. Own what comes from you, be it words, body messages, or actions.

4. Respond with "I" messages: "I am/I feel/I hear" and so on.

5. Clearly convey your ownership of what you say and do.

6. In descriptive (rather than judgmental) language, share what is happening within you as well as what you see and hear the other person saying and doing.

7. Pay attention to the physical distance or closeness you choose when you make contact with someone. Arrange yourself to be at eye level and at a comfortable closeness with that person.

In practicing congruence, Satir considered these components important:

BELIEFS	All people are manifestations of a life force.
	All people can grow.
	All people can be intimate.
	All people can be competent.
	All people can make sense and meaning.
	All people can stand on their own two feet.
	All people can be choosers.
POSITION	Face to face at eye level
	Eye to eye within arms' reach
ATTENDING	Consciously and in awareness, taking in fully with all your senses: sight, sound, smell, touch, taste, sensuality
MAKING MEANING	Understanding clearly the articulated words
	Understanding intended meaning
	Making the abstract concrete, and the covert overt
	Making the hidden obvious
	Making the general specific and clarifying its relationship to you, me, here, now, and specific situations
	Understanding sexuality: femininity, masculinity
SHARING	Reporting the inner-space experience
	Revealing, not exposing

Satir-based training devotes considerable time to helping therapists become congruent and communicate congruently. As a result, they empower their clients to a profound degree.

SUMMARY

Congruence refers to a state of being as well as a quality of communicating. At the first of its three levels, congruence entails acknowledging and accepting our inner experiences (sensations, interpretations, and consequent feelings about those feelings) and being able to express them. Congruence at Level 2 involves listening to our perceptions and expectations, and translating those into a responsible pattern of meeting our needs by tapping our yearnings. At Level 3, we move into harmony with our spiritual essence, or what Satir called the universal life force.

5

The Process of Change

Change is the cornerstone of therapy and education. This chapter focuses on changes, especially those involved when the process is in the hands of a therapist. In the Satir model, such changes frequently go beyond structural modifications. For example, if a family is concerned about the problem of a child's behavior, one intervention might be directed toward confirming the parents' roles and authority in relation to their children. The focus would be on boundaries and control issues within the family's structure.

The Satir model would instead focus on connecting parents and children at the level of yearnings, expectations, perceptions, and feelings. This would result in a system of sharing, acceptance, and respect as a matter of choice. It provides an internal shift for all family members and fundamentally changes each person's self-worth.

Change, then, as we use the term, is basically an internal shift that in turn brings about external change. This approach is not Satir's exclusively, but it represents a major difference from approaches that work on changing from the exterior or on changing behavior only.

Healing occurs through experiencing and learning about congruence. Satir used the analogy of a plumber, who does not sit down and try to get you to figure out how the hole in your pipe developed. He or she goes to the hole and does something to it. The repair has little or no relationship to how the hole got there. It may have developed through rust, but the plumber does not use rust to repair it.

Satir-model therapists evolve congruence in their clients from incongruence. This makes it possible for people to learn congruence without having to unlearn incongruence. To transform the survival stances into congruent communication, or to effect any other change, we need to examine the concepts of discovery, awareness, understanding, and new applications.

Discovery refers to what was in the past, to what exists now, and to how they are connected. For instance, we explore the picture of the client's events and the context in which a symptom developed. We also discover or uncover the coping patterns beneath the events. The person's reactions often include suppressed feelings of anger, panic, fear, and helplessness. From beneath these reactions, we find out about unmet expectations and unmet yearnings. These discoveries help us in the process of enhancing self-worth and congruence.

Awareness means developing a double listening attitude. We listen for content, and we listen for process. The content answers the question of what happened. It gives us the context in which to explore the process. We explore and listen to the internal process beyond the words. That process relates to meanings, feelings, feelings about feelings, family rules, and defenses.

We learn to hear what a client is saying without losing sight of his or her process. Communication that integrates content and process is the manifestation of high self-esteem, so it is important that we be aware of both levels when we work with people.

To *understand* means finding out, "How does the process work?" For example, "When my mother kissed my father, and my father then gave me a look that meant I should go out of the room, I thought he wanted to banish me. Now I can see he wanted privacy with my mother. I now understand." Understanding means learning how to make meaning of events and messages. Understanding means receiving the speaker's intent instead of judging the message based on our own projections.

New applications refer to what we have discovered, been able to appreciate, and now understand in new ways that support our growth. Some of these new ways are: that we need to gather information instead of making assumptions; that we are able to test our understanding rather than judging; and that we know how to negotiate and evolve rather than being competitive and demanding.

THE PRINCIPLE OF CHANGE

Working with the processes of discovery, awareness, understanding, and looking for new uses, we can help people transform their survival stances into more congruent forms of communicating. We use the word "transform" with specific intent to change rather than to extinguish or eliminate. Satir did not advocate eliminating placating or any other survival stance, for example. She added something else to what already existed, letting each stance come out as something new. This principle of transformation headlines all the therapeutic work we do and is expanded in detail throughout this book.

TRANSFORMING THE SURVIVAL STANCES

What can we add to the four survival stances to make something different? As the last chapter hinted, we add new perceptions, new ways of connecting, new feelings about our feelings, revised expectations, and new choices. The Satir vehicles show how to achieve this.

We don't ever have to focus on getting rid of anything. The idea is to add awareness, knowledge, manifes-

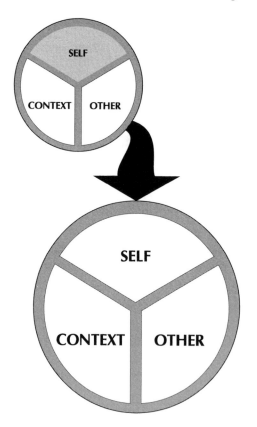

tation, and experience to make something else happen. Each stance already has the seed for wholeness and congruence. Adding an awareness of the self to placating, for instance, means caring about oneself as well as others. This transforms an old coping pattern to include a fuller sense of self-worth and equality.

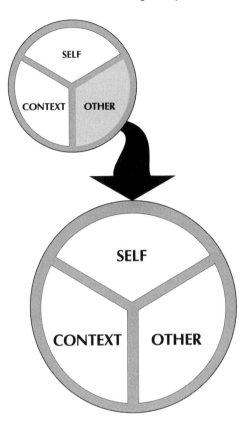

Adding an awareness of the other person to blaming fosters assertiveness without blame or judgment. This transforms the blamer's inner emptiness into self-validation and acceptance of the other.

When we add to the blaming response, we do not say, "Why are you always blaming? Don't you know nobody will come near you when you blame?" Instead, we figure out what to add by looking at this very phenomenon: nobody moves toward someone who is pointing the finger. So we add to that person's awareness by asking, "How does it feel?" This helps her get in touch with her loneliness.

Adding an awareness of self and other to super-reasonableness integrates the whole spectrum of affection, feelings, and body awareness with the person's existing

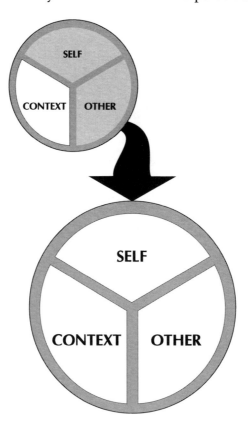

intelligence. Giving equal value to feelings and high intellect contributes great opportunities for harmony and wholeness.

Adding an awareness of self, other, and context to the irrelevant stance releases our flexibility, creativity, and openness to change within an appropriate context. This results in groundedness and presentness.

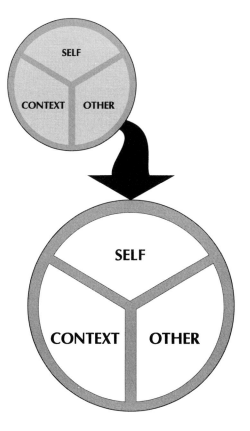

The process of changing these coping stances includes the following interventions. We ask for new pictures of possibilities and choices to extend our perceptions. We reframe old perceptions. We seek awareness of how the perceptions connect with our past learnings and how they contaminate our present perceptions. In this way, we separate our present perception from our past. We help the person make an internal decision to risk seeing him- or herself in a new light of responsibility.

When we look at unmet expectations and we let go of them, our *reactive feelings* (feelings about our feelings) change. Once we explore our expectations, they no longer control us. We can then respond congruently. Transforming our coping stances, which we once used to survive, leads to greater freedom and fewer restrictions imposed by our defenses. It also allows us more choices as to how we define and esteem ourselves.

Satir acknowledged that in certain circumstances we can choose to use survival stances in a congruent way. When we are stopped for speeding by an aggressive traffic cop, for example, we might choose to use our placating skills. In this sicutation we are not discounting the self, but placate in the interest of the self in awareness. Other situations may be well suited to our choosing anger, defensiveness, or super-reasonableness. We can use each coping stance in awareness instead of dealing with any threatening situation on automatic pilot.

THE CONTEXT FOR CHANGE

Virginia Satir believed change is possible for all of us. Even if no change is feasible on the outside, in our external circumstances—which is unlikely and rare—change is always possible on the inside.

At one level, change is natural and constant. The hours go by without our involvement. We merely decide how we spend our time. The seasons come and go. We decide merely how we experience them or how we want to react to them. Change at this "automatic" level is constant; change at the conscious level is more often potential or latent.

In itself, change is neither good nor bad. It can lead us to something that is either constructive or destructive. The question thus becomes what kind of change we are looking for. Satir clearly stated that *therapeutic change* provides greater congruence, greater freedom of choice, and greater responsibility for one's inner process, not only one's behavior.

Many individuals and families function at the survival level, sometimes for years, and firmly believe change is not possible. What brings them to our offices instead is their pain. The price for their status quo is getting to be too high, and they feel stuck.

Conscious change, including therapy, is the effort to develop a different sense of being, different expectations and perceptions, a different way of handling feelings, and more functional ways of coping. All this results in different behavior, of course, but the behavior represents only the visible, external form of the complex internal underpinnings.

Yet, as mentioned, the need for growth does not always call forth change. Newton's First Law of Motion states that matter continues in its state of rest or uniform motion unless it is compelled to change by forces acting on it. In human terms, most of us prefer our status quo over change. We need strong motivators to move from the familiar to a new state or place of comfort. These may be external motivators: a gun at one's head, a tornado on the prairies, a fire. Many less threatening external circumstances also catalyze change, of course.

Internal factors for change seem to be limited to three forces:

1. Threat, pain, or fear
2. Hope
3. Awareness

Individuals and families who come for therapy because of threat, fear, or pain make a major shift when they reframe their motivation into more positive goals. Rather than focusing on getting rid of something, they shift to working toward something. From needing help to reduce the fighting and possible family violence, for example, they reframe their goal into learning to accept each other more and achieving greater intimacy.

For example, imagine a family in which the father has been very busy for years establishing his business, leaving very little time for his son. The son behaved very cooperatively throughout elementary school. Now that the son is 15 years old, though, he becomes rebellious and argues with his father. The father becomes more and more frustrated and violent. The son is fighting back. Finally the wife convinces both to go for therapy.

Within the Satir model, the intervention would focus on the longings and yearnings for closeness, on caring and intimacy, and on the hurt and disappointment of unmet expectations. A closer connection between father and son at the level of feelings can result in expressing and negotiating new ways of accepting and understanding each other's needs. In other words, the intervention would not focus on their behavior but on new ways of relating and meeting each person's needs and expectations.

Other levels of motivation to change come out of our drive to survive. Threats at this level include:

"If I don't stop smoking, I will die."

"If I don't get help with this wound, I will bleed to death."

"If I do not stop physically abusing my spouse, I will go to jail."

These clients feel a sense of desperation. This leads to hopelessness, which drives them to "have to change."

Accepting Our Clients

As Satir-model therapists, we accept people's desperation, fear, survival threats, and pain. We connect with their inner selves and their yearnings. In effect, we accept their fears and desperation at the same time we reach out to them and validate them as worthwhile human beings.

For the family system to be open enough to change, its members need a loving, accepting atmosphere, a climate of trust and safety. The therapist needs to connect with each client at a level that is deeper than that at which the problem appears. In the Satir model, making contact and connecting with each family member is done through:

- Making direct eye contact
- Touching (i.e., shaking hands)
- Being at the same physical level
- Asking each person's name, and asking how he or she would like to be called
- Modeling equality of value by sharing

These elements of the process help family members feel more accepted, validated, and willing to take greater risks. Following this initial contact, the Satir-model therapist asks each family member what his or her hopes and wishes are for the session, paying full attention to each person instead of focusing on "the problem." It is important to remember that for coping and changing, the problem is not the problem.

Conveying Hope

People do not have to wait to undo a whole lot of stuff before they learn new and healthier responses. This is one of the difficulties many clients expect in therapy: they think they have to struggle with their many old learnings before they can learn and use something new.

Therapists can convey the hope that we all have the capacity to learn anew at any stage of life. At any time, people can say, "There must be a better way, and I will find it." This often helps move clients away from the attitude of: "Well, I've had this habit for thirty years, and there's no use in changing, and I probably can't," or "You can't teach an old dog new tricks." It isn't true of dogs, and it certainly isn't true of human beings.

Faith is an important ingredient here. People who believe something different is possible for them have faith, and are therefore willing to begin the process of change. But even when they know change is possible, that does not guarantee its success. Change requires an anticipatory attitude toward a positive goal, not just moving away from a painful or fearful state. It is far more useful to say, "I want to start a new class and meet people who are interested in that subject" than "I want to stop feeling so alone." A positively stated goal gives us a picture, a map, a desired outcome.

People often also need a considerable amount of help to bring about change. Hope alone will not do it. The past might still have a very strong hold on the present; old feelings might be unresolved or denied; and people might have very few skills to implement the changes their hopes generate.

Therapists can help them see they have the resources to learn those skills and make the necessary changes: to confront their familiar, dysfunctional, reactive patterns and make improvements. At first, family members often coattail on the therapist's sense of trust in this process of change. Gradually, one after another, they develop their own sense of trust in the therapeutic process, as well as in themselves.

Establishing Credibility

The context for change also needs to be believable. People need to find the desired changes plausible. The therapist needs to be credible. And the interventions need to make sense to the clients. The person who comes for help for depression does not develop a sturdy therapeutic relationship with a therapist who asks a lot of routine, impersonal questions about the client's toilet-training experiences. Therapists who neglect their credibility in this manner are like the alcoholic who looks for his car keys under the street lamp. He is searching under the lamp, he says, because there is more light there than where he dropped his keys.

In addition, the therapist establishes credibility by displaying confidence, competence, and high self-esteem. He or she creates a context of comfort, without interruptions and with a minimum of distractions. The therapist is open to questions about his or her background, qualifications, experience, and personal information. To add to internal awareness, he or she processes the family members' comments and interactions immediately without judging or diagnosing them.

Instilling Awareness

The third internal factor that motivates change is simply an awareness and acknowledgment that change is always happening. This contributes to the attitude that things can and will get better, and that we can make this happen.

In the first step of change, the person asks, "What can I add to what is already there to make something different?" The fact that we add something changes what was. We do not have to try to change it; simply putting something else into it starts the process. This keeps everything at a positive level, moving forward.

Following the Process

Again, the growing process depends on faith. This suggests a major shift from the *content outcome* to the *process outcome*. If I am angry because I did not get a promotion (the content outcome), dealing with my anger congruently will not get me that promotion. It allows me to deal more realistically with my expectations and requires me to define myself positively even without the promotion.

Once we follow process outcomes, we also follow our own sense of centeredness. If our expectations about the outcomes precede our process, we define ourselves accordingly. If the outcome follows our process, our congruence remains intact and we have a choice about how to handle any feelings of disappointment. When we are congruent, any outcome creates positive energy for our next step of growth.

For instance, when Sam expects to have supper prepared for his wife at 7 p.m. and it is not ready, he might feel totally discounted if she expresses disappointment. In this case, Sam has defined himself by a content outcome that preceded the process.

Satir used the metaphor that when we present something in a round way, we know there are no corners. Consider two balls that have come together. They can meet at any part of their respective surfaces because they are round. In other words, when we meet in our congruency, we have infinite possibilities.

To appreciate the complexity of change, we need to look outside the linear (one cause, one effect) model, as some physicists and biologists have done. The change process does not depend on a single variable. Things happen in clusters.

A cluster immediately implies a system: an action, a reaction, and an interaction. Change, then, is like an umbrella term for everything that happens in life and that has dimensions of differences. It is epitomized by the evolution of a larva into a butterfly.

SATIR'S STAGES OF CHANGE

Once therapists establish an accepting, positive context for change, they can help clients begin the process of change. Regardless of motivation, people who want to change go through a certain series of steps. According to Satir, this process has six stages:

1. Status quo: Within the person's or system's existing state, the need for change emerges.

2. Introduction of a foreign element: The system or individual articulates the need for change to another person—friend, therapist, or someone

else outside the system.

3. Chaos: The system or individual begins moving from a status quo into a state of disequilibrium.

4. Integration: New learnings are integrated, and a new state of being evolves.

5. Practice: The new state is strengthened by practicing the new learnings.

6. New status quo: The new status quo represents a more functional state of being.

Stage 1: Status Quo

When a system is in *status quo*, we can make reliable predictions about how it is operating. The system has set up a clear set of expectations and reactions. We can count on these. Their repetition is self-reinforcing and, through repetition, members of the system grow to feel these expectations and reactions are right. They have become familiar.

A family's status quo, then, is embedded in experience and results in powerful stances and beliefs. When a family is in a healthy balance, every member contributes or "pays" as much as he or she receives. For example, when a mother needs to stay late at work, her husband and/or children prepare dinner. Or, when a new baby is born, the older children still feel loved and wanted. If they do feel superseded, it lasts for a short time only before a healthy balance is restored. Thus, the exchange of values is fair and just. Few, if any, "residuals" are collected.

Similarly, in a healthy, balanced family, a child comes home with a note from the teacher stating he had cheated on an exam. In a nurturing way, the parents discuss the event with the child and the teacher. They make it clear that the child's cheating behavior is unacceptable, and they do so in such a way that his self-esteem is not impaired. He knows he is loved and that his cheating is not acceptable. They separate the person from the behavior.

With an unhealthy system, every family member has to contribute much more than he or she receives. Nobody comes out ahead, either. The exchange of values is unfair and unjust, yet stable. Over the years, residuals such as anger, fear, unmet expectations, lack of closeness, and limited intimacy are collected by various members of the family.

Some of these residuals turn into physical symptoms such as ulcers, headaches, and backaches. Sometimes one member of the family gets to be the black sheep or the scapegoat; this alleviates some of the excess pressure without changing the system's status quo. In an unhealthy system, numerous members can become symptom bearers of one kind or another.

We know a system is unhealthy when its members routinely cope by placating, blaming, being super-reasonable, or being irrelevant. We know that at least one person is paying more than he or she gets. In time, all individuals in an unhealthy system pay more than they receive. This is why, by the way, every member we interview is likely to tell us that he or she carries more burdens than the others and that the system is not fair.

Dysfunctionally balanced families continue their patterns until something relatively drastic happens. Something gives, and finally somebody in the system goes for help. The new pain might be too great, the behavior brought on by the crisis might be unacceptable, or unusual conflict may have erupted openly.

Therapy is only one of the possibilities for coping with crisis. Family members may also turn to friends, religion, separation, substance abuse, violence, or depression. These are all common alternatives and reactions to disruptions in the unhealthy system's balance. When a family system comes to the stage of unbearable pain, some members might try to cope through extensive use of alcohol or drugs, for example. After some time of alcohol abuse, that becomes the new problem. And when the family finally goes for therapy, the alcohol abuse is often the focus, while the original systemic family pain has gone underground. In the Satir model, the therapeutic task is to find the thread that leads back to the original systemic crisis.

Within this first stage in the process of change, when the family's status quo is disrupted, we see a lot of protection patterns. For example, when the father is abusing alcohol, we often find the mother using denial and excusing her husband's drinking with a series of alibis. In therapy, the family often presents a child's behavior as the problem. On one level, this deflects attention from the drinking; at another level, it distracts from the family's systemic dysfunction.

Protection, including our concept of resistance, is a survival resource for most members of an unhealthy system. It is an important basic belief of the Satir model that people do the best they can with what they know and what they perceive. Understanding this allows us to accept people's positions as a starting place and then help them move from there.

Stage 2: Introduction of a Foreign Element

Stage 2 marks the introduction of an element from outside the system, that is, somebody who wasn't there before. In the case of therapy, the foreign element is the psychotherapist or family counselor. For therapy to work, this outside person needs to be accepted by the majority of the system's members; this is why establishing a context for change is so important in initial sessions.

Making Contact

Beyond conveying acceptance, hope, credibility, and an awareness of change, Satir-model therapists find it vital to model congruence. Congruent communication is a powerful aspect of any intervention, and interventions in a family system need to be powerful. After all, we are asking family members to open themselves to entertain the prospect of deviating from their secure, familiar status quo.

The therapist needs to be in charge of the process, not the family. At first, some members may want to collect unpaid debts from other members or get even. The therapist therefore needs to connect very quickly with each individual, make contact, and validate each one's humanity. The most important aspect here is to make a personal connection below the level of the coping dynamics and survival stances.

Several dangers exist at this point. The first is colluding with one or more of the members, most frequently the parents (or whoever has the most power). Another is becoming enmeshed with the system and losing objectivity or, worse, having the system overpower and disempower the therapist.

A third danger involves the system's natural tendency to continue its status quo. This means the family may try to expel any foreign element during the early part of the change process. Therapists may feel quite alone if this happens and may consequently be tempted to placate, blame, be super-reasonable, or be irrelevant.

Instead, this is the time to be congruent. We want to facilitate the development of some new possibilities and work toward increasing the self-worth of each family member. By modeling congruence, we give them hope. With a physical metaphor, we might say we are helping them to know their backs even though they cannot see their backs.

Examining Expectations

One way we can help people know themselves in new ways is to explore their attitudes and expectations about change. One commonly held attitude is expecting another person to change and so solve our problems. This is a power struggle inherent in the hierarchical model of human growth. Rather than discussing the issue at hand, people who operate within this perspective care about (and argue about) who is right or wrong, who is up or down, who is the winner or loser, and who has the right to tell whom what to do.

Behind this struggle is the message of self-worth: "Do I count? If I count, you do as I say." This means we constantly adjust ourselves and our ideas to fit outside demands. We close off our insides for fear of being rejected.

Being whole has nothing to do with good or bad, right or wrong. It means we are connected with self and others in a harmonious way. Our words further our body messages and vice versa. We face and deal with whatever issues arise. We share our feelings. We take the risk of being vulnerable. We ask for what we want.

Examining Barriers to Change

Sometimes it is helpful for us and for our clients to look at the many ways we believe we cannot change. Doing this lets us see what kinds of barriers we are putting in our own way. Satir once worked with a lady who wanted to lose weight. "Carol" was very open and free in her therapy sessions with all kinds of information. She especially emphasized all the help she had sought to change her weight. Nothing had succeeded.

Satir finally asked, "What problems would you face if you did lose this weight?" Carol immediately replied that she would not be able to control herself sexually with all the men who might find her attractive.

That gave Carol's therapy a new point of reference, a contextual frame. The issue was no longer a matter of simply losing weight. It became a process of working with Carol's fantasies, fears, protective parts, her definition of herself (including her self-worth), and her choices.

Common barriers to change include attitudes about being "too much" or "not enough," be it in the realm of intelligence, age, money, size, energy, education, experience, fear, confidence, or self-worth. Two important barriers are:

1. Any rules that negate your feelings
2. Any feelings you have that you believe you cannot change

Rules that negate your feelings reach deeper than any particular feelings themselves. Usually family based, these rules result in not feeling integrated, being uninterested, feeling empty, never feeling quite good enough, and being driven in one closed direction. To allow our life energy to flow freely once again, we need to identify and change these rules.

Reframing Resistance as Dignity

What is this construct called *resistance?* According to Satir, it is people's way to say they are okay, even if they do not feel that way. They present themselves in this light, and our role is to accept them without worrying about "resistance." After all, resistance has served them well in the past.

The Satir model suggests we acknowledge our clients at the highest level of their dignity. We can then look at how they developed that and what they are protecting themselves against. This is far more effective than breaking down or overpowering resistance with a power trip. By turning on new light, we can notice what our clients haven't seen yet: that what they have been protecting, and has been purposeful in the past, no longer needs to be hidden or defended.

Let's look at a simple example. "Alex" indicates he would like to have more companions. He likes to have people like him. But every time somebody comes up to him, he seems aloof. Some people might say he is showing resistance. Others might ask Alex, "You said you wanted friends, so why are you behaving like that?" This approach tries to break down his self-protectiveness.

The Satir approach asks, "I noticed, Alex, when Carol came over to you and her hands were reaching out to you, you moved back. I wonder if you noticed that?" He can either say, "Yes, I did," or "No, I didn't."

If he says yes, we might ask the following questions, in sequence.

1. How did you feel when you moved back?

2. How did you feel about feeling that way?

3. Are you aware of a pattern that this suggests?

4. Have you ever experienced accepting such a reaching out, from Carol or others?

5. Knowing all this, how do you feel differently?

6. What new decisions are you willing to make?

7. What new activities are you willing to plan and implement? (For example, Alex might find it helpful to visualize himself welcoming and accepting people reaching out to him.)

Each of the above questions might require some exploration. We need to remember that people who show high resistance often interpret questions as blaming; they then frequently resist even more. To avoid this, we need to show clients like Alex a lot of acceptance and let them take their time. We are striving to have them be aware of, acknowledge, and then talk to us about their protective behavior at the survival level.

If Alex says, "No, I didn't notice myself backing away," his awareness is probably still missing. So we might say, "Is it possible that you withdrew without even being aware of it?"

"Yes."

"How does it feel, looking at the possibility you withdrew? How do you feel about that feeling? Any old patterns or experiences of withdrawal or denial that come to mind?" Explore these feelings and patterns; they often reflect an earlier time in the client's life.

With acceptance, gentle exploration, and trust in the therapist, people usually accept their protective part's value as "saving face" or preserving their dignity. With this new awareness, they can envision new possibilities of achieving what they actually want: closeness and companionship. They move to a new self-acceptance and willingness to risk.

So-called resistance contains all the ingredients for reframing. *Reframing*, in the Satir model, refers to interventions in which the therapist helps clients see themselves as capable and open to change. They can then explore more fulfilling ways to handle their fears and defensiveness.

Another way of looking at resistance is to compare it to getting out from under a blanket in a cold house. Rather than removing the blanket, we can start by heating the house. Once we feel warm, safe, and trusting, we will remove the blanket—our protection—and relax.

Often, the greater the survival value we place on the change, the more we push ourselves and the more resistant we become. This stimulates our fear and panic, and we feel less and less confident about changing. Eventually, or often after only a short time, we give up.

To change any habit—smoking, overeating, not exercising, and so on—we first need to accept the habit as a friend. As one of Satir's meditations says, take that which you no longer need, bless it for what it has done for you, and then set it free. In some "strange" way, many of these habits have protected us from something. We can accept them in that sense and reduce our fear through that acceptance.

Even better, we can replace our fear with acceptance, build a more trusting context for change, and then work to increase our self-esteem as it relates to that habit. We thus make our habit a friend before we change our need for it.

In the case of Alex, withdrawal had protected him from being pushed around. As a child, he had used anger to hold his life together. Anger became his protection for survival. By feeling his anger, he could avoid feeling his loneliness and his longing for intimacy. Afraid of being hurt, he separated himself from others and failed to connect with people.

As he grew older, people told him to stop being angry. He did not do so. Anger had become a form to hold himself intact. As long as people pushed him to behave differently, his anger got stronger and he withdrew more and more.

Since most such patterns are learned in earlier days, therapists need to help clients put their whole experience into a new context and find better, more functional ways of living and growing. For Alex, this means starting by recognizing anger and withdrawal as friends, his protection against people who did not (and did not try to) understand his feelings. Once he can acknowledge and accept this function of his anger and withdrawal, Alex can then talk about it in therapy.

Later, within a safe, here-and-now context, his therapist can help him look at new choices for protecting himself. These entail more effective ways of meeting his basic need to be understood.

If we can bless and let go of the habits and the judges within us, we can also let go of our resistance to change. Actually, both serve a similar purpose, and both can be transformed in similar ways. Blessing is a form of empowering ourselves—it does not descend from outside ourselves. And it enables us to go farther to find a more successful way of dealing with the Self.

Stage 3: Chaos

After the successful entry of a therapist, the family gradually starts to open up, at least to the extent of looking at itself. Simply by recognizing, acknowledging, and examining its routine expectations and reactive patterns, the system begins its process of change. Without necessarily even being aware of it, the family leaves its status quo (of taking its unwritten rules for granted) and ventures toward a new set of dynamics. A state of chaos inevitably results.

Chaos means the system is now operating in ways we cannot predict. For many members, not being able to foretell their family's expectations and reactions means they have lost their security and stability. They are in limbo, sometimes paralyzed by their fear of destruction. They may also feel a sense of loss or impending loss and consequently panic. Satir related the following example.

> *When I did my first successful family therapy work with a schizophrenic [in 1951], the status quo idea came to me while I was with the schizophrenic daughter. Chaos set in when the girl began to change. The mother was threatening a heart attack, the father looked like he was going out of his tree. In effect, all hell broke loose. And I said to myself, "Oh, my God, what did I do?"*
>
> *That is the time I became aware that chaos was a natural and necessary part of the therapy process. What I needed to do most was to steady myself, to keep myself centered and not panic. I simply continued to work with the individual and her parents through the chaos phase toward a new beginning. It was a great lesson for me.*

Normalizing Fear and Anxiety

In the early part of this phase, family members may feel as though the familiar ground is shifting beneath their feet. They feel they are losing control, and their fear of the unknown looms large. At this point, new possibilities are not obvious to the family.

Therapists normalize this chaotic stage by neutralizing clients' fear and anxiety. Opening up the opportunity for something new—new possibilities—lifts the taboo against looking at, feeling, and commenting about one's self. This helps family members to be open and aware of their internal processes. The therapist stays congruent, does not panic, and supports and accepts the family members as they go through the chaos stage.

During the most severe moments of chaos for a client, the Satir model suggests keeping the person very much anchored in the present. This phase is the time for only those decisions that can be executed in the next ten seconds. Making long-term plans during the chaos stage is like making long-term decisions during a state of rage.

Client levels of anxiety are the highest during this chaos stage. Feeling their vulnerability keenly, they are looking for safety. This is also the time when people are most likely to make categorical criticisms and protective categorical statements such as, "I'll never talk to you again," and "I'll see to it that you'll not be in my will."

When a client takes such a position, the Satir model advocates standing back, becoming grounded, and moving the conversation toward the person's feelings. Explore the expectations below these outbursts.

Satir practiced and encouraged a lot of physical contact at this stage of change. You may want to stay very much connected with the individual client or the family members, maybe even by touching their hands, or one shoulder, or whatever seems most appropriate.

To bring change out of the most severe moments of chaos, the therapist needs to remain centered, grounded, focused, and in charge of the process. Otherwise, clients may move back to their original unhealthy patterns. Of course, if they do, the therapist just starts the whole process over again.

The *therapist* also needs to be balanced physically, breathe *normally,* and approach the family and the therapeutic process with reverence and hope. If the therapist tries to avoid or negate the chaos, "therapy" can drag on for years with very little deep change. Some therapists don't like their clients to feel pain or anxiety, and therefore allow or even encourage their return to old, familiar patterns. Sometimes the therapist panics and the clients lose trust; they may not return for further sessions.

The chaos phase is when the healing begins. Clients let go of their positions or perceptions that no longer fit or that are too costly to hold. They consider a new perception of self and others. Only by working with chaos can the therapist help clients rearrange, restructure, update, and change their perceptions and expectations.

Simultaneously, the therapist showers clients with acceptance, love, hope, and encouragement. Integrity, honesty, and firmness are likewise essential. Humor can be helpful, and good jokes are often appropriate, especially the cosmic variety. A *cosmic joke* is a moment when we see the ridiculous or humorous aspect in what we had taken so seriously, namely ourselves in a situation we approached with a life-or-death attitude.

This is no time to avoid stress, however. For many clients, this phase is a very taxing time, sometimes lasting minutes, sometimes days. To help individuals and the family handle stress, it is important to:

- Acknowledge their stress and its underlying dynamics, such as fear.

- Normalize the stress by helping people accept it as part of the change process.

- Use it to move the process along: provide attention and acceptance, validate family members, and encourage each of them to use his or her resources, including support systems, to stay with the process of change.

- Keep the client(s) focused on their present feelings.

The depth of the change process relates directly to the skill of the therapist. To risk changing, clients need to trust the therapist. Trust depends a lot on a sense of confidence in the therapist. It develops as the system risks opening itself to new possibilities.

Getting Stuck

We have found that if a therapist gets stuck in the therapy process, it is usually at this stage. He or she begins to over-identify with the process of the client or gets enmeshed to some degree with an individual or the family. Most often this relates directly to an unfinished part in the therapist's life.

If this happens, we suggest the therapist get help by consulting a colleague. The most helpful and long-lasting step is to have one's own Family Reconstruction done (see Chapter 9).

Surfacing Family Rules

Satir raised people's self-worth by adding new dimensions to the rules they learned in their family of origin. One such rule might be: "I should never talk back to adults." This can be changed into a guideline that provides more choices, as in:

I can sometimes talk back to adults:
(a) When I want to express my feelings.
(b) When I feel I am being abused.
(c) When I feel discounted.

For more about how to change rules into guidelines, see Chapter 11.

Rigid rules and low self-worth often result in physical, emotional, and intellectual symptoms in family members. Congruent communication holds the opportunities for developing self-worth. A person's way of communicating reflects much of the information about what he or she has learned to date. We can also simultaneously explore the means by which he or she learned to cope. For instance, if the family rule is not to express anger, the child in adult life may avoid anger-evoking situations at any cost or, at the other extreme, use violence to cope with any feelings of anger.

Family rules also function to keep the *closed family system* operating. A closed system, according to Satir, is characterized by members who:

- Are guarded with each other
- Are hostile
- Feel powerless and controlled and are passive
- Are inflexible in their views and behaviors
- Wear a facade of indifference toward each other

Symptoms appear when the family's rules squeeze a member's self-worth to such a point that his or her survival is in question.

Providing the Context for Change During the Chaos Phase

As a whole, even dysfunctional systems generally have a predictable set of expectations and behavior patterns. Beneath each member's coping patterns lies a personal iceberg of unexpressed inner life. Once we see the balancing act of each member, we can zero in on particular possibilities for change.

Coping styles are person-specific. Their motivating dynamics, though, follow a universal process. To move the system toward less painful functioning, the therapist needs to address both the specific and the universal dynamics.

As therapists, we can use the story line that our clients bring to the session to help them consider areas for change. For example, if we see a family with teenagers who seem to fight a lot while doing the dishes, we might use that as the context to look at:

- Power struggles
- Parental conflicts
- Absence of validation
- Lack of intimacy

or a host of other possibilities that somehow affect the self-esteem of the teenagers. The point is that they are using dysfunctional behavior to meet their needs; using this content can help therapists create a context for change.

It does not matter whether the family's symptom is expressed semantically, nonverbally, intellectually, or in some combination. The individual's self-worth then has to find another way to express itself. Therapy can be a fruitful way to explore this, and steps in the chaos stage may shed light on the matter.

Steps in the Chaos Phase

1. Keep contact with the person or family.
2. Establish a contract.
3. Set the context for change.
4. Make connections with the internal process of each person.
5. If an "event" is the problem:
   a. Sculpt a scene (to increase awareness)
   b. Identify expectations (to work toward acceptance)
   c. Identify feelings (so that the person experiences them)
   d. Separate the past from the present (to achieve de-enmeshment, especially of perceptions, expectations, and feelings among and between family members)
   e. Refocus yearnings and tap inner resources
   f. Accept the past in memory, without expectations
   g. Return to the present: reframe present perceptions and expectations, and work toward transformation
   h. Honor the Self in present terms
6. Provide support, acceptance, hope, and possibilities.

One of Satir's major contributions in conceptualizing the process of change was that she recognized and used this stage of chaos. It is significant because it accepts people's fear of the unknown, anxiety, uncertainty, and panic. It also utilizes them in a positive, creative way to move the person or system from a dysfunctional status quo to a new, functional state of being.

Satir discovered that without this stage of chaos, no profound transformation of old, familiar survival copings could occur. Attaining positive, healthier, and more functional possibilities requires moving through a period of chaos.

Stage 4: New Options and Integration

Stage 4 entails developing new possibilities, using dormant resources, integrating our parts, and reevaluating past and present expectations. We accept new perceptions of our parents, our life experiences, our self-worth, and our future.

Letting go of many survival patterns of coping, we can accept new ways of being. If we never asked for what we wanted, we now begin. We break our long-time silence, decide how we want to perceive and accept ourselves, and ask for how we want others to perceive and accept us. We take charge of what we once did on automatic pilot, bringing our control back into consciousness, and becoming more responsible for our internal process of Self.

As we use new, healthy, open ways of accepting, feeling, sharing, and commenting on our inner experiences, we also learn to differentiate between body clues that go with our old experiences and those that accompany our new learnings.

For example, people in a closed system often do not differentiate between anxiety and excitement. They interpret everything as anxiety. As they transform themselves into an open system, they begin to notice and accept the difference and are relieved to discover that they feel excitement more often than anxiety. Joyfulness, new hope, and new or regained energy become part of their new status quo.

Stage 5: Implementation

Stage 5 is the practice stage. We need to remember that the power of past patterns is very strong. To maintain and practice our new options, we need to develop strong support. If we do well, we establish a healthy new status quo with a more present-focused life energy.

At this stage, therapists might need to have clients write things down, or have reminders in the car, on the refrigerator door, on the kitchen bulletin board, or in the bathroom. They also may want to encourage clients to use amulets, affirmations, meditations, and anchoring exercises to reduce the lure of past patterns.

People are often surprised that their behavior has become so automatic and so reactive. Simultaneously, as they practice what once was strange, it too becomes familiar and provides comfort. After some practice, systems and individuals once again develop predictable patterns of acting and being. This is also a time for people to practice new ways of:

- Looking and seeing
- Connecting and relating with others
- Enjoying intimacy
- Validating self and others
- Acting on their own behalf
- Feeling about self, others, and context
- Feeling about feelings

The underlying question becomes, "How do I want to be as I develop my life with congruence and high self-esteem, and feel integrated at various levels?" It is toward growth, wholeness, and functioning more fully that we can now give our attention.

The question is not, "Do I want to grow and change?" Rather, it is, "How can we get out of the way what has become a block in the natural flow of functioning more fully?"

To get your focus on change, we would like you to do an exercise. It helps if you do this with another person. If you do it on your own, it helps to share it with somebody later.

Think of a major change that took place in your life in the last twelve months, and write it on a piece of paper. You may have quit a job, taken a new lover, had a son or daughter move away from home, acquired a new car, had a close friend stop seeing you, decided to have an operation, or gone on a trip.

Next, go through the following questions.

- Did you choose to make this change?

- Was it an "automatic" change—something you didn't plan or think about much?

- Was it a change imposed on you from outside?

- If the change was imposed on you, what choices did you have but did not take?

- If imposed, what reactions did you have? What did you do with those reactions?

- Was the change a result of numerous consequences or events you did not attend to?

- Was it a result of pain? Of seeing new possibilities? Of being bored?

- Was it sudden, or was it in the making for some time?

- Was it connected to a deep yearning? Did it provide some fulfillment of becoming more fully functioning?

- Was the change connected with an expectation you had held for many years?
- Was it connected to your perception of what should be done?
- Was the change based on a strong feeling?
- Was it based on a reaction to a strong feeling, expectation, or perception?
- Was the change based on some survival issue? Did it give you some better coping opportunities?

These questions derive from the Satir model of change. They explore the various layers of process that are usually involved in making a major change. The next set is useful when the change has already taken place.

- Has the change left you with any guilt, anger, hurt, or disappointment?
- Are you pleased, happy, joyful?
- Are you relieved, less tense, less stressed?
- Do you see yourself in a different light (either better or worse)?
- Did you lose or gain any confidence with this change?
- Do you perceive others differently (more favorably or less so) since the change?

You may simply say, "It depends," and leave it at that. Or you may use this exercise as an exciting exploration of how much you decide for yourself, how well you manage your feelings, and how you motivate yourself to make changes.

We suggest you share your awareness and your learnings from this exercise with someone else. This helps you integrate the experience. We also suggest asking a friend or two to do the exercise and share their experiences, awarenesses, thoughts, and feelings with you.

Stage 6: The New Status Quo

The sixth stage provides a new status quo, a healthier equilibrium, and individuals and relationships that function more fully. A new sense of comfort has taken the place of the old familiarity. A new set of predictions develops about how the system operates. New self-images and new hopes emerge. Greater spontaneity and creativity are set free, and an enhanced sense of well-being radiates.

Many small changes take place in the process of therapy, of course. Clients or client families may need a lot of work—and may make many repeat trips from Stage 1 to Stage 6—before major transformations occur.

STAGE 1
Status Quo
Need for change indicated;
pain, unbalance, etc.

STAGE 2
Need for change articulated.
Foreign element enters.

STAGE 3
Chaos
Movement from
dysfunctional to
functional state.
From familiar
to unknown.
Fear, anxiety

STAGE 4
Integration of
new learnings.
New security
New comfort
New hope

STAGE 5
Practice
strengthening
of new state.

STAGE 6
New Status Quo
Equality
Harmony
Wholeness
Balance
Open to new possibilities &
comfort instead
of familiarity

SUMMARY

In the Satir model, the process of change has six stages. One builds upon the other, just as we build new learnings upon old ones. These stages are not singular; instead, they are multiphasic and repetitious. We might start by considering one thread from early childhood to the present. This focus widens and multiplies once we encounter the complexity of our human nature. We eventually graduate to working on numerous threads at the same time.

The process of change continues throughout life. It might become easier, more joyful, and more hope-filled every time we go through these stages. Perhaps there will even come a time when each individual can go through these stages with his or her own source of energy, with his or her own self providing the context, trust, risk-taking, and support to bring about further breakthroughs and growth opportunities.

Meanwhile, the next chapter looks at one of the more exciting vehicles for change, called the Ingredients of an Interaction.

6

The Ingredients of an Interaction

Instead of developing a set of simple techniques that were easy to learn, Virginia Satir developed what she called *vehicles for change*. These relatively comprehensive interventions bring about significant changes in the individual and the family system or various other systems. Her best-known vehicles are the Parts Party, which integrates a person's inner parts and resources; and Family Reconstruction, in which a person relives formative experiences that were influenced by three or more generations of his or her family.

During a later period, Satir developed a third vehicle, the Ingredients of an Interaction. This started as a close look at our internal communication process and evolved into one of the major change strategies in the Satir paradigm. We can use the "Ingredients" independent of any other technique or vehicle. It is also an excellent way to teach clients about process, as later sections of this chapter demonstrate.

The Ingredients intervention focuses on the pattern or sequence of our internal mental and emotional steps through which we process messages. For example, when we are confused, we might react from our internal interpretation instead of verifying the reality or intention of the message we received. This interpretation may or may not be present-based. In fact, most of us have patterns that are rooted firmly in the past.

The Ingredients of an Interaction explores two factors that influence our patterns of interacting:

1. The family rules we follow for processing information

2. Our coping style, which reflects our self-worth and gives us the basis for how we hear, feel, react, defend, and comment.

Satir saw a relationship between the way people perceive their own worth and how they cope, behave, and express themselves. Instead of focusing on their behavior, she paid attention to their perceptions, feelings, and expectations. She understood that people's behavior does not always match their internal condition or process.

She also knew that the way we behave and perceive represents what we learned in the past for our survival. Until we transform the survival patterns we developed as children, we continue to use them. These patterns include how we treat ourselves, how we treat others, and how we expect others to treat us.

We are all manifesting what we have learned, usually in our primary triad during our early years. Much of what we learned no longer serves us well. Yet, being familiar with certain coping patterns out of awareness, we continue to use them automatically.

THERAPEUTIC GOALS

The Ingredients of an Interaction is a powerful tool for identifying what we have learned and replacing our old learnings with more relevant, up-to-date, healthy ways to interact. It brings to light the process we learned when we were trying to survive in a dysfunctional system.

Once we learn about and can follow our internal process, we can change our defenses and rules for commenting. This raises our self-worth, allowing us to relate to ourselves, others, and our context in healthier ways. We can change our process and our communication into being congruent.

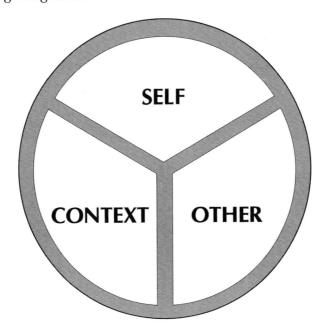

In other words, with the Ingredients process, we learn to:

1. Change our coping patterns, learning to communicate congruently

2. Increase our self-worth

3. Update our rules into guidelines

4. Reduce our defensiveness

The biggest hindrance to communicating congruently is that crippling aspects of our past still control us in the present. What we work toward with the Ingredients is a more fully functioning way of being. This means greater realness, wholeness, and connectedness; a free-flowing internal process; and less contamination from our past (especially from family rules).

THE PROCESS

The Ingredients intervention begins with six questions people ask themselves about specific interactions. They are:

1. What do I hear and see?

2. What meaning do I make of what I hear and see?

3. What feelings do I have about the meaning I make?

4. What feelings do I have about these feelings?

5. What defenses do I use?

6. What rules for commenting do I use?

Therapist and client then explore each of these questions in detail.

What Do I Hear and See?

Simply put, at this step of interacting we human beings are like video cameras. We take a picture and record the sound. We take in information with all our senses and assume we hear and see that information objectively and without bias.

However, few of us can actually report just what we hear and see. Some police officers learn this skill in their training programs. Very few therapy programs teach it. The most important part is to separate the sensory awareness from the interpretation. For instance, we need to use our senses to see, hear, smell, taste, and touch "what is." Usually we make the interpretation so fast that our sensory awareness gets distorted.

- This *differential awareness* or separation between event and interpretation needs to be taught. A simple way to start is to ask the client to state what he or she saw and heard. When Pat met Sue for the first time, for example, he did not look at her or shake hands. Sue immediately interpreted that Pat was not interested in her. Pat, on the other hand, was shy and thought he should not shake a lady's hand unless she invites him to. Without checking out Pat's intentions, Sue misinterpreted his behavior.

What Meaning Do I Make?

We humans have a very strong drive to make meaning out of everything we experience. This holds true from the simple level of making sense of a long, thin object lying on a dark street to deciding what life itself means.

Many of the meanings we ascribe to events, people, and experiences are based on our past learnings, past experiences, and our own level of self-worth. To base our interpretations on present reality instead, we need to recognize and distinguish how we ascribe meanings from "what is" or what others mean when they behave a certain way.

Continuing with the example of Pat and Sue, the therapist would ask Sue what she saw Pat do. Once Sue can describe this without interpreting it, Sue then asks Pat what he meant. Allowing herself to separate her meaning from his intent, Sue can hear the message differently.

How Do I Feel About This Meaning?

Very often our cognitive process is foremost when we decide on the meaning of what we see and hear. In this step, it becomes the background, and our feelings become the foreground—the center of our interest. We now personalize what we see and hear, getting in touch with our feelings about the meaning. We are no longer focusing "objectively" on what we see and hear.

In our practices, we find people have a difficult time distinguishing their feelings from their meanings. In terms of effective therapy, it is important in the Satir model to separate feelings from meanings. We have seen how, if Sue does not verify Pat's intent and responds according to her own interpretation, she might feel rejected and discounted. However, if she finds out Pat's behavior is related to his shyness and insecurity, she might reach out and invite him to shake her hand.

Separating what we perceive from what we interpret about it allows us to recognize that other possible meanings exist. Distinguishing our interpretation from our feelings about it allows us to check out the other person's intent before we choose a response.

How Do I Feel About My Feelings?

How we feel about our feelings indicates a decision or a judgment we have made about our feelings (e.g., "I shouldn't feel this way"). In congruent behavior and relationships, we accept and own our feelings without judgment, and we handle them (as well as other components) with a positive, open mind.

In our incongruent moments, we decide against accepting or expressing our feelings. If we feel angry, for example, we may feel terrible about it and decide not to let anyone know we are seeing red. If we are hurt, we may feel ashamed about that feeling. If we feel rejected, we may feel terrified. If we feel juicy and attracted toward the neighbor's spouse, we might feel guilty.

Recognizing how people feel about their feelings indicates most clearly where many of the therapeutic interventions are needed. People need a lot more help with these reactive feelings than with how they feel about the meanings they make. Feeling bad about their feelings gets people into all kinds of emotional dilemmas, inner conflict, and symptomatic body reactions.

Examining this reactive process with special care and attention is one of Satir's most innovative therapeutic interventions. It provides a chance to change dysfunctional decisions people have made about themselves and their feelings. Judging their feelings usually activates people's survival and coping behavior, which takes us to the next step.

What Defenses Do I Use?

Like the meanings we make, the feelings we have, and our feelings about these feelings, our defenses are usually based on our past learnings and experiences. The three major defenses are projecting, denying, and ignoring.

Projecting onto others means attempting to put our responsibility on somebody else. It helps reduce our guilt, but it abdicates personal responsibility. Projecting promotes the status quo, since nobody accepts responsibility or attempts to change anything.

Denial is a well-known defense mechanism. If we deny a problem exists, we do not need to give it our attention or take responsibility for it. Again, this defense is part of a survival pattern, often no longer necessary. We use it until we can replace it with more present-oriented perceptions, expectations, and behavior.

Ignoring is a defense in which we admit a situation or pattern exists but avoid facing any changes. Procrastination is often associated with ignoring. This pattern becomes familiar after some time, and therefore acceptable to us and hard to change.

During the Ingredients process, we work with clients to identify these defenses, explore alternative ways for perceiving themselves, and change their patterns into more healthy behavior.

What Rules Do I Use for Commenting?

Family rules alone often have enough power to influence our internal reality and even control what we say. Sometimes other significant people or institutions, such as the church, provide our rules.

In this step, we identify family rules that limit clients' self-worth, restrict their choices, and generally are no longer relevant or no longer fit. Once they identify their rules, clients can reevaluate, modify, keep, or replace and transform them. (See the discussion of transforming rules in Chapter 11.)

APPLYING THE PROCESS

We can use this sequence of questions about people's internal processes to help clients understand themselves. We can also help them change their coping processes to manage their lives much more satisfactorily. A frequent question, for example, is: "What are the dynamics of this person I know at work?" Using the Ingredients questions as a process format, we can help clients uncover the places they get stuck or derailed when they interact with others.

The accompanying diagram illustrates the internal process, the steps person B goes through before responding to an initial comment from person A. In addition to hearing the comment, B may also notice various non-verbal messages: A's facial expression, body position, muscle tonus, skin color, smell, breathing depth and rate, voice tone and pace, and other body movements.

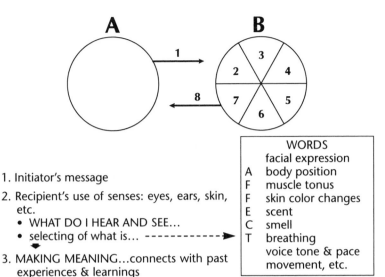

1. Initiator's message
2. Recipient's use of senses: eyes, ears, skin, etc.
   - WHAT DO I HEAR AND SEE...
   - selecting of what is... - - - - - - - - - - - ►
3. MAKING MEANING...connects with past experiences & learnings
   ➡creates
4. The FEELING about the meaning
   ➡activates
5. The FEELING ABOUT FEELING
   which activates the survival rules and
   ➡evokes
6. The DEFENSES: ⟵ projection, denial, ignoring
7. RULES FOR COMMENTING
   Re: roles, feelings, etc.
   - see what you should, say what is expected, feel what you ought
   - wait for permission, choose to be secure
8. Observable outcome: B RESPONDS TO A

A then goes through Steps 2 - 8.

	WORDS
	facial expression
A	body position
F	muscle tonus
F	skin color changes
E	scent
C	smell
T	breathing
	voice tone & pace
	movement, etc.

based on old learnings

Self
Other
Context

We often notice only some of these aspects of communication when we hear and see somebody talking. How we select our awareness is usually based on our own internal process: the meanings we make, the feelings activated by our meanings, our feelings about those feelings, our defenses, and our rules for commenting. Our awareness is also affected by our context and our relationship with the other person. The safer the context and the more trusting the relationship, the less biased our selection.

Presenting Problems

Our internal process goes rather quickly through the various steps. One way to look at the interaction between two people—the client's presenting problem—is to break it down into the six components that are indicated in the questions. When we take something apart and look at its many pieces, we see interrelationships between pieces that we did not see before. When we do this with an interaction, it becomes more clear and more amenable to change.

Susan and Tom

Let us consider a simple exchange between Susan and Tom, who has just come home.

TOM: Why isn't dinner ready yet?

SUSAN: Sorry. Oh, how can I be so stupid?! It will be ready in a few minutes. I am so sorry.

Superficially, this looks like an uncomplicated piece of congruent communication. As we take it apart, though, we can see it is a rather complex yet common transaction. Teasing out the many layers below each statement, and what each person's intention was, we can make a therapeutic intervention that helps both Susan and Tom recognize how they get stuck in their communication and why it is sometimes hard to make contact with each other.

When Tom asks about dinner, it is possible that Susan hears criticism. She sees a look on his face that she interprets as being critical and annoyed. She hears a tone in his voice that reminds her of a time when she was little and her father scolded her. She senses an energy in his body that feels to her as if he is ready to explode and hit her. His face is flushed; she interprets this as impatience.

The meaning Susan makes of all this is that Tom is angry at her and that she is going to be punished, told she has done something wrong, or told she is bad. She feels afraid of what is going to happen. Her feeling about that feeling is helplessness.

Susan thinks it is not acceptable to put words to her fears. One of the survival rules in her family as she grew up was that it was not safe to share her feelings. She had to behave as though they did not matter. Most of the time she pretended nothing ever happened to her, and she often went to bed with a stomachache.

Susan's learned rules are that it is not okay to comment and that she should not show fear or anger. Today she therefore ignores or denies what goes on between her and Tom.

All these steps—seeing and hearing, making meaning, feeling about the meaning, feeling about the feeling, following rules, and using defenses—are internal. Tom sees Susan and is not necessarily aware of any of this.

Susan could make various responses:

- Ignore Tom's question, saying nothing but feeling hurt or angry
- Express anger and blame Tom
- Explain herself
- Respond without feeling hooked, expressing herself positively and congruently, in tune with herself.

In this example, Susan apologizes to Tom while denying and ignoring her feelings. The point is that she actually had choices. How she uses these choices depends on how she perceives Tom, how she perceives their mutual context, and how she perceives herself.

We can use the same six Ingredients to analyze the internal journey Tom takes in response to Susan's apology. He hears a whiny, partially placating voice. He sees an apologetic, guilty look on Susan's face. He had intended to have an evening out with her and had bought theater tickets as a surprise.

Suppose his meaning for what he sees and hears is that she is trying once again to avoid intimacy with him. He feels disappointed about this. His feeling about being disappointed is that he is unworthy and hopeless: he feels like giving up, as in, "What's the use?"

Tom comes from a big family, and he was the oldest child. There was not enough emotional nurturing to go around, and he often felt deprived. His rule for surviving was not to ask for what he needed or wanted. People might say no. Instead of asking, he projected his (anticipated) rejection onto others around him.

Consequently, he learned to protect himself by blaming people. His rules for commenting are to hold back what he really wants and needs, and to not share his feelings. Therefore, instead of expressing what he really wanted to do—to have a pleasant evening for Susan and himself—he responds with blame.

TOM: Too bad you never can find time to be available for me. I bought theater tickets, and you'll be too tired to go. I'll ask Jeff to come with me.

Both Susan and Tom are either denying, ignoring, or projecting their feelings. Neither has stated how he or she feels or how he or she feels about those feelings. Neither checked out the other's intentions or the meaning of the other's statement. Susan is placating him, Tom is blaming her, and their argument will probably escalate into a situation in which he blames more and she placates more. The more she tries to apologize, the angrier he will probably become. So they can easily get into a never-ending loop of blaming and placating.

When this happens, they no longer talk about the issues at hand (plans for dinner and the evening). Both feel rejected, separated, misunderstood, not heard, and not validated. Neither feels intimate. They both feel low self-esteem and operate at a low level of coping.

Where did they get off the track? What happened to make two well-intended people's transaction result in more distance and feelings of rejection? If we go back to what they saw and heard, we immediately see the meaning each made was based on past experiences and decisions. Dysfunctional communication is often rooted in early childhood and our learnings at the survival level.

When many of the meanings we make are based on our past learnings about survival, we do not esteem ourselves very highly. When we are contaminated by the past, we understandably repeat our old patterns over and over again. Making meaning this way also activates a corresponding feeling from the past. Our feeling about this feeling, in turn, activates our survival rules, which activate our defenses.

We thus react defensively instead of clearly and congruently. Our defensive response's verbal and affective parts do not reflect the present.

Generally speaking, we select from our internal and external environments what we have programmed ourselves to see and hear. Whatever we expect or fear is what we believe we hear and see. Our response is based on our selection.

If Tom's father often looked at Tom in an angry way, it is possible Tom remembers that about his father more than other things. He may therefore select those pictures and those voices in his memory that show his father as an angry man. Many years later, when someone in his environment uses that kind of voice-tone or look, it immediately triggers feelings Tom experienced in the past. If he had been afraid of his father and felt inadequate and guilty about being afraid, Tom will cope with the present situation in the manner of his old learnings.

The present is the only place to live, if we are free. If the past contaminates our present, we continue repeating our old patterns, if not our behavior. The Satir model uses the past to illuminate the present—not to live in the past, deny it, or get rid of it. Out of the lessons of the past, we can learn to change the course of our present. We can provide ourselves with a more fully functioning life.

In working with families and couples, we need to identify such patterns and help clients bring their dynamics into conscious awareness. Once they acknowledge a pattern, they can disengage their emotional triggers and expectations from their early perspective. And they can then build a solid, self-responsible, present-focused view of themselves and each other.

Max and Ellen

Let us take another two short examples to track the internal process. The first involves Ellen, twenty-four, and Max, thirty-five. They have lived together for two and a half years, and Max has just moved out. The argument that precipitated their separation went as follows.

Ellen came home from work and told Max she planned to go to a show with a girlfriend that evening. Max told her not to go. His voice sounded harsh, his face was tight. What Ellen saw and heard reminded her of her father telling her what to do. She felt angry and helpless, yet decided not to go (just as she had customarily obeyed her father). It was her old, familiar way. She phoned her girlfriend and said, "Max won't let me go." Max heard this statement, packed his bag, and left.

Max's behavior does not make sense until we look at his internal ingredients. He saw Ellen's jaw getting tight and her eyes narrowing. Her voice was high-pitched and her words did not fit her affect. Even though she was cancelling her plans, her behavior did not fit his expectations. Max was thinking of their earlier plan to go and look at houses that evening.

He thought the show was more important to Ellen than keeping her promise to him, that he was not important, and that their life together was not a priority for her. He also took her words as sarcastic. These were some of the meanings he ascribed to her communication.

The incident also triggered an old picture of Max's ex-wife, who used to go out by herself and leave him at home. His interpretation was, "It is happening again. I must be careful—I'm in danger." This activated his anger, fear, and disappointment. His feelings about these feelings were helplessness and a sense of failure. He decided to protect himself by withdrawing, by leaving the situation.

This example again indicates that people have difficulty with unexpected behavior if it triggers their low self-esteem, their past experiences of failure, and their automatic coping responses.

Peter and Lucy

In the next example, Peter and Lucy are in their car. Peter is driving.

LUCY: Peter, you are such a rotten driver. Why can't you stay in your own lane?

PETER: You sound just like your mother.

On the surface, this sounds familiar enough, even though rather disrespectful. In terms of her internal process, Lucy is really saying she is uncomfortable and afraid of Peter's driving. Peter hears an angry voice and sees a tense body, a twisted face, and a trembling hand. The meaning he makes is that Lucy is angry at him.

Notice his selective interpretation: anger. He misses that she is afraid. He thinks her opinion is that he is not a competent driver and that she knows how to do it better. He feels attacked and put down again, like a "nothing." One of his defenses is to attack and project onto her.

His rule about commenting is that it is not acceptable to talk about his feelings. The only way he knows he can keep control is to stay behind his defenses and blame her.

Lucy's response is: "You are always blaming me," and so it goes, on and on.

To describe their relationship, we could say they blame each other, do not discuss the subject, and do not share their feelings. The transaction escalates into a power struggle, a win-lose relationship. Both feel rejected, misunderstood, not heard, lonely, and empty.

For many years the helping professions have tried to help people change their communication patterns without looking at or changing their internal process. Some professionals use Satir's coping stances to improve people's communication without using her more significant, powerful Ingredients of an Interaction. The stances are dramatic and elucidating, but this vehicle is what facilitates people's congruent communication.

Satir did not accept the idea that people would say or do something that did not make sense. As others had done earlier, she found that we can understand most reactions if we know "where the person is coming from." She believed that whatever a person communicates has meaning and purpose for that individual, even though it may not make sense on the surface.

As we go through the Ingredients of an Interaction, we can expand our understanding of how difficult it is for people to make meaningful contact. So much contamination from the past and so many automatic coping responses interfere.

We can also use the Ingredients to help clients understand how their interactions can become congruent. That way each can feel good about him- or herself, be vulnerable in terms of articulating his or her feelings, and build the opportunity for their contact with other people to be ongoing and positive.

Exploring New Meanings

In the case of Tom and Susan, we might explore new interpretations and meanings (once they have recognized and agreed to change their survival patterns).

TOM: Why isn't dinner ready?

Susan sees a perplexed, disturbed look on Tom's face. His body looks as if he feels tense. His voice sounds angry. The meaning she makes of what she sees and hears turns into a question: "I wonder what is going on inside Tom. It doesn't make sense that he would be angry."

Instead of reacting or letting her system panic, she decides to check it out. She feels puzzled and accepts this feeling. It does not trigger any of her defenses. She acknowledges her feelings, owns them, and consciously chooses how to comment to Tom in the present.

SUSAN: Tom, I am puzzled that you are in a hurry for dinner. What's the rush?

By checking out what Tom really means, she finds out about his intentions. She does not become stuck with her feelings, and her response is not ruled by unresolved past experiences or automatic patterns of coping. When she permits herself the freedom to comment on what she sees and hears, she can choose from among many response options.

Tom, on the other hand, sees a puzzled look, hears Susan's question, and decides this means he has not given her enough information. He feels fine about Susan wanting more information. He also feels it's acceptable to share his intentions.

TOM: I bought two tickets because I wanted to take you out. I thought it would be a nice surprise. So I thought we would have dinner early and go out.

This illustrates that making the same content more explicit, more direct, and nonreactive can transform this interaction into being connecting and nurturing. What at first sounded like an attack can now be an opportunity for understanding and connectedness.

Breaking the Defensive Habit

When we react to what we think we hear and see without confirming the other person's meaning, our disagreements usually escalate into arguments. Rather than focusing on the issues at hand, we react to protect our feelings, perceptions, expectations, and self-worth. When we feel attacked, even if only because someone disagrees with us, we go into our automatic coping cycle of defending instead of dealing with self, other, and context.

When we get into difficulties, we usually are stuck at the content level: "You did this or that, and you shouldn't have." The whole cycle of right and wrong, fair and unfair, gets triggered once the reactive self-defense pattern is in process. To break this defensive pattern and understand someone's communication, we need to look at that person's intent. The content only provides the context in which the self's and other's needs are met or not.

Let us take an example from Ellen and Max. When two interactions are far apart and a third interaction does not clarify the situation, we can assume pieces of the past and the present are confused. Perceptions are not obvious, and clarification would be useful. The following is part of the counseling session one of the authors had with this couple.

ELLEN: I wanted to go to the show with Ruby.

THERAPIST: [*To Max*] What did you hear?

MAX: I heard her saying that she wanted to go with Ruby.

THERAPIST: What did that mean to you?

MAX: That going to the show was more important than being with me and doing what we had decided.

THERAPIST: How did you feel?

MAX: I felt angry and rejected.

THERAPIST: [*To Ellen*] Were you aware that Max and you had plans for the evening?

ELLEN: Yes. I also knew that we had the next day free.

THERAPIST: [*To Max*] Did you know that Ellen had made plans for the two of you for the next day?

MAX: No.

THERAPIST: How do you feel, finding this out now?

MAX: I feel ignored. She makes her own plans.

THERAPIST: [*To Ellen*] Did you remember that you had plans for the evening?

ELLEN: Yes.

THERAPIST: How do you feel, knowing that it was important for Max that you and he be together for the evening?

ELLEN: I feel good about that, but I didn't feel he would mind me going out with Ruby when he is so busy.

THERAPIST: How do you feel now?

ELLEN: I feel confused.

THERAPIST: How does that feel?

ELLEN: I feel angry when he leaves.

THERAPIST: [*To Max*] What did you feel, hearing Ellen now?

MAX: I feel confused.

THERAPIST: What did you do when Ellen told you she wanted to go to the show?

MAX: I told her she could not go.

THERAPIST: How do you feel about this now?

MAX: Confused. That's why I'm here.

At this point the therapist continued taking the couple through their confusion step by step. Confusion is the stage of chaos necessary to move from the dysfunctional status quo through the stages of change to a healthier way of being. Confusion is a good indicator that both have moved from the familiar to the unfamiliar, that change is taking place.

THERAPIST: [*To Max*] When you felt angry and disappointed that Ellen planned to go out with Ruby, what picture came to your mind?

MAX: [*He thinks for a while, then speaks in a softer voice.*] The picture of my ex-wife going out often with her friends and leaving me behind. . . . It ended up in divorce.

THERAPIST: How do you feel now, as you are becoming aware of this connection?

MAX: I don't want the same to happen. . . . I feel scared.

THERAPIST: And how does that feel?

MAX: I am afraid to lose her. . . . I love her.

THERAPIST: [*To Ellen*] How do you feel, hearing this?

ELLEN: [*With tears in her eyes*] I didn't know he felt like this. . . . I feel sad. Also angry that he doesn't trust me.

THERAPIST: [*To Max*] Do you trust Ellen?

MAX: Yes, I do.

THERAPIST: [*To Ellen*] Do you believe him?

ELLEN: No, because he left.

THERAPIST: [*To Max*] What was going on inside you that you chose to pack and leave?

MAX: When I heard Ellen saying to Ruby, "He won't let me go," I don't know what it was, I just got so upset, I felt everything came to an end.

THERAPIST: [*To Ellen*] How did you feel when Max said you couldn't go?

ELLEN: I felt like a little girl and my father wouldn't let me go out. Because I felt like Max treats me like my father did, I was angry. I wanted him to know I was angry, and I defended myself by saying yes to Ruby.

THERAPIST: [*To Max*] As you hear this, can you recall your tone of voice, your posture, your feelings when you told Ellen not to go?

MAX: Yes. I was angry.

THERAPIST: Is it possible that you sounded like her father?

MAX: Yes. [*Raising his voice*] Whatever her father says is more important than what I say.

THERAPIST: How do you feel about this?

MAX: I feel I am never going to measure up.

THERAPIST: How does that feel?

MAX: That I can never win with her.

It became clear that their argument had become a win-lose power struggle. Even though Ellen decided not to go because Max told her not to, she was also responding, on another level, to her father. Max picked up and responded to this and concluded that he was not important to her. He obviously had felt low self-esteem and a need to protect himself.

The therapist followed the Ingredients process to bring about some changes for Ellen and Max. Here are a few more interactions from their same session.

THERAPIST: [*To Max*] Could you believe the possibility that Ellen wanted to stay with you?

MAX: No.

THERAPIST: Ask her now. [*The therapist shifts to the present.*]

MAX: Why did you decide to stay at home?

ELLEN: Because I remembered we had plans, and going to the show was not so important.

MAX: Why did you say what you said?

ELLEN: Because I was angry that you were telling me what to do in that tone of voice, which I didn't like in my father, or in you.

THERAPIST: Do you believe her now?

MAX: I understand more now what has happened. I didn't know that she would make that choice . . . not to go with Ruby and to choose to be with me.

THERAPIST: [*To Ellen*] How do you feel now, hearing that Max feels so insecure about your relationship?

ELLEN: I didn't know, and I'm sad. I love you, Max.

Following this exchange, the therapist continued using the Ingredients to explore the couple's assumptions, feelings, feelings about their feelings, defenses, and rules for commenting. Initially the session provided Max and Ellen with an opportunity to look at their own processes, hear what each other had done, and gradually connect with their own fears and past experiences. They could then move to their present longings and yearnings, namely to love and be loved.

Both had come into this relationship with low self-esteem. Max had already been through the demise of a prior painful relationship. Following this session with Ellen, which evolved from attack to understanding to acceptance, the couple decided to continue working on their relationship. In subsequent sessions, they worked on sharing their feelings, trusting each other, differentiating past and present, letting go of their past pain and coping dynamics, and accepting each other openly in the present.

Using the Ingredients as a tool to introduce change, the therapist helped this couple see, hear, feel, and finally live in the present. When we do this congruently, our defenses and rules from the past are no longer activated in our present interactions. We validate ourselves, and we accept whatever feelings we have. We own our feelings, share them, and consequently do something about our true longings.

Exploring New Options

Considering three choices, three meanings, three responses, and three actions when looking at changing old patterns is very helpful for clients. Satir encouraged people to have at least three choices. She said to have one choice is no choice; to have two choices is a dilemma; and to have three choices offers new possibilities.

The rules for commenting thus get transformed into guidelines, opening the door to choices for whatever fits. When transformed rules allow choices, we are not stuck with just one response. We have many options. (See Chapter 11.)

When clients begin recognizing how conditioned they are, how they lose their sense of wholeness when they attempt to protect the familiar from the flow of change, and how they live their lives as though there were only one possibility, they finally can get in touch with the flow of never-ending possibilities available to them. Awareness, acceptance, and connectedness become important avenues for growing toward wholeness.

Working with Process Versus Content

One basic reminder: we work with process, not content. Content gives us our clients' context, within which we look at the reactions of individuals and family members. Using the content as context also adds familiarity and validity to the process.

Referring back to when Max left home after Ellen had plans to go out with her friend, for instance, we use Ellen's story about her situation not as the issue to work on, but as the setting within which to change the dynamics between the two people. In that way, the therapist uses the content as the context for change. This helps make it easy to detect where clients are stuck and then work toward resolving this stuckness by helping them explore and accept new alternatives.

Working at Different Levels

Once we have identified all the ingredients of a client's interaction, we can decide to enter the person's inner system at any level: feelings, perceptions, expectations, or yearnings.

How you use the Ingredients of an Interaction depends largely on the level at which you want to work with your clients. You might want to start very simply, with feelings. Many therapies have used this vehicle just to help people look at what they see, hear, and feel.

Actually, most therapists we have worked with are quite good at clarifying what people see and hear, and identifying and reflecting how they feel. Very often, though, they skip the point about what meanings their clients make of what they see and hear.

Another aspect we suggest strongly is *asking* how people feel, not telling them. Likewise, ask about their meanings and their interpretations. Meaning is made from an internal point of view, not an external one. Meaning is subjective.

Feelings flow from the meanings we make of what we see and hear—or, more often, what we think we see and hear. If a client's feelings about the meaning are based on here-and-now experience, the client simply decides what to do with those feelings. In other words, he or she considers various choices and acts (rather than reacting).

Regardless of how much a client recognizes links between past experiences and currently dysfunctional reactions, the resolution of this needs to be present-based. This means we need to help our clients verify the meanings they make, affirm that their feelings are congruent with their meanings, take ownership of their feelings, and be free to make choices about how to respond. Finally, we need to help them comment about what they really want.

The powerful impact of the Ingredients can be useful in one-on-one counseling situations as well as couple, group, and family therapy. It is a very effective means of helping clients identify their perceptions, feelings, expectations, and yearnings. We have also started to use this vehicle for changing organizations, employer-employee relations, and cross-cultural conflicts.

So far, we have looked at tracking people's internal processes, starting with what they see and hear, and proceeding through the various steps to the point of commenting. The next chapter looks at how we can help clients change perceptions, feelings, and expectations through Satir's transformational interventions.

7

The Transformation Process

After many years of training with Virginia Satir, we three co-authors felt we had still missed something. We knew how to do Parts Parties and Family Reconstructions. We knew how to sculpt family relations. But these and other Satir interventions tapped into something more than we could identify initially. Participants looked different. Their faces were more radiant, they displayed more self-confidence, their ambience changed.

For years we just credited Satir's magic and power, or her interventions, for such major transformations. Then, as we worked together more intensively, we decided we could no longer give only such partial answers to what we saw and did. Gradually, we added to our understanding. It did not come in one sudden moment.

We first took a look at how Satir dealt with feelings. She did not follow the Freudian way of gaining insight and understanding. Freud focused on people's feelings in relation to past experiences. Nor did she use the encounter movement way of endowing feelings—any feelings—with godliness. That movement encouraged people to express their feelings without any expectation to do anything else.

We also saw a major difference between what she did and what Carl Rogers taught and believed. He elicited people's feelings and asked them to own their feelings to be in charge.

Satir not only had people acknowledge, own, and express their feelings. She also encouraged people to make choices about how to act on those feelings in the present.

Satir used this metaphor: "Feelings are like a human thermometer. A thermometer tells us what temperature it is, which in turn helps us decide what to wear. Feelings tell us about the temperature of our internal processes and help us decide how to be and what to do."

Satir also advocated the transformation of people's feelings about their feelings, as discussed in the previous chapter. This chapter examines this transformation in greater detail.

THE SIX LEVELS OF EXPERIENCE

With the Self at the core, as the source of our inner experiences, Satir found various layers or levels of experience:

1. Yearnings
2. Expectations
3. Perceptions
4. Feelings
5. Coping
6. Behavior

These experiences all take place within our specific context at the moment. People usually present this as content. For instance, we often hear clients say, "My father did not love me." Exploring the content statement leads to one or more specific events, such as the father taking only one son fishing and the second son concluding that his father did not love him.

The second son's yearning was to be loved equally. His expectation was that if his father loved him equally, he would have taken him fishing, too. His interpretation was that his father did not love him. His feelings were disappointment and hurt, and anger toward his brother.

This is a specific example of how the Satir model uses the content to discover the six levels of someone's experience. The content of a client's problem is simply the context within which change seems plausible and relevant. The content also helps provide the context to identify the person's coping process. As Satir often said, "The problem is not the problem. Coping is." If we can help clients cope well at the levels of their expectations, perceptions, feelings, and fulfilling their yearnings in the best possible way—if we can help them take all levels into consideration—then we help them make progress. Context anchors changes in the reality of their experience.

The figure on the next page shows distinct levels of experience. In real life, the Self affects external behavior, and the context affects the Self. Effects flow inward and out. The levels are interdependent and do not operate in linear sequence. Often they are all affected at the same moment.

Each level of experience contributes particular kinds of processes to the person and to his or her relationships. Each layer needs checking out, although Satir's process of transformational therapy can start with an intervention at any level.

Other schools of therapy emphasize one layer over another, or even choose one layer to the exclusion of all others. Some therapies work on behavior only, hoping it will change the whole system. Some work on the feeling level only. Satir advocated working at all levels (even though many people think of her in terms of her coping stances and communication work). Her model of growth addresses all six levels, and her vehicles for change facilitate transformation on all levels.

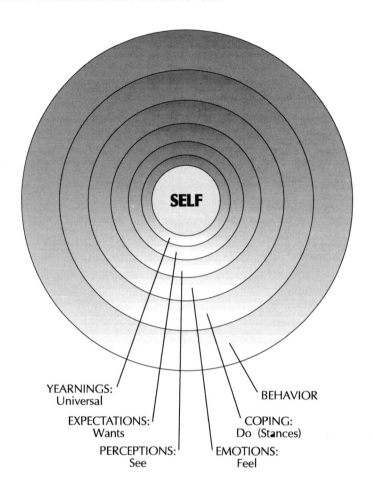

The previous example indicated all six levels of the second son's experience. The process of identifying all these levels gave that client an opportunity:

- To express hurt.
- To widen and expand his perceptions by remembering other experiences or events with his father,

or some specific qualities and resources his father had.

- To identify and own similar qualities and resources in himself.

- To increase his understanding and acceptance of his father as a person.

- To discover and own his own unmet expectations, and to say, "Yes, I wanted to go fishing with my father. I own this expectation. He didn't live up to my expectation. Can I let it go now?"

- To fulfill his current yearnings and expectations now and to own them without putting them on others.

When we explore these levels, we often find them loaded with material that needs changing. Much of the material and many of the patterns are past-based. Each level might need some changes and interventions for it to function more openly and congruently.

Yearnings

The level of yearning is each person's longing to be loved, accepted, validated, and confirmed. These yearnings to love oneself, to love others, and to be loved by others are universal. How yearnings were satisfied or not satisfied when we were growing up has a major effect on how we develop, mature, and deal with our feelings. In early life the Self can get so bombarded with trying experiences that it defines itself through them and limits its development. Life then becomes just a survival process. If a child's yearnings are met, on the other hand, that person has the opportunity to develop high self-esteem, congruence as a way of being, healthy patterns for coping with stressful situations, and the ability to love self and others.

Expectations

Much of the "unconditional love" literature of Carl Rogers and others addresses people's universal longings for closeness, wholeness, intimacy, freedom, excitement, and creativity. We found that these yearnings show up in all kinds of expectations.

For example, we usually expect to be happy. Many of us expect the external world to meet our needs. We expect other people to provide for us, very much as our early childhood taught us when we still depended heavily on others for our survival.

Let's say Tony is a child who longs to be close to his father for intimacy, validation, and acceptance. If those expectations are met, Tony has no difficulty. If not, he needs to accommodate that unmet expectation. During childhood, he might just bear it. Later, his unmet expectation is likely to move into the feeling level and translate into hurt, loneliness, and possibly anger. In later years Tony may bootleg that longing into another relationship or just carry around the discomfort of his unmet expectation. If it gets fulfilled at a later date, present relationships take on their own value, and the discomfort and longing of the past disappear.

Many times people do not voice their expectations. In therapy, then, clients need to tap and transform their unmet expectations of the past. Expectations are usually formed from universal yearnings. For example, consider the Self that is not validated or is validated only under certain circumstances defined by others. To survive, that person constantly has to give up his or her own expectations and needs to be loved. These experiences lead to low self-worth, pain, hurt, and self-devaluation. Consequently, the person decides, "I am no good. I am not lovable."

People also form expectations from a sense of external comparison: "They have it, I want it." Their hidden hope is that they will feel better about themselves, have a better perception of themselves, or increase their self-esteem. If a man buys a Jaguar with the expectation that this will help fulfill his need for validation from others, he might be disappointed once he has the car. Did he buy it to feel better about himself? Or so that others would feel better about him, and he could then feel better about himself?

Self-worth involves more than meeting our own expectations, especially those expressed externally. It is also based on our own sense of empowerment and importance. In the case of the Jaguar-buyer, this would sound like: "I want it, I deserve it, and I can feel good about me." The value of owning the car thus reflects a personal want rather than a means to raise his self-esteem.

Another common expectation concerns people's belief that things have not been fair. They therefore feel their reactions are legitimate, and that they do not need to change. For example, one son may say he is not treated as well as his older brother. He therefore feels he does not need to do any household chores; he has the right to be sloppy.

Fairness for this son can mean fulfilling expectations of equality and justice. Or it can be some other expression or reflection of his own perception of the reality of the situation. Expecting fairness means expecting the outside world to change first, while the person's inner world remains the same. Obviously, people often need to let go of their "fairness" stand before they can make major changes and transformations.

In family therapy, most of the expectations that need attention are based in the past. If we wanted to sit on our dad's lap when we were five years old, and we still hold that unmet expectation, maybe as a resentment, we need to deal with it. We cannot go back and satisfy it. What we can do is accept our expectation, let go of it, and then look at how we can fulfill our yearning in the here and now.

For instance, "I had this expectation when I was a child. I own it. It is mine. I now can let go of it and no longer blame or judge my father for not living up to it. I accept that I cannot fulfill that expectation of the past. However, I have choices about how to fulfill my expectations and yearnings in the present."

Sometimes Satir-based therapists in a group setting role-play a childhood scene and allow the family member to experience sitting on "Dad's" lap (the lap of a group member chosen by the person to role-play the father). This helps some people let go of their expectations and move into the present.

Clients need to recognize and work on the interplay between specific unmet expectations and universal yearnings. When they reevaluate their expectations, they need to make a connection with their underlying yearnings. This helps them meet their yearnings in a realistic way in the present. It transforms the contamination of the past and frees the person to deal in the present with new choices.

In her many vehicles for change, Satir developed a process of separating the impact of the past from situations in the present. We are calling this process *de-enmeshment*. While others have written about enmeshment within a family, we needed a de-enmeshment process to separate people's past-contaminated material from their present experiences. Satir's transformation therapy (described in the next section) provides the theoretical and practical bases for this to happen.

Perceptions

The third level of experience is called perceptions. These are also known as beliefs, attitudes, values, or pictures. Our perceptions are bound up with our sense of self; this interconnection is very strong, stable, and hard to untangle.

We usually form our perceptions from a very limited base of knowledge, especially when we are young. When we were small and Mother told us to go to our room while she and Dad were talking, we might have assumed we were not wanted. In fact, though, they just wanted privacy.

Our limited information leads to a different, more narrow picture of what actually happened. We therefore have a distorted idea of that reality. This leads to interpretations and conclusions based on incomplete information.

We each have our own perceptions about the same event. Each child in a family describes the same event in a different way. In the Satir model, one therapeutic task is to help people expand this limited perception. This leads to a new interpretation of the experience and the multiplicity of events taking place at the same time.

For example, a person might say, "I know my mother stopped loving me when I was three years old." In exploring what happened at that time in the family's chronology, the person discovers that her mother had another baby at the time and that her father lost his job. The family had had to move.

The reality also was that this child did not have this information about the stress on her parents. So she decided her mother did not love her, instead of having the information and understanding to realize her parents' preoccupation with their situation was not related to their love for her.

Feelings

The fourth level of experience is that of feelings. Feelings are often strongly past-based. Even if our present feelings are triggered by a present event, we usually use our accumulated feelings to react. And these accumulated feelings are the ones we need to deal with in therapy. Our reactive feelings—how we feel about our feelings—are based on expectations and perceptions that relate to our self-worth or self-esteem.

The most prevalent reactive feelings are hurt, fear, and anger. Our culture still differentiates between women's and men's reactive feelings. Women are readily allowed to feel hurt and to cry, and men to be angry and to yell. These two feelings might be the opposite sides of the same coin: one cannot have anger without hurt. Within our culture, it might still be easier to enter the feeling level of women through hurt, and of men through anger. Therapy needs to deal with both.

Coping

Coping patterns are the so-called defense or survival mechanisms. Under stress, they appear in the four survival stances. As symptoms of stress, these stances become dysfunctional solutions to conflicts on a deeper level. They often serve as protection, a way to survive. They also indicate how a person sees him- or herself in relation to others. Helping clients become aware of their stances gives them a "thermometer" for checking their levels of self-esteem and their perceptions about how to survive.

Behavior

Behavior, the sixth level of experience, is the outcome of coping and the external manifestation of a person's internal world. In other words, behavior is the external expression of our self-esteem.

TRANSFORMATION

This section first explores the process of transformation and then describes some techniques.

The Transformation Process

The Satir model emphasizes process. For many people, process used to mean the opposite of content. It meant how things happen, not what happened. It also referred to the order of events. People would discuss what they had seen and heard, and they would call its sequence the "process." Many people still think of process in this way.

Satir used the concept of process as the major avenue for change. This concept indicates that the flow of a person's energy is transformed from a dysfunctional pattern or dynamic to a more open, free, and healthy pattern. Metaphorically, this kind of transformation is like clearing the river so it flows freely and is not obstructed anywhere between its source and its end, the ocean.

Satir thus discouraged people from focusing on the story about a problem. Instead, she focused on helping their entire internal process. This allowed them to tap their yearnings and to change:

- Their perceptions
- The meanings they make
- Their feelings
- Their feelings about those feelings
- Their expectations
- Their motivations and actions, which stem from their yearnings

These changes are significant, and the client definitely goes through some sense of chaos. It is thus very important that facilitators are firmly grounded in their own energy so they can provide support and stability for clients as they take risks during the process of change.

To transform existing material at each level of experience requires three steps:

1. Explore each level to find the dysfunctional material that it might contain from any period within the client's whole lifeline of experience.

2. Transform the dysfunctional material. Some de-enmeshment might be needed.

3. Move to the present in an accepting way, validating the self in a positive manner and honoring the level for its positive contribution.

The following discussion looks at each of these levels and steps in detail, since transformations take place at each level of experience. Limiting ourselves to one level of intervention is usually not enough.

The transformation process includes tapping yearnings: helping people become aware of, acknowledge, and accept their yearnings. This is a basic process of connecting with our inner core or life force.

We also help people identify their unmet expectations, usually held over from the past. Having acknowledged these, they can then:

1. Let go of the ways they expected or wanted their expectations to be met.

2. Return to their more universal yearnings and find present ways to meet those yearnings.

3. Let go of their unmet expectations (e.g., still wanting to be the valedictorian at high-school graduation), acknowledging that they cannot be met any longer.

4. Develop expectations in harmony with their yearnings and the present-day reality.

Reframing perceptions is another aspect of the transformation process. Part of the transformation of perceptions involves adding new data to correct or update people's interpretations and decisions. New perceptions, in turn, usually influence and possibly change their expectations and feelings.

Reframing perceptions was one of the more powerful interventions that Satir used frequently. Using metaphors to reframe people's perceptions is especially powerful because it engages the brain's right hemisphere, bypassing the usual circuits that resist change or rationalize the status quo. (More on reframing in a later chapter.)

Feelings and feelings about those feelings usually need a lot of attention in the transformation process. They are interrelated with expectations and perceptions, and a change in any of these influences possibly changes the others. Tapping feelings involves the following steps:

1. In a safe, accepting environment, have clients re-experience feelings from their past. Linear, cognitive "understanding" is not enough here: they need to connect with actual feelings from the right side of their brains.

    One of the easiest ways to tap feelings is to sculpt the client's picture, relationship, and stance. Then let the wisdom of the body help the process.

2. Have them acknowledge and accept those feelings.

3. Have them let go of feelings that get in the way of being congruent. To do this, bring their expectations and perceptions into awareness also, and connect these to their feelings. In other words, create the appropriate context for working with their feelings. Releasing expectations and perceptions clears the sources of reactive feelings, so the client spends little time just bathing in past feelings or self-pity.

    Once you have introduced new perceptions through, say, reframing, the feelings usually change too. The same is true for any pictures of reactive behavior created by those reactive feelings.

Transforming Feelings About Feelings

In our respective clinical practices, we had seen most clients either submit to their feelings in a fairly unaware way or fight their feelings with fairly strong rejection or denial. We learned from Satir that our feelings belong to us. We can choose either to have our feelings run us, control us, or we can use them to oil the system, ride the waves of life, and intensify our joys, excitement, and enthusiasm.

To learn how to manage and enjoy our inner experiences seemed like a new and exciting challenge. When we start with the conviction that these feelings are ours, that they belong to us, we establish a new relationship between them and the Self, the owner, the "I am." If we own our feelings, we take a step toward managing or riding them with awareness and appreciation.

To help the many people whose past experiences contaminate their present feelings, Satir developed her Family Reconstruction process (see Chapter 9). This complex vehicle for change connects, updates, and transforms people's past-generated feelings into a system of self-care and self-management. Taking charge of their feelings empowered these people, got them to live in the present, and gave them a sense of being whole.

At this point in our study, we realized some process was taking place between people's selves and their feelings. Satir's process questions gave us some interesting clues to what was actually happening. For example, consider a workshop participant standing in front of a large group for the first time and being asked about his or her hopes and wishes for the workshop. Satir's process questions might include the following:

SATIR: How do you feel?

PARTICIPANT: Scared.

SATIR: Close your eyes and see what picture comes to your mind.

PARTICIPANT: Being up front in a class in grade school.

SATIR: How old are you?

PARTICIPANT: Ten.

SATIR: What were you scared about?

PARTICIPANT: People would laugh at me.

SATIR: What meaning did you make of that?

PARTICIPANT: That I am stupid.

SATIR: What happened?

PARTICIPANT: I tried to stay away from the front of the class.

SATIR: How old are you now?

PARTICIPANT: Thirty-two.

SATIR: Now open your eyes and look around. What do you see, and how do you feel?

PARTICIPANT: I see people being attentive and supportive. I feel relieved.

Sometimes it is helpful to have the participant ask the audience if anybody else feels the same way. This shows that the person is speaking for many other people.

When the facilitator asks, "How do you feel now?" the grown Self makes the connection that the present scary feeling belongs to a past context and not to a present reality. The person can then separate the past from the present. That usually changes the feeling of being scared and empowers the person to take charge of the present.

Satir's questions made people aware not only of their feelings and their feelings about those feelings, but also of the processes occurring beneath those feelings. We eventually found layers of processes, much like the old metaphor of the many onion layers of hidden experience.

The transformation process proceeds to explore new ways to cope. The Satir model teaches people alternative ways of behaving, being, and becoming before asking them to give up their protective survival patterns.

Once new coping patterns are explored, people can let their behavior change. Behavior is usually the outward manifestation of a complex internal process. Changing behavior alone often has limited success. The

Satir model believes behavior changes as a consequence of change at the other levels. If someone's behavior is violent, of course, then behavioral restriction is appropriate and helpful.

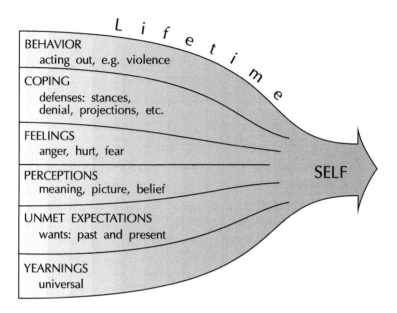

The Satir model suggests that therapy and change need to occur at all levels, during the person's entire lifetime. There is no rule about starting the transformation at a certain level. When the therapist is in tune with the client, has good rapport, and is in process with the possible changes, either the therapist knows at what level to start working, or it actually might not matter.

Cognition alone has proven not very helpful in making transformations work. Satir therefore engaged right-brain capabilities through her use of humor, trance, meditation, music, physical touch, and vocal tone. She made the change process more comprehensive by adding experiential learning to the cognitive process. Therefore all her vehicles use a lot of experiential role-playing, sculpting, and metaphors to bring about change. We suggest using the client's logical, rational, cognitive side for providing the context within which the change occurs. This is explained in the next chapter.

Having had an opportunity to deal with past material at each level and having de-enmeshed it from the present, the person can now start integrating self, other, and context into wholeness and congruently flowing energy. This encourages the person to use his or her resources and to make appropriate choices in the immediate circumstances. Released from attending to and coping with the past, the client can live in the present with more energy and curiosity.

Some people have called this process of de-enmeshment *second-level change*. Moving beyond the content of the problem and the behavior of the person moves us into Satir's concept of second-level change. This usually includes changing our expectations, perceptions, and feelings. To make transformation possible, it may also mean going back to our own basic yearnings.

TRANSFORMATION INTERVENTIONS

Satir took great care to caution people against adopting any technique in a rigid, unbending way. With these cautions in mind, one simple transformation intervention is to add to what is. Instead of fighting darkness, metaphorically, we can add light. The darkness disappears in the process. Likewise, when we add a new perception, a new feeling, and a new expectation, then a new coping pattern emerges. We have thus transformed something by adding to what was.

Another analogy is the chemical reaction in which a new compound forms when we add to what exists. By adding hydrogen to oxygen, for example, we get water. In therapy, we help clients add helpful or healing parts to their existing resources. The first healing additive is awareness. After a particular pattern, even a painful one, becomes automatic, it sustains itself without conscious help. Through the process of becoming aware, clients move from the automatic to the conscious level of responding, giving themselves choices and new possibilities for change.

One recurring pattern is that clients use their parents as models. Even if people consciously decide not to follow the example their parents provide, they still do. They may not copy their parents in the same context, and therefore for some time seem as if they act differently, but the similarity becomes obvious once we look at the patterns they follow.

A common example is when parents have strict rules about attending regular worship services. Their children must always attend, regardless of other activities or intents. On becoming parents, these offspring might not ever take their own children to services, possibly in reaction to their own experiences and possibly because they want to be better parents. However, their rigid pattern might manifest itself as forcing their children to attend school, sick or not. In this way, the rigid pattern continues in a different context.

This supports the importance of looking back at old learnings and how we still use them to cope in present circumstances. Sometimes therapists need to spend considerable time and effort helping clients de-enmesh from their parental modeling. Of course, if the model has been of a congruent nature, with high self-esteem, the client has a head start that provides many positive results.

A lot of interest exists in our society right now in dealing with sexual abuse and alcoholism. We are finding that the transformational approach of the Satir model has a very powerful effect on people trying to resolve their sexual abuse experiences, as well as helping people with their alcohol dependency. The transformational approach goes beyond helping them deal with what happened to them and with their feelings. It helps them deal with all six levels of transformation and brings success and happiness into their lives.

With alcohol dependency, the transformational approach quickly moves to the inner yearnings and then helps individuals and families examine their survival patterns. Replacing survival patterns with coping patterns and coping patterns with healthy self-care patterns brings about major transformations instead of changing some simple behavioral pattern.

Self-esteem is based on more than feeling good. It entails being in tune with all levels of our personhood. Valuing ourselves includes being realistic in the present. We all have the capacity to feel feelings. It is how we deal with them that really matters. There are times, for instance, when we feel angry. Anger in itself is a natural feeling. It is also an example of feelings that can drain or redirect our energy. How we work through it is thus important when we are trying to live congruent lifestyles.

ANGER TRANSFORMED

To deal with ourselves in a responsible, conscious way is probably one of life's most important tasks. One component of this task is to deal with our feelings. Anger is one of the most commonly experienced yet most poorly managed.

Anger is a reaction. It is not that we become angry but that we feel angry. Anger belongs to us: it is not us. Yet some of us look at anger as coming from outside ourselves, perhaps because of an event. Some of us look at anger as a result of something happening within ourselves.

Nonetheless, it is a reaction. When some event occurs, we interpret it and ascribe meaning to it. That results in or turns into our reaction. What events outside yourself get you hooked most easily into an angry reaction? What do you do then? How do you get yourself out of your angry feeling?

When we look at our angry feelings objectively, we might notice all kinds of choices available to us.

- We might hit the other person.

- We might acknowledge our anger by saying so, or by simply acknowledging our feeling to ourselves.

- We might blame someone else by stating that that person "made us angry."

- We might keep our anger inside and gradually suppress it.

- We might look at a deeper level of experience to see what actually sparked our anger.

- We might move our anger to the other side of the coin—hurt or fear—and face those feelings first.

Anger accumulates. People can experience it over the years and collect their angry feelings. Some people who have collected anger this way have short fuses; almost anything sets them off. Usually it appears to be an over-reaction to a simply annoying event.

Turning to part of the personal iceberg, we need to look at what lies below the level of anger. Anger's partners are usually hurt and fear. In bringing clients to an awareness of their anger, we also need to tap their hurt and fear and deal with all three. One of these feelings is usually more active, more engaged, more powerful than the other two. Nevertheless, all three need therapeutic attention.

Below these feelings, as indicated earlier, are perceptions and expectations. If we perceive an external event to discount us, we might feel angry. If we had an unmet expectation, a promise not kept, we might panic and then get angry. So to help people deal with their anger, we might need to help them transform their expectations or perceptions, or both.

When people have high self-esteem, they are less reactive to the behaviors of others and therefore have less need to get angry. Accepting that anger is a natural feeling we all have, there are alternatives to feeling angry. To find them, we look at our expectations and perceptions and find ways to handle both congruently.

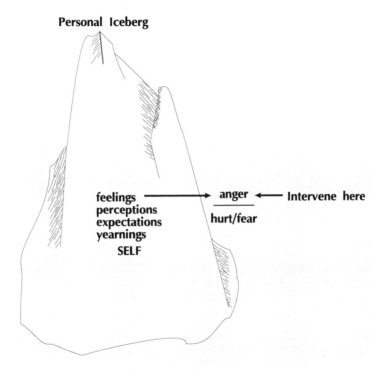

Personal Iceberg

feelings ⟶ anger ⟵ Intervene here
perceptions
expectations   hurt/fear
yearnings
SELF

In terms of the Satir coping stances, people with placating stances usually hide or suppress their anger. When, through some therapeutic help, the placating person starts the process of dealing with his or her self-esteem in ways that do not try to please everybody else, that person starts to release years of pent-up feelings, especially anger. People who have accepted such a person are often upset when their formerly placating friend starts unleashing anger. Fortunately, if the transformation is completed, the angry period does not last long.

Placaters often find their release of anger very difficult. With so much anger stored up, it feels more like rage. The possibility of becoming totally out of control once the flow starts can be threatening. We need to remind placaters that acknowledging their anger still allows for choices about their behavior.

Blaming people have the opposite problem. They express their anger indiscriminately. Some of us still remember much of the "encounter movement" of the sixties when people were encouraged not only to express their feelings but to act on them as well. With people who blame, we suggest helping them acknowledge their feelings and accept them. Then, in a state of high self-esteem, they can decide what to do, both with themselves and with their feelings. In other words, we can help people be in touch with how they feel, deal with those feelings, and not jump into some type of reactive behavior. Just because someone feels something does not mean he or she should act on it.

The accompanying figure indicates the steps to take in dealing with anger. This process of second-level change includes transforming those feelings. Again, this means working at all other necessary levels of experience. Depending on the person and circumstances, you can start at any of these levels and move back and forth until all areas are covered, cleared, and changed.

Anger Transformed

BEHAVIOR   –   What action did you take when you were angry?

COPING   –   What were you trying to communicate to the other
                   person? How were you using anger to cope better?

FEELINGS   –   How were you feeling? (Angry) Were there other
                   feelings you felt, associated with anger? (Hurt, Fear)

FEELING ABOUT

FEELING   –   How do you feel about feeling angry?

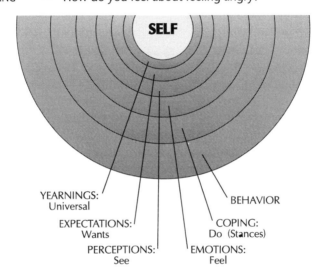

YEARNINGS:
Universal   BEHAVIOR

EXPECTATIONS: COPING:
Wants   Do (Stances)

PERCEPTIONS: EMOTIONS:
See   Feel

PERCEPTIONS –   What do you think would happen if you put words
                 to your angry feelings now? Did you have other
                 choices than becoming angry?

EXPECTATIONS–   Are you aware of what you were expecting that
                 might have precipitated your anger?

YEARNINGS   –   Underneath your expectations, what were your
                 yearnings or longings? How could you acknowledge
                 and express these yearnings differently?

SELF   –   What is your level of self-esteem?
                 a) prior to your anger?
                 b) during your anger?
                 c) following your anger?

The following partial transcript is from a session we observed with a counselor under our supervision. He was seeing a couple who were having "marital problems." During their second session, the wife expressed strong anger toward her husband about how he "always" put her down and how terrible she felt about it.

COUNSELOR: Does this remind you of anything in your earlier days?

WOMAN: Yes, he's just like my dad.

COUNSELOR: What did your dad do?

WOMAN: Well, he thought I had no brains and no looks, and he made me feel worthless.

COUNSELOR: What had you hoped for from your father?

WOMAN: More love, more acceptance.

COUNSELOR: What would you like to do about it now?

WOMAN: Well, maybe I can let go, let go of those expectations. But my husband still brings out those worthless feelings in me, and I get angry.

COUNSELOR: How could you let go of your feelings about yourself?

WOMAN: Well, maybe I don't have to see myself the way they did.

This counselor and client were doing two important tasks here. They were separating the present from the past, and the client was beginning to change her expectations and perceptions. Following some further work, the husband and wife started a new communication pattern. He started to hear his wife more clearly and could validate her importance. This started a process of communicating more openly and creating greater intimacy. She made a shift in her own sense of identity and worth. Perhaps her husband would make a similar shift before long.

TRANSFORMATION AND CONGRUENCE

Anger is a feeling that can be dealt with in a deeper transformational process that leads people to become more genuine, more whole, and more congruent at the level of Self. Congruence was initially identified with being in tune with our feelings and accepting them. The Satir model identifies three levels of congruence, as described in Chapter 4. All are important to becoming more fully human.

To recap, at the first level of congruence, we accept our feelings as they are. At Level 2, we are in harmony with our Self. If there is a discrepancy between having a certain feeling and being in harmony with our Self, we need to look at and possibly change our feeling. Feeling anger, hurt, or fear indicates a discrepancy at this level.

The third level of congruence is being in harmony with our Self and our life energy, spirituality, or God. This level of congruence has not received much attention in the literature or in practice. Satir incorporated this dimension more and more over time, first through her meditations and gradually throughout her general practice and training.

Change at any of these levels produces an internal shift that lets the person feel more responsible. The shift produces several other by-products: self-confidence, an awareness of more choices, and access to more inner resources. These in turn help change the person's dealings with the outer world, including making his or her relationships more intimate and his or her communication more effective.

People around this person often change too. In families with a delinquent youngster, for instance, we sometimes work only with the parents. After they have some success transforming their own lives, they report considerable improvement in their relationships with the youngster and in his or her behavior.

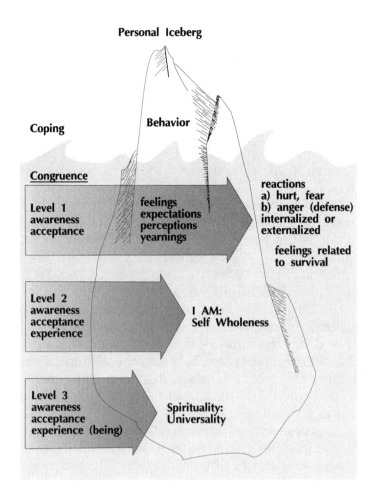

Personal Iceberg

This typifies the way systems change. Altering one component or member invariably affects every other part of the system. Likewise, as this chapter describes, our six levels of experience interlink and change in response to each other. Once we establish a therapeutic relationship and a supportive environment, the client provides the context for change.

Using Satir's creative methods, we can assist the transformation process with any particular intervention at any level of experience. Transformation on any of the levels can create chaos at any other level. This follows Satir's principle of change. Working through this eventually brings clients into more self-integration and congruence, which is the general therapeutic goal of the Satir model.

The next chapter addresses self-integration at length in terms of a vehicle for change called the Parts Party.

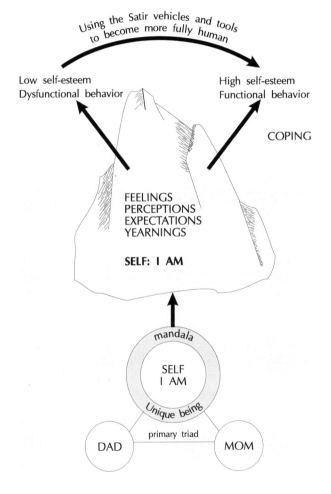

Satir's Transformation Process

8

The Parts Party: Integrating Inner Resources

Whenever we meet people, we assume that whatever they are expressing is the whole person. Yet at that moment we experience only one part of what they are. As we become better acquainted, we learn more about their other parts. For example, we see them at 4:30 in the afternoon when they look absolutely magnificent, and we see them at their worst first thing in the morning. They don't always seem the same people, yet they are.

One of Satir's major vehicles for change is called the Parts Party. This chapter describes it and looks closely at the many parts we human beings have, how we handle them, and how we can transform them into resources for being whole and congruent. The Parts Party is a process that identifies, transforms, and integrates our inner resources.

Our tendency to think of one piece as the whole brings to mind the story of four blind men each touching one part of an elephant—the tail, leg, trunk, and ear— and generalizing that part to make meaning of the whole.

A related concept—that people have many dissimilar facets—underlies the Parts Party process, which Satir used to create a new learning context.

The classical way to do a Parts Party is to have a group of 15 to 40 people who are willing to play the roles representing various parts of the "Host" (the person whose parts are to be transformed and integrated). A fairly large room provides space for an imaginary party room; the Guide (facilitator) needs a flip chart and may use other props to create a party atmosphere or strengthen the visual characterization of the parts being enacted.

Many of us deny the parts of ourselves we don't like and pay attention to the parts we consider acceptable. We try to be one thing—such as good, right, confident, or funny—as though we could embody only that one quality. In our efforts to hide what we find unacceptable, we deprive ourselves: we are unaware that our every ingredient is capable of many transformations and uses.

One way to accept and transform our "unacceptable" facets is through the Parts Party, whose title is paradoxical. Juxtaposing serious concerns with an entertaining party framework allows us to stand back and experience something other than the pain we have always associated with certain traits, circumstances, or events. Satir also worked in a way that excited people and appealed to their sense of the dramatic. This created a new learning context. We enjoy and remember great movies, for example, because they contain dramatic scenes. These dramatics make new learnings possible, exciting, and comfortable.

The Parts Party has five major steps: preparing the Host, describing how his or her parts behave, developing the inevitable conflict between the parts, transforming the parts so the conflict can be resolved, and following through with the integration ritual. These steps are detailed later in this chapter. The intervening sections provide their theoretical background.

PARTS AND RULES

We all have many parts or facets, which Satir called our "many faces." This actually means we have many possibilities. With every face goes a voice, a set of images, and a set of expectations related to our early survival. This concept of different faces parallels Roberto Assagioli's theory of psychosynthesis, in which different parts are called subpersonalities.

Most of us have labeled these parts positive or negative, good or bad. Some people label some of their inner parts—such as their Judge, Little Child, Old Person, Fear of Death, and Desire for Fun—as bad. These people have to use all their energy trying to keep these "bad" parts from showing.

To make all our parts available as resources, instead, we can transform them. We can also transform the implicit and explicit rules we have. These rules are resources too. Everything we have is a resource, but some people do not perceive parts of themselves this way. As long as we have to put down, hide, reject, or deny anything about ourselves, we cannot use our energy freely.

We constantly integrate numerous parts within us. We assign these parts different meanings and survival values. For instance, we may have assigned our child part a low or negative value, which means we should never let this facet show. Simplistically speaking, this value usually corresponds to what our parents considered unacceptable while we were growing up ("Don't be so childish!").

It is as though we looked at ourselves and made two columns: a "good" one and a "bad" one. Usually, when we make this kind of separation, we do it to get rid of the "bad" parts by ignoring, denying, or distorting them. Therefore, our energy goes toward presenting our "good" parts. When we try to hide the parts we consider bad, we eliminate possibilities of growth. Our inner Manager organizes our other parts to fit our perception of ourselves, not necessarily our inner wisdom.

We can expand the condition or state of any part at any time. We can also transform any we consider negative.

Some people think they don't have many resources. When they discover their resources, they find they have many sleeping parts that need reawakening. In many of us, our parts fight among each other continually, often to the extent of incapacitating us. Short of that, we end up procrastinating, saying one thing and doing another, and not feeling wholehearted. Consequently, the Parts Party's value lies in enabling us to amalgamate our resources into a harmonious state. Examining how our parts operate demonstrates our internal processes and provides the means to increase their effectiveness.

Meanwhile, our rules prevent us from acknowledging, integrating, and transforming our parts. These rules govern our human relations and tell us what parts of ourselves we can express. All human rules have a positive goal: to preserve self-worth. For example, if we have a rule that says we shouldn't be angry, we envision ourselves living by repressing our anger. The positive, life-preserving goal thus often has negative results.

We developed our rule against anger because we believed that if we express anger directly, we put ourselves in a vulnerable or dishonorable position and can then be rejected or punished. We learned our rules in childhood, usually in our relationships with our parents. During childhood, all the behaviors and knowledge we internalized were based on our parents' expectations. Therefore, if our mothers said, "Don't be angry," we acted accordingly. We internalized her messages, thinking we would be lovable as long as we acted according to these rules. (On the other hand, if our self-worth was smothered with too many "shoulds," we may have rebelled or withdrawn.)

To keep from showing the rule-breaking parts of ourselves puts a heavy burden on our wisdom. We cannot express our wisdom because we have overwhelmed it by worrying and attempting to maintain one particular image of ourselves. The jokester who channels all his energy into being a clown is an example of someone who depends on just one part of himself for survival. The same is true of someone whose identity lies in being intelligent and confining herself to being called only a "professor." Devoting ourselves to one image represses our other parts, leaving us feeling perpetually poverty-stricken and often lonely and empty.

Failing to acknowledge our parts keeps us from evolving. For instance, a person who grew up in a political system in which power was perceived as dangerous, cruel, manipulative, and controlling might perceive his or her own power as negative and be fearful of it. Another person may fail to acknowledge a part by saying, "I couldn't be brilliant because there was already a brilliant one in my family. She got all the good grades, and I didn't." When we dismiss or deny the parts we perceive as unacceptable, we eliminate growth possibilities. For instance, many of us pretend our anger does not exist ("I'm not really angry"). We may not realize our anger contains the basis for asserting ourselves. When we deny our anger, we do not acknowledge or exercise our assertiveness. Our rights continue being violated, and we continue feeling angry without exploring the possibility of growing in a different direction and developing communication patterns that break this cycle.

Rejecting our parts is like amputating our limbs. The more parts we deny and the longer our list of how we "should" be and behave, the more we cripple ourselves. And we do so in vain: the parts we decide we should not express eventually surface in devious, often destructive ways. This usually entails emotional or physical pain, or both.

Unexpressed anger at someone else, for instance, may result in feeling horrible about ourselves and treating ourselves badly. And if we meet someone who also denies his or her anger, we may find ourselves speaking politely on a superficial level while we battle each other on an unspoken level through our respectively denied parts.

Disowning parts of ourselves also shows up in the four imbalanced forms of communication: placating, blaming, being super-reasonable, and being irrelevant. Satir therefore intervened in ways that addressed people's internal processes and conflicts, not their words. When she heard placating responses, for instance, she discerned that people were discounting themselves in favor of others. Simultaneously, they were putting their own sense of worth into the hands of these other people.

When we make our self-worth depend on how others value us, we also make our self-image contingent on how they see us. In the process we amputate parts of ourselves according to what we expect will win their approval. An analogy is the person who finds a portrait in an art gallery that suits the image he or she wants. It is a picture of someone with green eyes, five foot two, and 101 pounds. Looking at him- or herself, the onlooker sees someone who is brown-eyed, five foot eight, and 170 pounds. He or she wishes it were possible to cut off the parts that do not match.

Participating in a Parts Party awakens the desire to acknowledge parts we have ignored, reevaluate parts we have kept hidden, see clearly any parts we have distorted, and re-evaluate parts that demand more attention. Through acknowledging our distorted parts, we can integrate ourselves into whole beings. Acknowledgment includes being aware of present reality rather than living in the past or in the conditional future. Accepting all our feelings brings us out of the panic and anxiety we feel when we deny, distort, or ignore our disliked parts. Obviously, this reduces the stress we put on ourselves.

Feeling tense is a clue that we may need to transform our internal process. Tension indicates a gap between our present state and our ideal self, what we consider we "should" be. Not being able to maintain ourselves in the narrow confines between our condition and our rules about that condition ("I feel angry, but I'm not supposed to") immobilizes us. And if we panic at this stage, we explode.

Identifying, acknowledging, examining, and employing our parts, rules, and inner wisdom help us transform our internal process and deal with present circumstances. By removing our self-made limits, we expand our choices.

INNER CONFLICTS

We each have myriad parts, resources, and characteristics, even though they manifest in many variations. Some parts are universal and need to be acknowledged in some form during a Parts Party. For example, we each have wisdom. Our wisdom cannot operate as long as we feel little and worthless. Often we do not notice our wisdom; it may speak to us through a still, small voice. We need to empower our wisdom and use it for our own growth and development.

Another universal part is the inner judge who says, "You shouldn't have done that." Our judges and our "shoulds" often go together. Satir reminded us that we can elect our own judges. We can specify the kind of judge that will help monitor what we are doing and support what we do. Most of us have a critical, censuring judge. We each need to develop our judge part as a friend.

We also each have a little child, a grown-up, a manager, an older person, a sexual part, the wish to continue our life force, the fear of death, the wish for fun, and a singing part. These parts don't always get along; for instance, sometimes the love of life and the fear of death conflict. The singing part is usually silent when the fear of death and the concern for hanging onto life dominate. The little child may want to play and the adult part says, "No! I'll keep you in jail forever."

Satir searched for the inner dialogue among people's parts, knowing that conflicts often are resolved through greater awareness and acceptance of these inner dynamics. Our conflicts arise because most of us label our parts as positive or negative. It is as though we looked at ourselves and made two columns, one for "good" attributes and another for "bad" ones. As mentioned earlier, the values we assign usually correspond to what our parents considered acceptable and unacceptable when we were growing up.

Usually when we make this kind of separation, we do so to get rid of the "bad" parts by ignoring, denying, or distorting them. For example, we may have assigned the little child a low survival value, which dictates that we should use all our energy to keep this "bad" part from showing.

Repressed, our "bad" parts clamor to get out. Their noise is so loud that our inner wisdom can't come through. A heavy burden also falls on the manager and the grown-up parts, who are responsible for hiding our unacceptable aspects. After all, they think it's terrible to be this or that.

Extremely worried that some undesirable part of us will come to light, we tighten up and eliminate certain possibilities for growth. Simultaneously, we squeeze out our life force.

DISCOVERING INNER RESOURCES

We can change this inner conflict at any time in our lives by relabeling and reintegrating our parts as inner resources. For instance, we find that our devalued little child played a vital part in our being here today. We are alive, we have made it, and we have survived no matter how destructive or painful our experiences were in growing up. That little child survived, and his or her history of coping became a learning experience.

The next chapter relates the story of a thirty-six-year-old man who felt isolated as a child, convinced that his father wanted to kill him. The boy grew up with anger, pain, and low self-esteem. In spite of his environment, he had strength and developed ways to cope. When he learned to recognize and validate himself as a child and his strength to survive, he started treating his own children and himself differently.

Our little child provides our largest platform of possibilities; our experiences as children were very broad. Many of us got more and more narrow in our views of ourselves as we got older. We may feel we have little, if any, inner wisdom, creativity, and abundance. When we rediscover our many parts and see how they all connect with each other, we realize we can reawaken our resources. We no longer have to limit the little child's foundations. If we label or deny parts of ourselves, we feel a lack of resourcefulness. And if we immediately remember that all our parts connect and depend on each other, we can experience an image of diversity with unity.

Most people who have participated in a Parts Party use this image constantly. No matter how lonely they may be, they never feel as poverty-stricken as before. It is important to know that we can go through the cycle of life and grow and expand—a process the inner older person is also capable of relishing. Experiencing a Parts Party means breaking our taboos about how we "should" be, so it frees us to become more resourceful, connected, and congruent. We acknowledge and express more of ourselves more comfortably.

Acknowledging Our Parts

In the acknowledgment process, we learn about those hidden parts that bore the title "should not." Feeling angry, vulnerable, sexual, fearful, or boastful are commonly denied or distorted parts. This includes using euphemisms or modifiers for them, such as, "I'm frustrated" or "I'm a little bit irritated" (rather than angry).

By acknowledging them, we also give clear form to parts that previously felt nebulous or vague. In addition, we may find parts that say, "I ought to behave as if I felt uptight about this" or "I ought to behave as if I were offended, but actually I like it." We also have parts we already acknowledge and accept. These require nothing further than allowing them to evolve, since all our parts are capable of further growth.

Still other parts are sleeping. Like dormant buds, not only do they need to be acknowledged and awakened; we also need to nurture and use them. The transformation process continues toward this end.

Accepting Our Parts

Once we acknowledge a part of ourselves, we can work on accepting it. This begins the process of transforming it into a piece that can relate to and enhance our other parts, which is a major function of the Parts Party.

Satir often used the metaphor of people treating parts of themselves like vicious dogs, confining them in a small area with locked gates and high fences. Our hungry dogs howl continuously and bite ferociously when we open the gate. Then people tell us, "You see?" or "I told you so." But if we care for our dogs, nurturing and accepting them, we can let them out safely. They may bark, but they won't bite.

In the acceptance phase, we pay attention to our dogs and feed them. From our immobilized condition of polarizing our "good" and "bad" parts, we shift to a state in which each of our parts is equally eligible for being integrated and valued.

Transforming Our Parts

Between accepting a part and integrating it, we may need to transform it. This does not mean eliminating anything; every part is capable of being transformed and contains growth energy for us if we discover how to use it.

In its primitive state, the energy of negatively valued parts is not always particularly useful. Anger, arrogance, destructiveness, and manipulation have potentially creative powers, but not in their existing expressions. The Satir model helps us liberate these parts, allowing their captive energy to be used in cooperative, nurturing ways.

Having access to every part's energy is like being in command of a series of switches. We can activate the switch to any of our parts—our child, our hedonist, our judge, our wisdom, and so on. We can also deactivate any switch ("I don't want that kind of judge any more") without affecting the system's electrical current. With practice, we become so well acquainted with our switches that we can turn them on and off according to our capabilities and needs.

Using this kind of metaphor helps us realize how much power we can exercise over our inner lives. Satir also used the image of a seed, which contains tremendous latent energy. Although it starts small, it soon evolves into a thriving plant if we give it light, nutrients, and a place to grow. Imagining our parts as seeds that are ready to flourish under the right conditions helps us visualize our own power and our capacity for transformation.

We can use this power creatively or destructively. If we feel powerless, we usually try to obtain a sense of mattering from other people. That shows in this inner plea: "I'm nothing, and you have to help me. If you go, I'm nothing." Or we may base our psychological survival on material items, such as monetary wealth. We then find that if we lose our money, we lose our sense of value and purpose. We may even commit suicide.

The Parts Party works toward a balanced concept of power that requires acknowledging our own resources and using our resultant energy creatively. It transforms hostility, for example, which is a combination of helplessness, effort, and projecting our pain onto another. If we stay with our hostility—"Isn't this awful?" or "Poor me!" or "It's all your fault!"—we stunt our growth. If we transform hostility slightly, we find our ability to be helpless. Transform this further and we have the capability to take action. Hostility can actually provide us with energy if it is transformed.

We can likewise transform jealousy. Unchanged, it causes us to mutter, "You've got something I haven't, and you're terrible for having it. I'm nothing for not having it, and that's not fair." Jealousy transformed becomes our ability to see ourselves in relation to someone else for growth rather than competition. It can become an opportunity to learn from the other person, to discover that we have similar or different resources to feel good about, and even to share our resources.

Many of us fail to transform parts of ourselves because we accept our "correct" feelings and deny our "wrong" ones. Accepting only the "good," "clean," and "right" parts of ourselves usually results in feeling dry, uninteresting, and empty, however. We are repressing a lot of potential energy. This detracts from our entire being, since each part is significant to the whole and helps it be more efficient. Despite its specialized function, each of our parts is a hologram of our being. It is like each cell in our body, which contains the specific message for its own function as well as the genetic program for our whole body. Each of our parts contains the wholeness of our being. Conversely, this wholeness can become characteristic of the different parts once we integrate them.

Integrating Our Parts

The Parts Party's goal is to transform and integrate our various parts, using what Satir called our *life force toward wholeness*. In many people, this inherent force toward integration is in a dormant or budding stage. It gets stronger during the Parts Party as we begin to gain a holistic perspective about our parts. Without feeling inferior or superior to anyone, we come to see that we can understand each of our parts, each has its place in us, and each can relate to every other part. We also realize it is immaterial whether we derived any parts from our parents or other family members.

Gaining this sense of unity about our parts, we can begin to behave differently, in an unfragmented manner.

Our parts no longer fight continually, our heads pulling one way and our hearts another. When one part triumphs over another, we splinter ourselves. We also promote fragmentation if we confine our work to one level. An example is examining how our mothers treated us without looking at how our fathers treated us, how our mothers felt about how our fathers treated us, and how our fathers felt about how our mothers treated us.

In the integration process, we need to work at all these levels and examine all our parts. The point is to discover how our parts can support, help, and love each other as they perform their individual functions. Some parts need help with their tasks, and integration allows us to muster our resources so that happens. For example, our fingers cannot do what our hearts do, yet our fingers and our hearts have a relationship with one another. We can use our fingers to caress someone; they help us carry out our hearts' intent.

STRUCTURING THE PARTS PARTY

Having outlined the basic processes of the Parts Party—acknowledging, accepting, transforming, and integrating—we can now examine how its context and structure express these stages.

Context

Satir placed great importance on creating a context of good humor and enjoyment. In her work, enjoyment often entailed dramatics and humor. She also used paradoxes. Dealing with serious issues in the framework of a play, game, or party, she would create a paradox by asking people to discover humorous aspects of what were otherwise threatening experiences.

In addition, she infused a comprehensive perspective into new learnings. For instance, in working with a woman who talked about her horror of kissing in public, Satir asked, "Will it kill anybody?" The woman laughed. Referring to death in a situation like this can be an easy way to elicit someone's sense of humor while adding greater perspective to their situation.

Although we often treat events as if they were life-and-death matters, this is rarely a reality. If someone agrees with us and says, "Oh, my, yes, that's really awful," we may get reinforced, but we also feel suffocated right away. If someone lightens our outlook with humor, the context becomes fun and creative, and we can take in new learnings much more easily.

Old learnings often hamper us from seeing new circumstances. Our left brain tends to draw conclusions from single incidents. If a dog bit us in the past, we may have decided that all dogs bite and we should avoid them forever. We may have discounted that this dog was an old bitch with a new litter, and that we had interfered with her pups. We also may have ignored the fact that some dogs do not bite. Therefore, we sometimes need help to see new learnings in a larger context, such as the one the Parts Party provides.

Steps

Here is a summary of the Parts Party's five steps.

1. Prepare the Guide and Host for the party.
   a. Identify the Host's parts in terms of famous people.
   b. Select adjectives for them.
   c. Categorize these adjectives.
   d. Select role-players.
2. Have the parts meet each other.
   a. Initiate the party by having the parts meet and interact.

    b. Have the parts freeze and then identify their feelings.

    c. Verify these with the Host.

    d. As they resume interacting, have the parts exaggerate their expression of subsequent feelings.

    e. Have them freeze again and identify these feelings.

    f. Verify them with the Host.

3. Develop a conflict.

    a. Have the parts try to shape the party in their own image.

    b. Have one part dominate the party.

    c. Have all the parts freeze and identify their feelings.

    d. Verify with the Host.

4. Transform the conflict.

    a. Have the parts interact and achieve cooperation.

    b. Have them build harmony with each other.

    c. Have them accept each other.

    d. Verify this process with the Host.

5. Perform the integration ritual.

    a. Have each part present its many resources and transformations.

    b. Have each part ask the Host for acceptance.

    c. Have the Host accept and integrate all the parts.

    d. Have the Host take charge of these parts with new choices and new energy.

Prepare the Guide and Host

You, the therapist, are called the *Guide* of the Parts Party. The person who wants to accept, transform, and integrate his or her parts is the *Host*.

To prepare the Host, talk with him or her beforehand and find out what he or she hopes to achieve through the Parts Party's integration process. The clearer the goal, the more forceful the experience.

To prepare yourself, also get as much information as necessary to form clear images of the parts the Host wants to integrate.

Before the party starts, clear yourself of any distractions so knowledge can flow unhampered from your left brain to your right brain. Parts Parties are spontaneous, action-packed experiences that need both your formal and your improvisational talents, so this is important.

As the person who directs the action—the Guide— you have many responsibilities in the Parts Party. These include pointing out meaningful events in the role-playing and making their significance more obvious to the Host by asking pertinent questions. The manner in which you guide instigates and colors the transformation process.

For the party to succeed, it is essential that you develop trust in the Parts Party process. This originates in acknowledging that every one of us has pieces that constitute a greater whole. Out of trusting and out of the process comes the reawakening of hope in the Host. This releases energy and excitement, creating a vehicle for change with dramatic appeal.

The high level of trust you develop with the participants is also important. It enables them to go into an altered state of awareness during the Parts Party, which is necessary for becoming fully aware of inner parts. Satir did not use hypnotic techniques to establish trust. Rather, she created the context in which trust thrives. Trust develops through the Guide's attentive contact with the Host, which displays a sense of excitement and provides a sense of security and acceptance.

Novice guides often become overly concerned with small details and with directing all of the parts too rigidly. This may make the role-players anxious about their performances. To create a more comfortable atmosphere, Satir told guides not to focus on analytical details but to encourage the flow of information from the Host and to observe the evolution of this information. Since participants do not know how this will be expressed, you need to be aware of how to develop each of the steps in the party.

Identify the Host's Parts

Have the Host select six to eight parts to work with, and then think of well-known characters or people to represent these parts. They can be characters from nursery rhymes or literature, historical or political figures, movie stars, and so on.

Extreme examples are especially useful. Some should be characters who make the Host's hair stand on end; some should make him or her feel juicy inside. Questions you can ask include: "What famous figure makes you think, 'Oh, I can't *stand* that person!' or 'That person makes me feel good'?"

The more parties you guide, the more you will discern the universality of the parts that Hosts choose. Regardless of culture and language, we humans share similar experiences and similar difficulties integrating them. One commonly chosen character, for instance, is Adolf Hitler. Untransformed, our inner Hitlers destroy. The point is not to discard this part indiscriminately, however. Transformed, it becomes a source of power and energy for creative and relevant methods of self-protection.

For the purposes of this discussion, we will suppose your Host gives you the following characters:

- Buddha
- Marilyn Monroe
- Satan
- Snoopy
- Richard Nixon
- Albert Einstein

Hosts are not restricted to choosing characters to represent those parts. You can invent variations to suit individual needs for integrating different aspects of the Self. For instance, let's say Thomas wants to work on body image. He may want to choose parts of his body—arms, legs, head, heart, face, and stomach—to represent parts of his image that trouble him. With blind people, Satir used sounds as guests at the party.

Nor is the Parts Party restricted to a particular population. Satir was able to develop trust relationships and do Parts Parties with psychotics, bringing them to an astonishing level of integration. Actually, everybody is a good candidate for a Parts Party, especially people who are having considerable internal conflict, those who want to know themselves better, and those who need more significant integration than other therapeutic processes provide.

Select Adjectives for the Parts

Have the Host say the first adjective that comes to mind for each character (or body part). Buddha may thus be pure; Monroe, sexy; and Satan, evil. These adjectives correspond to the way the Host processes things internally, so it is important that he or she supply the adjectives without "help" from you or other participants. Our parts are universal, but we each experience them differently and so use different adjectives. And it is these adjectives that the Parts Party seeks to transform.

In this example, the Host first thought of these adjectives:

Buddha	Pure
Marilyn Monroe	Sexy
Satan	Evil
Snoopy	Funny
Richard Nixon	Deceitful
Albert Einstein	Intelligent

It is important to note that we are like carousels, our many faces turning continuously. Often unaware of what parts are facing the outer world, we frequently show parts of ourselves that we do not know we have.

Categorize These Adjectives

Ask the Host to indicate which adjectives he or she considers positive or negative. For example:

Pure	Positive
Sexy	Positive
Evil	Negative
Funny	Positive
Deceitful	Negative
Intelligent	Positive

To start the transformation process, ask the Host to consider situations in which each positive adjective would become negative and vice-versa. This challenges any kind of all-or-nothing linear thinking; it also gives the Host a sense of having choices, which is a major goal of the Parts Party.

An example is the use of lying. We may describe other people as liars, and we may rate lying as negative. When challenged, though, most of us can think of a good situation in which to lie. One would be when lying would save someone's life.

This kind of realization simply lets people acknowledge that a negative act or quality can sometimes become an ally and be used positively. Recognizing such choices signifies that the Host is beginning to separate particular events from his or her use of them. In other words, events (or people) do not cause our responses. How we respond is a choice we make and is not controlled by events outside us.

Select Role-players

By this time, the Host may be in a slight trance or at least have opened his brain's intuitive side (right hemisphere), and is flowing with the process. (For more on trances, see Chapter 9.) At such a stage, ask the Host to select and invite participants from the audience to enact the characters.

Give each person selected the opportunity to accept or reject the invitation explicitly. This allows for an important interactive process between Host and role-player. Once someone accepts a role, the Host explains how he or she thinks each particular adjective is manifested in terms of body movement, interactive behavior, voice, statements, and so on. For example, the Guide might ask the Host how Buddha's purity would be manifested, in the Host's perception.

The impact of the part is increased if each individual has some simple props or costumes to highlight the character he or she represents. Before beginning the party, Satir usually scheduled time for the role-players to find clothes and props.

It also helps to suggest a setting for the party, which people can then imagine. Sometimes music adds to the illusion of being at a party. As the Guide, you will also be able to make a conscious attempt to raise the proceedings' level of fun, laughter, and humor. Stay in the intuitive, emotional sphere as much as possible.

For instance, when people reconvened and before the party started, Satir would lead a short meditation focusing on breathing. This let participants give themselves permission to act, observe, and be in touch with all the parts they would encounter. During this meditation, Satir would tell the role-players they had been mailed invitations to a party. After closing the meditation, she would announce the start of the party.

Have the Parts Meet

Initiate the party by having the parts meet each other and interact. The Host and Guide stand on the sidelines, observing how the role-players behave. Guests arrive randomly, just as they would at any party. The Host remains "invisible" to the guests, who make their own introductions and engage each other in terms of their stereotypes or caricatures. Watch each one for several minutes after his or her entrance; role-players' gestures, posture, and speech should exemplify their assigned characteristics.

Satir clarified that we are looking for how our parts behave, not how we "should" behave. This emphasis is especially important for people who fail to realize that they own their parts. Once we understand our ownership, we can observe our parts and say, "Yes, this happens with me," rather than, "My parts are making me do it."

Have the parts freeze and identify their feelings. At some point as they continue meeting, you (the Guide) announce a complete freeze on the action. Usually there are three such freezes during this part of the process. At first, you help the Host see how these parts are managing, how they cluster, and how they separate. Watching our parts interact is like watching ourselves internally. You may give directions to the parts so the Host can see specific groupings. Check with the Host, however, to make sure these groupings fit his or her experience. You need to make sure you do not shape the parts according to some preconceived design. Your directions need to emanate from watching the role-playing and taking into account how the Host responds. Then ask each part what he or she is feeling personally in this role.

Verify these feelings with the Host. Consult with the Host to ascertain how closely each role-player's feelings—as well as verbal and body languages—match the Host's perceptions of that part. For example, to emphasize his despicable quality, the Richard Nixon actor may have to be told to sneer, avoid eye contact, glance around quickly, and hunch his head forward in an exaggerated, tense way.

As they resume interacting, have the parts exaggerate their expression of subsequent feelings. We can do little on the outside that matches the more intense emotions we feel inside. The more extreme the parts can be as they continue mingling, the more helpful and successful they are in contributing to the transformation of the Host's parts.

For example, Buddha might preach world peace, Monroe might try to seduce Nixon, and Nixon might pretend to be listening to Einstein, while watching Satan. Satan might try to destroy Snoopy, and Snoopy might find the whole scene amusing. Einstein might try to connect with Buddha to make sense of what is going on.

If role-players are in an altered state of awareness, they spontaneously reflect the Host's inner workings. This uncanny mirroring is not surprising when we remember that the Host intentionally chose all the parts and their adjectives. In this process, the Host and each role-player established a subconscious agreement. What follows can only be explained in terms of common human experiences, the subconscious, the universality of inner life.

Whatever the main feelings the characters reveal at the first freeze, the next move is for them to continue the party, exaggerating their feelings as they continue mingling.

Have them freeze again and identify their own feelings. As Guide, you need to stay in charge of the process. The party becomes the playing out of parts. It is an external manifestation of the Host's internal workings.

Verify these feelings with the Host. Pay close attention to his responses. See whether what is happening is familiar so that the Host can make connections with his or her own internal process. Have the Host internalize as much of the experience as possible. Satir often hastened the Host's recognition and assimilation of experiences by characterizing what he or she might be feeling, in as few words as possible.

After the sharing, ask each character to identify which of these new feelings he or she will exaggerate. Then have them all resume interacting while you and the Host watch.

Develop a Conflict

As the Parts Party unfolds, it becomes obvious that certain parts will have to collide. While you will see certain parts evolving, others develop a stalemate with each other; they are not able to proceed in tandem.

Have the parts try to shape the party in their own image. This time, when you ask the parts how they feel, also ask them how they want to change things to improve the party. Then, for the next scene, instruct them to take action to control the party. In effect, you are asking them each to dominate the party.

What this represents is our trying to integrate at a point of great stress when, instead of reducing conflict and increasing cooperation among our parts, all hell breaks loose.

Have one part dominate the party. For instance, if "Anger" dominates the party, it may yell, blame, sit on others, or bind people up. In the process, the other parts obtain new information from each other in an effort to coexist. Having one of our parts dominate the party represents the effort most of us make when we try to get a linear focus.

Full domination of the party by one part is unsuccessful. The more one part tries to dominate, the more chaos and division occur. After this had unfolded for a time, Satir would sometimes ask three different parts to try to dominate. This proves equally unsuccessful.

Have all the parts freeze and identify their feelings. You can ask each part what has to be done for him or her to dominate: "You all intend to dominate, so how is it that it's not happening?"

Anger might typically respond, "Well, I can't dominate because Satan won't allow it."

"So what are you going to do about Satan? And Satan, what are you going to do in relation to this?"

The point here is that the effort to integrate behaviors begins the process of parts living in harmony.

Verify with the Host. Throughout this domination process, check the validity of the role-playing with the Host. Cognition is not vital at this stage, so Satir usually asked, "Does this scene say anything to you? Is it familiar?" Checking in this way lets you know if anything ill-fitting has entered the scene. If so, it may mean the Host is denying some new information; or that the information does not fit. In either case, you need to continue the process by moving on to something else.

Satir often asked the parts to pause and then move again in whatever direction they wanted to go. Again, whenever it fits, you can freeze the action and have each part share his or her experience, thoughts, and feelings.

Extremely infrequently, the Host struggles so much internally that he or she cannot identify with the parts at this stage of conflict. (If so, you can encourage the Host to stay with the struggle.) More commonly, the Host finds that observing and verifying the parts is very helpful; this process often offers new insight into our internal workings.

Transform the Conflict

The next stage requires transforming the parts so the conflict can be resolved. Satir often suggested that someone from the audience take notes on each transformation. If the Host has written material to refer to later, he or she can integrate knowledge that may not have been triggered during the actual party.

When dominating the party was unsuccessful, Satir asked each part for specific suggestions regarding desired behavior from the other parts. Typical responses include: "I've got to get Intelligence to shut up," and "I've got to get Sex to stop being so dominating."

Have the parts interact and achieve cooperation. After eliciting these responses, Satir asked each part what it needed to enable it to cooperate with the rest of the parts: "Whom do you need to help you? What do you need from them? What are you willing to do?"

Guides need to help Hosts to become knowledgeable about and accept their parts. This is the crucial first step toward integration: to move freely and in harmony with each other, all the parts need to show how they can cooperate with and be useful to one another.

When we see a part of ourselves (such as anger) released and translated into another resource (such as assertiveness), we no longer have to be afraid of that part. By allowing ourselves to express a previously repressed part, we receive feedback that enables us to act differently. We still retain our parts, but we have transformed them by adding new dimensions.

Have the parts build harmony with each other. As all our parts begin relating harmoniously on some level, we see how they initiate their relationships. For instance, our Nixon part may begin as dishonest, may evolve through desperation and loneliness, and may end by wanting to reach out and make meaningful contact with others. Through each transformation, other parts assist.

The rudimentary attitude of dishonesty, when pressed, turns to desperation. Underneath the desperation we find loneliness and, beneath this, a sense of help-lessness. After all these transformations, dishonesty becomes congruent in that it becomes an honest call for help.

In one Parts Party, when Satir felt the Host was ready, she drew attention to a connection other than the ones the parts themselves had made. The Hostess, June, had evolved to a point in her loneliness where she was fully aware of it. Meanwhile, she was paying attention to a power part that had evolved into wanting to protect. When Satir heard the power part—"I am now your ability to protect yourself"—she asked June, "Are you hearing about loneliness over there, saying 'I am lonely'?"

Satir timed her question for when June could form new perceptions. June saw the new possibilities: that her power part had another dimension and could now become her protection, and that she could accept her lonely part.

Have the parts accept each other. When the Host has recognized the new possibilities, have the corresponding parts act this out.

Verify this process with the Host. Satir then said, "Now all your other parts are hearing what's going on. Does that fit where you are?" Struggling to reconcile her many parts and have them be in harmony, June had been neglecting her lonely part. With this intervention, she recognized and integrated it.

Perform the Integration Ritual

The Parts Party leads to an integrated experience which cannot be dictated. It must evolve out of the Host's own inner world. If we stop the party at the point where we just see how the parts cluster, we merely duplicate the way the Host is now ordering him- or herself. People cannot perform the integration until the parts are ready and the transformations have taken place. Sometimes this whole process takes several hours.

The integration ritual is the last phase of the Parts Party. This relatively short, powerful process requires the Host to acknowledge his or her parts and their transformations. This reinforces the acceptance of each part in a symbolic way. The ritual also helps us integrate as a complete entity the transformation processes we have witnessed and accepted.

Have each part present its many resources. To integrate learnings from the Parts Party, we need to make all our parts available to ourselves, even those dormant ones that have just reawakened. Many of our dormant parts had previously been denied or ignored. When we see the possibilities of transformation, we open ourselves to a process of regeneration.

As Guide, you arrange all the parts side by side in a circle around the Host. Have the first character reach out toward the Host with one hand, identify the part and all its transformations, and ask if the Host will accept that part. If the Host answers yes, the role-player gently places a palm on the upper chest or shoulder of the Host, or owner. This does not exert much pressure; it is a light physical touch that anchors the experience.

Then, with the Host remaining stationary and the first part maintaining contact, all the parts move a few steps sideways. A new character now faces the Host and repeats this process of identifying the part, requesting acceptance, and making physical contact. In the end, a necklace of hands encircles the Host's chest and upper back. (Your job is to make sure the Host remains unweighted and balanced physically.)

Have each part ask the Host for acceptance. You also need to make sure that the Host's recognition of each part involves thought and acceptance. When each part requests acceptance, make sure that all of that part's possible transformations are included in the request.

For example, the Nixon part might say, "I am your Nixon. I am your ability to be despicable. I am sometimes pitiful and sometimes confused about my power and the good of others. Will you accept me?" Stopping here, the owner might reply with hesitation, as in: "It's kind of hard to deal with him."

You would need to ask the Nixon character to come up with other possibilities: "I'm your power and your ability to have energy, and to have others work with me. I have the capacity to relate to others. I am also fearful, and my fear sometimes interferes with what I want to achieve. Will you accept me?"

A fuller explanation from the part about further possibilities and transformations usually results in whole-hearted acceptance by the owner.

Have the Host accept and integrate all the parts. The result of a successful Parts Party is the Host's full acknowledgment and ownership of all of his or her parts. This enables the Host to feel complete and to be aware of all the resources available to him or her.

Some of us find it difficult to accept the different states of our parts. We do not want to admit to viciousness, vindictiveness, anger, or vengeance. Many of us try to integrate these parts through force, not evolution, by omitting necessary acknowledgment and transformation steps—an enterprise devoid of lasting benefit.

Despicable and "negative" parts are not the only ones we may find difficult to accept. However, putting any part or ability into a positive framework—such as its wise, comfortable, creative, or benevolent uses—generally lets the Host recognize that part more readily in the integration ritual.

When we look back at ourselves, we often see our own absurdities. We may wonder how we ever thought or acted a certain way. When we realize our potential to be friendly and loving toward ourselves, we may view some of our past acts as surreptitious and vindictive. When we see ourselves as caricatures of absurdity, though, we can laugh. This combination of tragedy and comedy reinforces the realistic quality of what we learn in the Parts Party. Before experiencing our own transformation, we may be afraid to expose all our parts; afterward, we can show them easily and be friendly toward them.

Transformations fail if any part has been neglected or omitted. You will know whether a part is missing if the Host cannot claim all of his or her parts. One part we often overlook is our sexuality (not necessarily referring to genital sex). Until we take sex into account, our parts are not in harmony. When we discover what we lack, we can find the part we need. We have all the resources we need; however, we may have to awaken them or see them in a new form.

If the Host has trouble owning all the parts, you can ask, "What objection do you have to what your part is presenting to you?" Once you know the objection, you can ask the Host to enlist other parts to help with the objection. If the Host cannot accept the Nixon part, for instance, Loneliness might say Nixon is needed to feel protected. This may help the Host overcome his or her objections.

Another tack is to ask, "What aspect of this part would you feel comfortable claiming right now?" You can then work on building the Host's acceptance of this part. All our parts have energy, and they are potential troublemakers until we understand, care for, and transform them. Then they become pieces of our internal resources.

Have the Host take charge of these parts with new choices and new energy. Once the Host has accepted all the parts in the circle, lead him or her in an appreciation of the ritual. Satir often equated the Parts Party process with a spiritual experience, and she used the following appreciation:

> *Let your body be balanced. Allow the hands of all your parts to be balanced just as they are . . . and I would like you at this moment to be in touch with the fact that you have seen many parts. You have seen them in their many states of interaction. You have seen them in all their possibilities for transformation.*

I would just like you—at this moment, as you feel the physical representation of each hand around your shoulders—to be in touch with the meaning that you feel in these parts. All of these parts can appear at any time with you, in any state. Your parts will move and change as they transform completely.

What I would like your parts to do is to move in a light way around you while you remain in one place. You will feel the many parts as they move around you, leaving the meanings that you take from their presentation. Feel this in your body and let yourself be in touch with the energy from the earth and from the heavens. Let your lovely eyes close, and at this moment be aware of what you're feeling right now. You are in contact with all your parts.

When you have words, could you share them?

Satir's closing words in the ritual directed the Host to look at all the parts as they moved slowly around, being aware of his or her richness of resources and the ability to be in charge of all these parts. Then Satir advised that, as the parts remove their hands one by one, they leave meanings in the owner's body. When the Host wishes, he or she opens his or her eyes.

It often helps all participants if the role-players discuss how they felt during the transformations in the party. Usually the role-players identify strongly with the parts they played, so they gain insight from the Host's remarks and vice-versa.

This chapter describes the classical form of the Satir Parts Party. Many variations use its essence and process, such as the reframing techniques of neurolinguistic programming. In individual therapy, it is also possible to have the Host experience each step through visualization and imagery. This is a useful way for clients to make contact with and integrate their parts and inner process.

9

Family Reconstruction

Family Reconstruction is an intervention developed by Satir for reintegrating people into the historical and psychological matrix of their own family of origin. One of the major Satir vehicles for change, it provides a way of seeing ourselves and our parents with new eyes, and thus seeing the present and the future in a new perspective. This includes giving ourselves greater possibilities and more freedom, and being responsible.

PREPARATORY SESSION

The Star—the person whose family will be reenacted—is usually picked in advance of the reconstruction session. The Star and the Guide (the facilitator) devote about three hours to preparation beforehand, completing the Star's family maps, a family life chronology, and a "Wheel of Influence" (all described in later sections). These tools help clarify what the Star wants to change and help explore certain facts about the Star's family of origin.

This preparatory meeting between Guide and Star also serves to make a good and trusting contact and contract, to become familiar with all the material (in terms of both its contents and its process), to clarify the specific changes the Star wants to make, and to start the process of change (i.e., the therapist enters the family system).

The Family Map

The universal map, or most basic family plan, consists of three people: an adult male, an adult female, and a child. The Satir way of presenting this is:

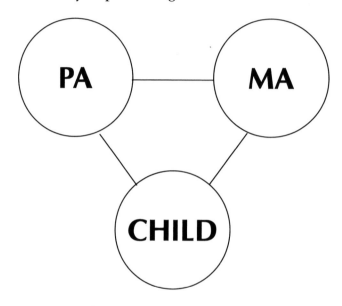

As Satir's concept of family spanned three generations, we expand this map to include the Star's maternal and paternal grandparents.

The analogy of a map is useful for outlining the territory of Family Reconstruction and making its route easier to travel. It helps to remember, though, that the map is not the territory. The family map simply helps us learn about our internal and external reality by illustrating who was involved in the Star's early existence, even though these relatives may no longer be present. The family map symbolizes most of the "cast of characters" who will appear in the Family Reconstruction.

Preparing family maps takes place in four stages. The first stage asks for details of the Star's parents:

- Date of marriage
- Name of each parent
- Birthdates and birthplaces
- Current ages or ages at death
- Religious affiliations
- Occupations
- Ethnic backgrounds
- Education
- Hobbies

For ease of illustration, we use a biologically intact family here. Adaptations can be made for single-parent families, stepfamilies, and other families that are not biologically intact.

In the second stage, the Guide asks the Star to add these elements for each parent:

- Three descriptive adjectives
- His or her primary coping stance under stress
- His or her secondary coping stance under stress

The Star's construct of reality is what operates in Family Reconstruction, so objective accuracy is not critical. If the Star does not have certain information, the Guide encourages him or her to "make it up."

Stage 3 is illustrated below. The Star adds:

- All the children, from eldest down
- First-stage information for each child (*listed above*)
- Second-stage information for each child (*listed above*)

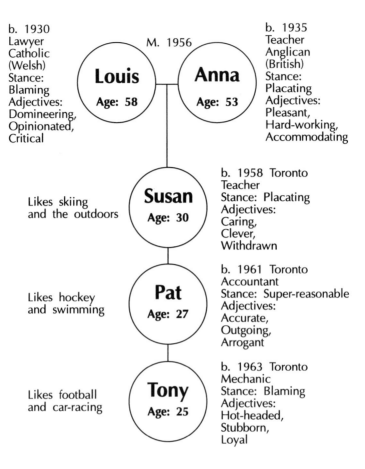

b. 1930
Lawyer
Catholic
(Welsh)
Stance:
Blaming
Adjectives:
Domineering,
Opinionated,
Critical

M. 1956

Louis
Age: 58

Anna
Age: 53

b. 1935
Teacher
Anglican
(British)
Stance:
Placating
Adjectives:
Pleasant,
Hard-working,
Accommodating

Likes skiing
and the outdoors

Susan
Age: 30

b. 1958 Toronto
Teacher
Stance: Placating
Adjectives:
Caring,
Clever,
Withdrawn

Likes hockey
and swimming

Pat
Age: 27

b. 1961 Toronto
Accountant
Stance: Super-reasonable
Adjectives:
Accurate,
Outgoing,
Arrogant

Likes football
and car-racing

Tony
Age: 25

b. 1963 Toronto
Mechanic
Stance: Blaming
Adjectives:
Hot-headed,
Stubborn,
Loyal

In Stage 4, the Star creates three separate third-stage maps: for his or her maternal grandparents, paternal grandparents, and the Star's own family of origin. In addition to third-stage data, the Star indicates (from his or her perspective):

- Family rules of parents and grandparents
- Any family patterns (e.g., occupations, illnesses, coping stances, causes of death, etc.)
- Family values and beliefs (e.g., value of education, money, etc.)

- Family myths and secrets
- Family themes

For presentation to the group, the Star usually puts all these maps on large flip-chart paper, to be displayed or hung during the actual Family Reconstruction.

Compiling the family maps smoothes the way for constructing the next tool, a chronology of the family's life. (See Appendix B.)

Family Life Chronology

The family life chronology is the second step necessary before the actual Family Reconstruction begins. It covers three generations, beginning at the birth of the Star's oldest grandparent and ending when the Star comes of age (eighteen, nineteen, or twenty-one, in most jurisdictions). For example, the Star's oldest grandparent may have been born in 1901, and the Star may have come of age in 1975.

The chart integrates the following information in chronological order:

- Birthdates of each family member
- Dates of important family events (e.g., moves, marriages, divorces, deaths, reunions, tragedies) and achievements (e.g., graduations, promotions)
- Dates of important historical events (e.g., wars, natural disasters, economic upheavals)

The family life chronology usually takes four or five sheets of flip-chart paper.

Wheel of Influence

The Wheel of Influence chart shows every person who influenced the Star intellectually, emotionally, or physically during childhood and adolescence. These people gave the Star many learnings, and the Star responded or reacted to them in some way. The Star also responded or reacted to these people's interactions with each other.

The more people the Star names in his or her wheel, the more influences and resources that person had to draw on in his or her development. People to include are: family members of three generations, others who lived in the Star's home (or in whose homes the Star lived), special teachers, and friends. Other influences include: imaginary playmates, pets, treasured toys, and person-specific events and items.

The Star writes his or her name in the center, surrounded by circles representing the other people—like a wheel with spokes. The spokes can vary in width, with thicker lines indicating greater closeness.

Below each name, the Star lists three adjectives that describe that person. (With family members, it is enough to use the same adjectives as in the family maps.) Then the Star labels each adjective as positive or negative, as shown in the accompanying illustration.

Many Stars worry about not being able to remember or ask relatives about childhood events and their family's chronology. The Guide can provide reassurance on this. When we are young, we store everything we learn or experience in our brain's right hemisphere (sometimes called our subconscious). Consequently, we believe that we can also recall it. Family Reconstruction provides the process through which this is possible.

The hope in a Family Reconstruction is to integrate the knowledge and wisdom of the Star's left and right hemispheres. Our cognitive understanding often provides the context of what happened, even if we were not particularly aware of it as children. Likewise, when Satir talked about an altered state, or trance, she was talking about moving beyond our cognitive part and using our intuitive part to tap the wisdom of the Self and to provide the process for change. Even if the Star did not remember some childhood details consciously, the material necessary would be available at another level of awareness.

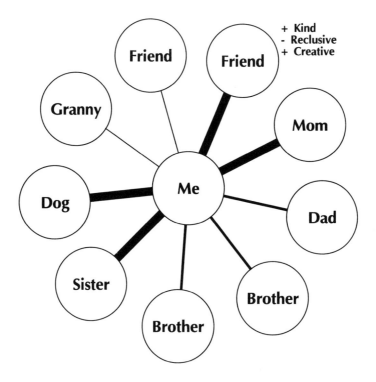

The body's ability to register information regardless of circumstances explains how we have ready access to it. We may qualify such information by saying things like, "If I had to guess, I imagine things would have happened this way," or, "I don't know but I would guess. . ." Nonetheless, experience in Family Reconstruction shows that many of people's "guesses" can be verified later by other family members.

In other words, people who have no conscious recall of their personal history can still provide data for a Family Reconstruction. Satir asserted that every human being knows everything about him- or herself and that it is only a matter of tapping into that information. For "unknown" facts, she would tell people to "make it up." Operating from the brain's right hemisphere, or in a trance state, the Star would usually be able to give accurate information—accurate at least in terms of the family dynamics and their coping process.

Whether right-hemisphere "guesses" are objectively accurate is not crucial. It is the Star's construct of reality that is being tapped, and Family Reconstructions are conducted within those perceptions. Any changes also transpire there.

FAMILY RECONSTRUCTION PROCESS

Once the Guide is familiar with the Star's family maps, chronology, and Wheel of Influence, these are hung on the workshop walls for reference. The Family Reconstruction can now begin.

A classical reconstruction is done in a large group (of fifteen to hundreds of people) and takes one to three days (6 to 20 hours). After a few introductory statements, including a time frame for the day's activities, the Guide tells the Star's life story. The Star usually sits and listens. This provides an easy avenue for tapping the brain's right hemisphere, which helps the Star enter the process of experiencing the reconstruction.

Telling the story involves more than the on-the-surface information about the Star's family. Other purposes include:

- Providing the context in which the Family Reconstruction will take place

- Providing an overview of the Star's lifeline and making some important connections between current issues, family patterns, past events, and people who influenced the Star's development

- Showing how the family coped and handled stress, anger, conflict, and pain

- Highlighting the family's resources by reframing many of the Star's negative experiences into terms of how people handled stress

- Raising useful possibilities, such as noting that certain names appear over and over in the chronology and therefore might be significant to the family

- Preparing participants by fostering a frame of mind that helps them join the Star's journey of discovery

- Indicating the Star's yearnings, expectations, perceptions, and feelings as the story is told in terms of a "personal iceberg"

- Indicating family values, beliefs, and rules, and how the family defines itself and its members

- Identifying the patterns that need to be changed and the negative effects of the past that still need to be transformed

- Revealing the hopes and wishes of the most significant family members, especially the Star, and whether they have been fulfilled

- Demonstrating the sacredness of life and celebrating new possibilities, choices, and growth opportunities

Once the story is told and the Star takes in the many messages contained in its telling, the Guide asks the Star to select and invite other workshop participants to play the roles of relatives and other people who were significant in the Star's childhood. The cast usually consists of the Star, a stand-in for the Star (so the Star can watch him- or herself during enactments), the Guide (or a triad of guides), and people who play the Star's siblings, parents, grandparents, and other important figures and/or resources.

Satir believed strongly that, given our universal connectedness, anybody could play every role. Nevertheless, it is important that the Star does the selecting of individuals to portray each family member or significant other who will become part of dramatizing the family's dynamics. Initially, the process of selecting role-players also helps the Star see family members as separate beings, managing their own lives as best they can.

As members of the group, participants are both encouraged to accept the Star's invitation and given the choice of declining. Those who accept then have an opportunity to "enrole"—to get in tune with the particular family members they will portray, respectively. They do this by familiarizing themselves with their respective adjectives and coping stance(s), and by hearing about the other members and the context in which they lived together. Little else is needed to assure that each role-player is ready for the reconstruction.

Satir often encouraged players to improvise props that would strengthen the characters' visual identity and reality. Usually during a coffee break or lunch break, people could find a hat, a ribbon, a briefcase, or some other prop to enhance their portrayals.

Meanwhile, this early part of the reconstruction includes making some contracts between the Guide, the Star, and the players. These understandings highlight trust, openness, and willingness to work. For instance, the Guide assures close emotional contact with the Star and asks participants to join in the Star's life journey. Then the Guide asks the Star to indicate the goals he or she wants to achieve through the Family Reconstruction— what changes he or she hopes to make.

Family Reconstruction works on two tracks, as it were. One involves releasing pent-up feelings and overcoming the impact of the past: dysfunctional patterns, perceptions, and expectations. The other involves going beyond the limits of what we know. This helps us move toward growth, wholeness, and healthy and optimal functioning.

So as the reconstruction begins, it is important to spend time clarifying the Star's goals and recording them for everyone to see. The Star can usually talk about a goal that involves moving toward a new state of being. These goals usually evolve, however, from simple behavioral changes into something more process-based and more strongly related to deep personal yearnings. For instance, in a Family Reconstruction we did with Bruce, he said his goal was to have less contempt toward his father. When the Guide explored this goal with him, it became clear that what Bruce really wanted was to feel closer to his father, to have greater acceptance and less critical judgment of his father's behavior. He longed to be with his father. The Guide then explored what effect that would accomplish for Bruce. He realized he would feel better about himself and his father, and that would allow for a healthier relationship between them.

Once the introductory phase is complete, the classical Family Reconstruction follows a four-act format, namely:

1. Sculpting the family of origin

2. Sculpting the families of origin of the Star's mother and father

3. Sculpting the Star's parents' meeting, courting, and wedding

4. Resculpting the Star's family of origin

As shown in the following descriptions of each part, dramatizing the dynamics of the family's last three generations gives the Star a chance to achieve the personal and universal goals identified earlier.

Sculpting the Star's Family of Origin

The Guide asks the Star to describe a time when the family was in stress, when family members did not see eye to eye. It is best to pick a significantly traumatic event that happened before the Star left home. Often it is some incident the Star talked about during the preparation session.

The purpose here is for the Star to externalize his or her construct of the family dynamics and to identify the perceptions and feelings that arose under stress. This also gives the Star an opportunity to use an adult point of view in looking at some possibly painful coping patterns in his or her family.

After the Star relates the event, the Guide asks how the Star feels. This anchors that feeling or any new awarenesses. Once this is done, the second part begins.

Sculpting Parental Families

The Star first sculpts his or her biological (or adopted, or foster) mother's family of origin. The purpose here is for the Star to focus on what it was like for his or her mother to grow up. What were her major learnings within her own family of origin?

To do this, the Star and the Guide ask various questions about that family. Some of these questions may be about things the Star has never known or asked before. The answers are usually related to the experience of the respective family member (as when the Star's uncle, who was still living at home, is able to talk about his parents' reactions the night the Star's mother eloped). This gives the Star a new perception of, feeling about, and sense of connection with those maternal grandparents. It also allows the Star to identify some parts of him- or herself that might have come from them. This can be an empowering experience.

This process also lets the Star connect with his or her mother at a younger age. What were her dreams, hopes, and struggles? The Star often comes to a new appreciation of his or her own strengths and a greater acceptance of his or her mother. Any stored negative judgments or resentments may decrease.

The Guide then leads a similar process with the family of origin of the Star's father. Every opportunity needs to be used to deal with any unfinished business. For example, the Star may need to experience saying goodbye to his or her paternal grandparents and others who were significant during childhood.

The Guide also encourages the Star to connect with his or her father at a deeper level of caring, intimacy, and acceptance. In the case of Bruce, introduced earlier, this deepening was started by asking the role-player father what his wishes and hopes were for his son. Hearing about these yearnings helped the Star connect with his own yearning for closeness. It also opened a connection at a deeper level between him and his "father." Family Reconstruction is often the first time a son or daughter shares deeper feelings with his or her "parent." Such new experiences and awarenesses lead to greater wholeness.

Sculpting the Star's Parents' Meeting, Courting, and Wedding

In this act, players reenact the meeting and courting of the Star's parents. This is when the first relationship patterns developed in the Star's family of origin. Sculpting it also gives the Star a chance to hear the hopes and dreams of each parent, both as individuals and in terms of their relationship with each other.

Most people watch the courtship act with delight. Its purpose is to connect with the couple at a time before the Star was born, with their respective yearnings and expectations, and with the coping patterns they each brought into their relationship. This provides a background and deeper appreciation for these two people, who later in the drama become the Star's parents.

Next, a special sculpting lets people experience the wedding of this couple. Possible conflicts between the two families may be enacted.

Following the process carefully means the Guide asks questions about the Star's perceptions of earlier family history. Since the Star was not part of that wedding, these questions can lead him or her to new information about and new insight into the dynamics and forthcoming struggles for this marital couple.

Resculpting the Star's Family

After the wedding, players develop the Star's family of origin by portraying the birth of the Star and of each sibling. The Guide and Star pay careful attention to how each child's arrival changes the family system and the relationships among family members. The Star also experiences how he or she participated in the process: his or her stand-in manifests the Star's own coping and survival in relation to other family members and within the family's dynamics.

The Guide usually asks the Star to recall and sculpt a traumatic scene or significant experience and to receive comments from the players about how it was for everyone. The internal process of each member is thus manifested, and the Star gains new awareness and appreciation for him- or herself and all other family members.

To achieve the goals identified earlier by the Star, the Guide may also ask the players to act out specific scenes. For example, suppose a woman in her fifties wants to be more assertive and to connect with her older sister, who had raised her. The pattern between them has been a controlling older sister with a placating younger sister. Now the Star wants to move to a more equal power balance. Although she now looks after her ailing sister around the clock, the Star still acts like an accommodating and placating two-year-old when in her sister's presence.

In this case the Guide chooses a scene that manifests this relationship in an earlier time. Dramatizing that scene in an exaggerated or extreme form triggers the feelings of helplessness and anger that the Star could not act on until now. The Guide encourages and supports the Star to direct her stand-in (the Star's younger self) to select new choices and to stop using the old coping pattern. The younger self stands up to her older sister, telling her how she feels and sharing this new decision about what she will and will not do.

The preceding process uses the past to change a pattern the Star still practices in the present. However, it succeeds only when the Star's decision to change is made at the level of self-esteem. That is why the Family Reconstruction is designed to help us get in touch with who we are, what inner resources we have, and what we can become. Family Reconstruction is an effective method for helping us recognize and acknowledge our own infinite possibilities and unique beauty.

The final part of sculpting the Star's family of origin is for the Star to:

1. Verbalize and own any unmet expectations and yearnings

2. Relate and express his or her feelings about unmet yearnings and expectations

3. Identify strengths and weaknesses of the parents, relate these to him- or herself, and thereby form a new connection between self and parents

4. Work toward a new level of acceptance of his or her own personhood and those of the parents

5. Accept the similarities and differences of him- or herself and his or her parents

6. Accept his or her parents as people who did the best they knew how

7. Accept the self with high self-esteem and share that with his or her parents, knowing the Star no longer needs to crave validation and approval that was missing in the past

This requires the Guide to weave delicately between past and present, strength and weakness, differentness and similarity. It also means the Star lets go of unmet expectations and takes increasing charge of him- or herself.

Closure

When the Star has achieved a state of higher self-esteem, empowerment, and hope, the Guide brings the Family Reconstruction to a close. This involves deroling the players and taking some time for each player to share his or her experiences, in terms of both playing the role and having the reconstruction affect them personally.

Nonplayer group members also have the chance to share their experiences of how the process affected them. The observers usually participate in the Family Reconstruction on three different channels: relating the process to their own experience, focusing on the Star's process, and focusing on the Guide's process. Like Family Reconstruction in general, each of these can be a way to get in touch with the life process and release energy, either by igniting hope or by clearing some blockage.

ORIGINS OF FAMILY RECONSTRUCTION

We are the outcome of our thoughts, our feelings, our perceptions, and our met and unmet expectations. We are also the outcome of our relationships and our learnings, which are based on interactions with our survival figures (usually our parents). People's coping problems relate almost invariably to unreconciled child–parent experiences. Old learnings prevent us from defining ourselves holistically because they often keep us focused in the past and using the incomplete perceptions we had as children.

When we were born, we had to learn how to treat ourselves, how to treat others, and how to expect others to treat us. We also had to learn the rules we lived by within our families. By the time we began to talk, we had learned these basic survival mechanisms of how to define and protect ourselves (including using the coping stances identified by Satir).

Growing up does not necessarily reduce the impact of our childhood rules and relationships. The present is the only dimension we live in physically, but when the past contaminates the present, Satir knew, we continue repeating old patterns. One goal of therapy is to change this contamination to illumination: to use the past to see and live in the present more fully. This helps us move from being compelled to being able to cope, and from coping to recognizing our choices and our freedom.

As shown in the following description of how she developed the Family Reconstruction method, Satir knew that blaming our parents does not change our early acquisition of coping strategies. This is not a blame situation; it is a human situation. As Satir saw it,*

> *The universe is orderly. We as human beings operate that way, too. We cannot always see the order of our humanness, mostly because we do not look or we do not look with open eyes.*

> *To find that order was important to me. I knew it was there somewhere. For me, the basis of that order is the Life Force. I also found that things follow certain things and that everything has a consequence, and in that sense*

---

*Avanta Network annual meeting, June 1987, Mt. Crested Butte, CO.

*everything has a price and also a reward. And so I began
to look at things in that frame.*

*I began to see the universal in the specific of each indi-
vidual's pain. I saw the pain connected to the loyalty to
parents. That in itself was not new. Freud knew that. I
started to follow the relationship between what people
learned in their families and their behavior.*

*During the early days I ran weekend marathons where I
saw people try to free themselves from their negative experiences in ways that did not seem to be helpful. Nevertheless, I started to put things together, such as:*

1. *Parents were not natural enemies of children, as psychoanalysis had led us to believe.*

2. *People were doing the best they could. Why then
   would things turn out so bad for their children?*

3. *People carry the constructs of their families within
   them.*

4. *People were dealing with their constructs, not with
   the actual father or mother. It was the interpretation of their experience that needed changing.*

5. *Next I learned about traumatic incidents. It was not
   the traumatic incident that caused people's pain. It
   was the way people reacted to the traumatic event. It
   was the way people coped. I saw people experiencing
   identical events and being "affected" very differently.*

6. *I found that the problem is not the problem, but that
   the coping or lack of coping became the problem. I*

would look for ways of taking these constructs from within and externalizing them.

7. *Externalizing the internal process led me to role-playing. When I added the context to the process, I started having people play the parts of mother, father, siblings, and significant others within the three generations of the family of origin. The content became the context [that is, the story provides the setting or container within which the Guide facilitates the changes and transformations expressed by the Star's goal].*

8. *Then I equated this with a theater. I developed a dramatic form, which included fun and humor, and allowed us access to the brain's right hemisphere.*

9. *I also found that role players knew what to say even with very limited information. I realized the universality of the process and the ability of role-players to tune in to the process with very limited data.*

10. *I found this process to be multilevel, spiritual, and very powerful. By now the approach is well developed and is known as Family Reconstruction.*

11. *Parents are children grown up, and they do the best they know how.*

This section has described how Satir developed classical Family Reconstruction as a tool for change. She later developed two shorter versions, the Critical Impact Reconstruction and the Internal Visualization format, described at the end of this chapter.

GENERAL GOALS

One outcome of Family Reconstruction is the possibility of communicating with our parents as human beings of equal value. From watching others and from her own experience, Satir felt strongly that we cannot be totally whole until we have connected with our parents as people. If we had been born as independent beings, fully individualized, we would have known long ago that our parents were simply other people. Conversely, if our parents had not had to act as parents, they would have realized long ago that their children were people, too. We all would have had a holistic, equal-value perspective of each other. However, we instead learned to see ourselves and others in terms of roles and labels.

The first time we see something, we form perceptions of that thing based on our location, our understanding, and our feelings about ourselves. As infants, we form our first perceptions of adults when we are on our backs, looking up. These and other early experiences can affect or distort even our adult perceptions. And these first learnings are sometimes more influential than those that follow.

For example, Satir once wondered why so many of the people she worked with claimed to have devils, weaklings, or stupid people as parents. When she met these so-called monsters, they did not look horrible to her. She began seeing that people often developed these strong convictions from perceptions founded early in their lives. A little boy might think, "My mother was always weak," for instance. He arrives at this conclusion through his childhood understanding, his perceptions, and his feelings about himself. Change any of these three aspects and the person may arrive at a different, less limited conclusion.

Updating ourselves is another important aspect of Family Reconstruction. Although we exist in the present, we might still be experiencing inordinate expectations and pain from occurrences that happened many years ago. Family Reconstruction is a caring, effective way to help people release themselves from inhibiting childhood survival messages. Distinguishing past from present experiences is an essential step toward discovering life's abundance.

- Otherwise, Satir stressed, people will continue to limit how they express their life force. As a magnificent example of the universal energy that supports life, the human spirit is capable of many manifestations. Until people integrate their experiences and make sense of the world from a state of abundance, though, they limit themselves to expressing only a few aspects of themselves.

Family Reconstruction offers an opportunity to make sense of all the relational parts of our experience. How these parts are organized is specific to the Star's unique history, chronology, opportunities, and family rules.

Returning to Bruce: his unique history included having lost his mother at the age of five and having to live with his stepmother, whom he did not accept. He also did not have an intimate relationship with his father. Bruce's perceptions of these facts helped him organize his sense of self then as a person of low self-worth and feelings of being disconnected from others. He protected himself by pleasing others while discounting his own feelings and yearnings. His family rules that "Father must be protected at all cost" and "Don't show your feelings" reinforced his loneliness and worthlessness.

How we treat ourselves and others depends on what we learned in our family of origin and the degree to which we could express our uniqueness. In Bruce's case, his sense of uniqueness was crushed during interactions with his very controlling stepmother. As he worked through his painful past, he gradually began accepting himself and manifesting many of his suppressed resources. One such resource that blossomed was his ability and interest in writing.

Emotional pain results when we lose contact with ourselves as powerful beings—powerful in the sense of respecting ourselves and acknowledging that the world is a better place because of our existence. Aware of the pain associated with the old learnings and with how people perceived their parents, Satir found that it was not enough to portray only the nuclear family of origin. She added grandparents to the Family Reconstruction context, making it a multigenerational reenactment of learnings, rules, and patterns for interacting.

Another general thrust of Family Reconstruction is to reassess the weight we give positive and negative experiences. For instance, the major survival message children learn translates into: "I must always do what my parents want. Otherwise they will not love me." If pleasing does not work, children may cope by feeling angry or frustrated, blaming, or withdrawing. Parents may then react to this behavior rather than to the child's need to survive.

We human beings will go through much pain to accommodate reactions and feelings that don't make sense to us. Our defenses inhibit openness and block off the outside world from the hurting inside. We also adopt negative learnings more easily, taking positive ones for granted.

Our conclusions are often based on these negative experiences. For example, if we do seventeen things that turn out well and an eighteenth that turns out terribly, we may feel we have had a bad day. Another example could be that for sixteen years your father never spanked you, and on your sixteenth birthday he did. You later claim—in all sincerity—that he beat you all your life, because the memory of the negative far outweighs the awareness of the positive. The negative holds the door closed to the awareness of the positive, and our perceptions are often limited by our negative experiences.

If we examine most negative self-worth messages, Satir found, they are based on:

- Beliefs — related to Self and parents

- Ignorance — related to limited information

- Lack of awareness — related to a distorted way of making sense of the world

- Intent — related to mistaking the intent below the behavior

Satir used Family Reconstruction to give people a chance to see themselves and family members in a way that exposes their beliefs, ignorance, unawareness, and mis-understandings. It also lets people experience each other's real intents of acceptance and caring. Perceiving the human frailties of these patterns in relation to their own parents, most people are able to grow toward higher self-worth. And that is the level of self-esteem at which change occurs.

THE IMPORTANCE OF CONTEXT

To view the old learnings with adult eyes, we need to understand and experience their context. Satir's inter-vention reconstructs that context, the family, where our survival patterns developed when we were young and helpless. Its specifics—our place, time, and situation within our particular family—shape our learnings and simultaneously provide the means to change them.

That is, if we see our survival patterns were necessary for that time and place but do not fit for us in our present situation, then we can change. We can find ways to live more harmoniously and to appreciate and use our old learnings with a new understanding.

To use old learnings in the present is sometimes inappropriate. In Family Reconstruction, Satir identified old learnings and traced them back through three or more generations. This helps us recognize the circum-stances that gave rise to and perpetuate family rules. We can then make choices about keeping, revising, or discarding our childhood rules.

Family themes, myths, and secrets arise and thrive in much the same way. Many families sustain a shadow or ghost of someone who lived a hundred years ago and whose presence, fears, hopes, and beliefs are still felt by present family members. Such shadows or secrets often become very clear when we look back to the third generation past.

Even though many misunderstandings may show up in a Family Reconstruction, these don't invalidate the Star's earlier perceptions. Our perceptions were the best we had at the time, just as our parents' were. We all suffered from misunderstandings or faulty conclusions and yet made the best of what we had.

For instance, a woman who feels worthless throughout childhood and adolescence does not automatically feel differently when she has a baby. The man who has temper tantrums before becoming a parent will continue to act in this manner after he becomes a father.

During a Family Reconstruction, Satir did not question whether love feelings existed between parents and children. She knew people can best express love through congruence. As long as they express incongruent feelings associated with blaming, placating, distracting, or being super-reasonable, they cannot communicate love messages very well. Family Reconstructions clear away these blockages to help people see the love messages of the parents and to communicate, send, and receive these messages in a recognizable form.

We are whole when we come into this world, and our potential for wholeness remains no matter what happens. We are the outcome of our thoughts, our feelings, how we perceive all our body processes (especially since many of us have been taught that parts of our body and body functions are bad), our life force, and our behavior. Using all of these is a way of making meaning.

All the traps and pains in our past experiences contain the opportunities for new choices, new opportunities, and new possibilities. The trap is gone—it has become a part of history—and all that hurts today is what we have told ourselves about it. Being stuck in old perceptions that no longer fit is a choice. Our perceptions are ours.

Everything that ever happens to us is registered and available under certain conditions somewhere in our consciousness, as mentioned. The human body is always picking up and responding to the energy that others transmit. For example, a baby in the crib reacts to voices and touches. A strong voice feels tight, perhaps, or a hand feels anxious. The baby probably has no cognitive awareness of what this really means. The feeling is registered, however, and can become available to that person's awareness later in life.

Somehow we need to sort out these experiences and make sense of them in our conscious mind. There has to be a way of making meaning of these experiences and utilizing them. An infant does not differentiate between the outside world and him- or herself, and has no awareness of context. If parents are fighting within earshot, for instance, the child reacts and has feelings as a result of the sounds.

Going back and putting behavior into context can change our perceptions and attitudes. Part of Family Reconstruction involves looking at the conclusions we made about questions like these:

Who am I?

How do I feel about myself?

How do I cope with interactions between males and females?

Am I loved?

Can I trust?

How we answer these is based on how we perceive ourselves in relation to the world around us. Our perceptions also underlie how we are at any moment, how we
perceive what happened in the past, and how we cope. As
small children we learned through touch, tone, and eye
contact. We also experienced double messages. For example, Dad looked sad but refused to acknowledge that, saying, "I am fine. Don't worry about it." How do children
make sense of this?

Another example occurs in a context that involves
the relationship between two parents. Their two-year-old
sucks his thumb and his mother smiles. When only his
father is present, though, the boy is not allowed to suck
his thumb. When both father and mother are present,
the mother does not smile; she tells the boy to take his
thumb out of his mouth. The child's conclusion about
all this might include feelings of rejection, confusion,
and low self-esteem.

The idea in Family Reconstruction is not to try to
convince such a person that his mother or father really
loved him. Instead, by adding new information and perceptions, we hope to create conditions in which he would
experience a new awareness and understanding of his
parents' love, and realize that the problem involved the
relationship of his parents rather than his behavior.

Family Reconstruction is a journey that provides
human context. For example, when people are out of
control or in pain, we observe the outcome of their
behavior. Putting the behavior into context is a process
that can raise self-esteem. To do this, we can use questions such as:

- How did it happen?
- How does it make sense?
- How did it move from A to B to C?

Answering questions like these clarifies the context of the experience and promotes the person's energy and self-worth.

With all this focus on the past, we remind readers that the present is the only time in which we live, the only time in which we can change. We cannot change the events of the past. Therefore, we can change the past only in terms of its impact on the present.

LEVELS OF CHANGE

Three different levels of change are possible in a Family Reconstruction. At each level, the goals of the reconstruction parallel those of Satir's whole system.

Level 1

Level 1 characterizes a kind of change that occurs throughout the reconstruction, from the time the Star is selected until the reconstruction sessions end. The following paragraphs describe this level of change and its goals.

Make Connections. The Guide meets with the Star to identify the hopes and wishes the Star wants to address through the upcoming Family Reconstruction. They also prepare the family maps, chronology, and Wheel of Influence. This session helps the Star perceive some continuity of the life force, both personally and within his or her family.

In the preparation as well as the Family Reconstruction session, one goal is for the Star to picture his or her life in a more continuous form, more holistic, more cohesive. Sculpting is a powerful technique to achieve this goal during the reconstruction.

Release Feelings. This goal allows the Star to contact feelings and experience or re-experience them in a safe, accepting environment. It is a form of catharsis. Once the person can experience and own these feelings, he or she can also let go of them when that fits, at any time during the reconstruction.

Update Experiences. When the Star reviews the child's world during Family Reconstruction, he or she adds new information and an awareness of self, other, and context. This adult perspective allows for a here-and-now reality without the contamination of the past.

Toward this end, the Guide leads the Star to ask questions that never before felt safe to ask and encourages the role-players to respond to and converse with the Star.

Discover the Unknown. Working at the level of not knowing what he or she doesn't know, the Star uncovers and discovers distorted conclusions and important new thoughts. The Guide often raises new possibilities, new connections, new interpretations, and new insights.

Identify the Automatic. Much of our internal process has become automatic, including our survival patterns. In this aspect of the reconstruction, the Star attempts to identify and acknowledge his or her family rules, family themes, family myths, and dysfunctional patterns of coping.

Accept What Was. A large part of the goal of Family Reconstruction is to help the Star accept the feelings, perceptions, and expectations of his or her past and to let go of as much as possible, as well as to appreciate what was.

Change Behavior. Once the person can see what he or she does to belong, be validated, and be accepted, he or she often can change certain behaviors. Change is also based on achieving any or all of the other goals mentioned.

Family Reconstruction at Level 1 has an impact on people's lives and is considered a major therapeutic success. Many schools of thought consider achieving these first-level goals to be the totality of therapy. Satir found this level of change was not enough to achieve and maintain high self-esteem.

Level 2

Second-level change has a transformational effect on the Star. The following are goals at Level 2.

Transform Energy. Family Reconstruction changes negative energy into positive energy at the level of feelings, perceptions, and expectations. Rather than straining to suppress or defend against past pains, the Star who lets go of unmet wishes can free up immense energy to spend in meeting current needs and desires.

Raise Awareness. Through the various stages of the reconstruction, the Star becomes more conscious of his or her life energy, the level where the Self and its universal yearnings are being fulfilled.

Integrate Resources. In second-level change, the Star begins integrating his or her inner resources, his or her many parts. This takes place at the level of Self and leads toward higher self-esteem. The Star thereby reaches some greater degree of congruence.

Change Focus. Second-level change in the Star is characterized by a major transformation toward recognizing his or her freedom, choices, inner resources, and possibilities for greater intimacy. The person moves toward a more inner-directed focus and is freed from the contamination of his or her past.

Individuate. By reviewing his or her learnings and family context, the Star can begin de-enmeshing from dysfunctional patterns and self-limitations. Distinguishing his or her own values, needs, and resources, the individual can value his or her own human equality while respecting samenesses and differentnesses.

Level 3

Satir sometimes worked at a third level. When the Star had made a decision that did not promote survival and yet was struggling to stay alive, Satir would create a context for redecision.

This involves helping the Star go back to an earlier place or time when the Self decided his or her life was not worth living. For instance, take the case of a person who has been hospitalized several times for attempted suicide. The Guide first searches for the most significant context in which this Star reached this conclusion about worthlessness.

The purpose of recreating this context or situation is to examine the Star's life-or-death decision, which he or she may have made at an unconscious level while facing an untenable situation or event. Within this context, the Guide helps the Star transform his or her original conclusion into a more constructive, positive, hopeful choice for life.

The goal at this third level of change is for the Star to regenerate his or her life energy. This taps his or her biopsychological and spiritual levels of being.

THE CRITICAL IMPACT RECONSTRUCTION

During the last five years of Satir's life, she developed a shorter version of the classical Family Reconstruction. Called the Critical Impact Reconstruction, it is based on the classical format and orientation. Both use the same process of change and have the same general goals; both use family maps, chronologies, and Wheels of Influence; and both use role-players.

The Critical Impact format is usually much shorter, lasting about three hours. The process focuses on select survival copings related to the Star's goals. It puts more emphasis on transformation and usually concentrates on one or two major issues in which the Star feels stuck. The process also emphasizes the level of Self (as indicated in the personal iceberg model, Chapter 3) and on increasing self-esteem.

The reconstruction focuses on making specific major changes. Metaphorically, it is like clearing debris in a river. A competent engineer needs to dislodge one particular log jam to have the rest of the debris follow. In the

Critical Impact Reconstruction, a change in one major area may have a similar effect and precipitate many other relevant changes.

This process usually transforms a dysfunctional automatic pattern of survival. Or it may address a traumatic experience that needs healing at the level of the Self. The Critical Impact format can generally be used with issues such as the following:

The sudden death of a significant other

A traumatic, violent, or tragic experience

Rage and repressed anger

A fearful fantasy

A decision to make in the present that follows new patterns of coping

Chronically ill patients may also benefit from this format, especially when the initial medical condition originated in the Star's growing-up years. This process of discovery for growth and learning about Self is exemplified in the following case summary of Mr. A., who was seen by one of the authors.

Mr. A., 44, is a married, employed male who lives with his wife and two children. He first presented to the Department of Psychiatry in 1979, at age 32, with the complaint that he could not hold on to a job. He had had a dozen jobs in the previous twelve years since leaving high school. He had sold real estate, been a taxi driver, and held other positions briefly.

He had quit his most recent job, as a stock-keeper and parts manager for a trucking company, because he was upset and depressed. He suffered tension headaches, had had crying spells off and on since high school, and couldn't sort out what he wanted to do with his life.

When he was first seen, his father was 70; his mother, 67. He described his father as "distant" and his mother as "very close." He said his one brother, eight years older, also suffered from depression and had once attempted suicide.

He said he did not drink or abuse drugs. His major interests were weight lifting, photography, and reading. He was eating well and sleeping well. He was not suicidal.

Mr. A. was referred to the day treatment program for group therapy. He was not given any psychotropic medication. He also started attending the pain clinic because of severe, chronic lower back pain. He continued attending the outpatient department until 1982.

He attended group therapy for one year, but he continued to be very weepy and was unable to verbalize his feelings. He began expressing violent sexual fantasies, and he informed his group therapist that if he saw a woman with long hair sitting on the bus, he had an impulse to go up to her and cut off her hair. A year later, in 1980, Mr. A. took an overdose of sleeping pills.

In 1988 he returned to the outpatient department. He was fearful, angry, frustrated, and irritable; and he was having marital problems. He was also losing his temper with his two sons, ages six and eleven.

Referred for marriage counseling and group therapy, he continued feeling very shaky and weepy. Eventually he started on antidepressant medication. In his individual therapy, he became preoccupied with early life experiences. He felt guilty for being angry at his sons, because his father had always been angry. He recalled the following scene. Standing up in his crib when he was an infant, he was sobbing and choking, and someone was yelling at him.

At this point he was referred for a Family Reconstruction. The Guide first had three meetings with him, developed trust and rapport, informed him in detail about the process of Family Reconstruction, offered to show him a videotape of another such intervention, and offered him the choice to participate in his own reconstruction.

When he agreed, the Guide assisted him in compiling his family maps, life chronology, and Wheel of Influence. Between meetings, Mr. A. filled in the gaps with more detailed information when needed. During this time of preparation, he requested frequent visits with his psychiatrist, because doing his family maps triggered his anxiety and fear.

The Family Reconstruction group consisted of approximately thirty people. Hospital staff came by invitation (most of them knew Mr. A. from his previous visits), as did several professionals who had previously participated in a Family Reconstruction seminar given by the Guide.

The time had been set for three hours maximum. After people introduced themselves, the Guide asked Mr. A. to present his family maps and the story of his parents' background. Role-players selected from the group then enacted a brief sculpture of the father's family and the father growing up, then the mother's family and her growing up. Next players sculpted Mr. A.'s family of origin and a scene described by Mr. A.: his two-year-old stand-in heard arguments and felt afraid and alone.

Throughout the process, the focus was on finding new learnings about Mr. A.'s father, his struggles, his coping, and his pain, and on connecting these awarenesses with the Star's copings and struggles in the present. Special attention was paid to the father–son relationship in the here and now.

Mr. A.'s father was the oldest of three children. Mr. A.'s grandfather was a farm worker, and the family was very poor. Later they moved to the city, where the grandfather worked seven days a week for the railway. The grandmother died when Mr. A.'s father was twelve years old. This left Mr. A.'s father responsible for looking after his younger brother and sister. The grandfather remarried twice, but had no time to spend with his children.

Mr. A.'s mother was the youngest in a family with three children. Her mother also died when she was young, and her grandmother lived with the family for a long time. Her father was described as "mean."

Mr. A.'s parents met at a school social. They dated for a few years and married in 1939. Their first-born was a son. Mr. A.'s father was drafted during World War II and had traumatic experiences at the European front. When he came back, he was "a different person." Mr. A.'s mother recalls he was bitter, sad, and depressed. He very seldom talks about these experiences. Mr. A. was born in 1948.

One of the vignettes focused on Mr. A.'s father's loss of his mother at age twelve. The context is the father's family-of-origin sculpture.

GUIDE: So I think it is still a pain for him. He had lost her very early, and then he had to take over. I just wanted you to get in touch with that. I don't think he got very much help with that pain when he was twelve from his family because his father had to go on working and looking after everything, so where was that little boy getting support?

STAR: From nowhere. He was pretty much by himself. His father would catch a train to work at seven o'clock in the morning and wouldn't come back until seven o'clock in the evening.

GUIDE: How do you feel, getting in touch with that? A twelve-year-old boy, just the age of your son? If he lost his mother suddenly and you had to work twelve hours a day, and he had two children to look after? That's what your father went through.

STAR: It's very scary to have to think about that. The way he coped was to push it away.

GUIDE: And that certainly shaped him, how he coped with difficult situations. We are saying one thing he used was to push it away, not to talk about it; and then later in his life he had to do that too with his family. So that's maybe when he started to learn it, how to deal with pain. Is there something you know about that, that you push away things that are very painful?

STAR: Yes. When I was small, if things didn't work out. We were talking about this in group last week. I pinned all my hopes on a few people, and if things didn't work out the way I had hoped, I would be extremely disappointed. My youngest son is six, and he has a habit of when things don't work out for him, he starts to cry. I used to do the same thing. Why he's like that, I don't know. He hasn't learned the crying from me, because he hasn't seen me cry. So somehow we are very, very similar.

GUIDE: Maybe you are also similar to your father. He probably couldn't cry.

STAR: No, he couldn't.

GUIDE: I don't think he could afford to cry with this hard-working life he had to do.

STAR: No, he couldn't. He didn't have time.

After weaving these similarities and establishing opportunities for connecting, the Guide turns to the twelve-year-old father in the sculpture. The time is after his mother's death, which had left a big empty space. Standing too far from his father to lean on him, the twelve-year-old was being pulled on by his two siblings.

GUIDE: [*To the twelve-year-old father*] How do you feel? You are twelve years old and your mother is suddenly gone.

FATHER: I feel lost, empty—and what am I going to do? My mom is gone, and she was all I had. Who am I going to depend on for support? And now she's gone, and my arm is getting heavy.

GUIDE: How do you feel?

FATHER: I feel really scared—really, really scared that she's not here, because she was the anchor. She held us all together. Now she's gone.

GUIDE: How do you feel?

FATHER: I feel like grabbing onto somebody's leg. I am falling forward over here, so I just grab like this. [*He reaches toward his own father.*]

GUIDE: That is probably true. [*To the Star*] So he is grabbing onto him [the grandfather], and what do you think your grandfather does?

GRANDFATHER: Well, I feel I've never been here, so I can't really do anything. I am so busy with work that I cannot do anything for the kids.

GUIDE: [*To the Star*] Now I think your father learned something from his father. What do you think your father learned?

STAR: I think, Father, that you learned not to express your feelings. You learned to hide your feelings. You learned to cope, to be very independent; and I think you were independent before, from what you told me last weekend. Being independent, you were able to do the things you did, but you had to hide the feelings that a twelve-year-old would have, having to do all those things.

GUIDE: [*To the Star*] I think you did something like that. You know how to hide your feelings. You cried a lot. Can you tell me how you were hiding your feelings from him? How you know what he knew?

STAR: [*To his father*] When I was small, I was so afraid of you. You used to have such a temper, and you would get so upset at small things. Come home from work in a nasty mood. I couldn't tell you because if I cried, you called me a crybaby. So I couldn't do that.

GUIDE: He probably couldn't cry with his father either.

STAR: No.

GUIDE: So he didn't want his son to cry. He didn't know that it is okay to cry? Always? So you learned differently. Tell him: your son can cry. Teach him. You are not doing that with your son.

STAR: Okay. I get mad at him [the son] for other things, though.

GUIDE: That's okay. I think there is no father who doesn't get mad at his child. The question is, how?

STAR: Okay, I allow my son to cry when he is hurt, but I still get mad at him when he does things that I don't like. I try to tell him that I am mad at him, and I try to tell him why I am mad, although sometimes I don't always know . . . Quite often I am not mad at him; I am angry at something or someone else.

GUIDE: Tell your father how you deal with your anger.

STAR: When things go wrong and I think I can't do something, that's scary. I don't admit that I am afraid. How I recognize it is I get a feeling that I don't belong here any more. Wherever I am. And so I leave. If it's a job, or a place where I am, I just get up and leave. That's how I used to do it. I don't do that any more. Several times in my life, I have come within a hair's breadth of killing someone because I was angry at you. [*To the Guide*] A couple of weeks ago I went to see my father, and he put me in a spot that I didn't like, and I came very close to squeezing the life out of him.

GUIDE: Come back here. Open your eyes, look at me. There is nobody in this world who didn't sometimes have the feeling to kill someone. I want you to know that. Especially when there is so much anger. It is okay. You didn't kill anybody, did you? What do you want to do with that anger?

STAR: Grab it by the throat and squeeze the living heck out of it.

GUIDE: And that is what you are afraid of?

STAR: That's right.

GUIDE: Because?

STAR: Because he can't do that.

GUIDE: Because he didn't what? Because he didn't nurture you, he didn't show life to you the way you wanted it? He didn't live up to your expectations. What did you expect from your father? What were your expectations? Every little boy has expectations. Tell me.

STAR: Somebody who would care. Somebody who would care if I thought I was dying. Not somebody who would ignore me if I thought I was dying.

GUIDE: How did you survive? How did you do it? Just tell me.

STAR: How did I survive? I didn't.

GUIDE: You did. Yes, I think a child can expect Father and Mother to do nurturing, to help not to die.

STAR: Yes, I did survive.

GUIDE: [*In a strong voice*] So I at least think you should tell your father that you did survive in spite of him, damn it.

At this point, Mr. A. went inside to his core and for a few minutes showed no connection to anybody, or even to the context. The Guide stayed close to him, repeatedly asking him to come back.

Then an enormous transformation took place. From the space of a frightened child, he suddenly opened his eyes, turned around, and demonstrated a relieved energy. He kicked the wall with his left foot, danced around, and then looked at his psychiatrist, across the room.

STAR: He [his father] didn't say he would kill me. I said I would kill him.

GUIDE: Tell him.

STAR: [*To his father*] I thought I heard you say you would kill me, and you never said it. I said that I would kill you. [*His voice is shaking, and his affect is very happy.*]

GUIDE: But you didn't. But you felt like it.

STAR: Many times.

GUIDE: Can you tell him the times you felt like killing him? Because that was legitimate. Please tell him.

STAR: [*To his father*] When I was a baby and when I cried and you wouldn't come and pick me up. When you wouldn't take me with you. When you were mad but wouldn't tell me why. When I cried because I thought you were mad at me, and you wouldn't tell me what you were mad at, just stayed mad.

GUIDE: When he ignored you.

STAR: When you ignored me. When you expected me to go and do things like you did when you were young, but I wanted you to come with me, but you wouldn't come. When you sent me to Sunday school but you wouldn't take me. When you wanted me to go and play baseball and I wanted you to take me, but you wouldn't. You tried to show me how to catch a ball; I didn't catch on. I just wasn't athletic, and you gave up and went into the house in disgust and left me standing in the back yard in tears.

GUIDE: Tell him how much you are yearning for being loved by him, and that was missing for you. He probably loved you, but he didn't know how to show it. I don't know; he will tell you. What did you feel?

STAR: [*To his father*] For most of my life, all I wanted was for you to accept me. To say I was your boy, the way I tell my boys. That they are my boys, and I love them.

GUIDE: Can you tell him what kind of a father you want to be? How you learned how to be from your experience with him?

STAR: I want to be the kind of father who doesn't get mad because my fishing line gets stuck and I lose a lure, or something like that. Who will do things because he loves me but won't act like he is doing it grudgingly or he is doing it because he has to—it's his duty—and he doesn't enjoy doing it. I'd like to be the kind of father who could laugh at kids' jokes and take them for what they are.

GUIDE: Can you tell your father that sometimes you feel you do something similar to what he did, and that now you are aware of it?

STAR: I know that I do things, that I do more things with the kids than you did with me. I still sometimes do it grudgingly. I take them places and sometimes get angry because I have to take them there. I know that I do it, and I try not to do it.

GUIDE: So you know that feeling, not to do it. He did that; [so] you are not doing that. But there is a feeling in every parent sometimes not to do something they [the children] want you to do. I hope you are not doing everything they want you to do, just because your father didn't.

STAR: No.

GUIDE: You are using your judgment. Is there anything you can tell your father that you have learned from him? That you can appreciate? As a man to a man? He certainly wasn't living up to your expectations—that, you can tell him. Whatever his life was before does not condone that he wasn't the kind of father you expected him to be. That was your loss. But when you look at him as a whole person, is there anything that you can appreciate?

STAR: I appreciate the value of your family and why it is worthwhile to keep your family. Why it is worthwhile to go through all of this.

GUIDE: Anything you learned from him? I have a feeling there are lots of similarities you are trying to sort out yourself: how to cope with that, and how to be different, and how you want to be different.

STAR: Are you talking about the good things, or the things I don't like? There are more things that I don't like.

GUIDE: So tell him what you don't like first.

STAR: I don't want to be snarly and angry all the time. I want to be able to give my kids a hug when I come home from work. I want to be able to do things with the kids, and do things for the kids, and not to be mad for having to do it. I want to be able to help them do things and however it turns out, that's the way I think it should be done. I want them to be able to do things in their own way, and be able to accept what they did. I want them to be able to know that I accept what they have done, and that they did their best, and that they can accept it. I don't want them to get from me the feeling that nothing they do is good enough.

GUIDE: What do you want for yourself? You can give that all to the kids, but yourself—do you appreciate yourself? And you can see your own steps.

STAR: I want my kids to be able to think if they have a problem they can come and see me about it.

GUIDE: So you will share with your kids.

STAR: It's really difficult, but I try to share with my kids.

GUIDE: What would you like for yourself? You are doing this for yourself. Can you tell your father who you really want to be? You. Not only as a father but a person yourself. Because you have so many beautiful resources to be a whole person. You decided you don't have to be angry all the time. Can you be angry and then accept it when you are angry, but not being angry all the time? What are you going to do with your anger?

STAR: I want to be able to recognize when I am angry. To know what I am angry at, and to deal with it at the time.

GUIDE: Do you recognize your anger? I appreciate that. You told him how angry you were, and how does it feel right now?

STAR: It is still scary.

GUIDE: Can you tell him how you feel?

STAR: My father and I actually are fairly close in some ways. We are as close as a seventy-nine-year-old to a forty-one-year-old, father and son. We are close that way.

GUIDE: What about your mother? She had something to do with all that. Are you angry at her? Where was her nurturing?

STAR: I am not any more. It was eight years ago that I went through that in group. [*To the mother*] Eight years ago, I was very angry, and I was angry with you for Father, I guess. [*To the guide*] Not being able to deal with the problems that I had and with my father, not being able to talk about feelings, not being able to find some way to get out of the mess I was in. All she could say was, "Yes, he treated me the same way."

GUIDE: Now I would like to ask you to do one thing which is very hard, I know, because you told me that before. I would like you now to hear me. You are forty-one years old, you have lived a life, you have raised children for twelve years and six years, and you have a loving wife. You have your own family, and these people are your father and your mother. That's their role. They didn't live up to your expectations. They had their own hard life. Can you look at your father as a person, as a man, living his role as a father? As a father, he didn't live up to your expectations, and probably his father didn't live up to *his* expectations. He had a tough life. That doesn't mean anything in terms of your expectations.

The only thing I want you to do is to accept that that's the way he was and he is. That you do not have to contaminate your life now and continue to be scared and afraid because of what happened. Can you let those expectations go?

You expected him to be a certain father. Has nothing to do with him. Has to do with your expectations. What I am asking you to do is very difficult, to own your own expectations and to let them go, and to say to yourself [that] today you are a pretty okay person in spite of all that. And he is who he is, and you are who you are.

And there is pain involved, and there is sadness involved, but you coped with it. Can you appreciate it, that you coped with it, and that you have been working very hard for years to have coped with it?

STAR: [*To the father*] I can accept you the way you are, and I can accept that you didn't do it on purpose to hurt me.

GUIDE: Can you stand on your feet and say to your father [that] he lived his own life in his own way, and for you to be the kind of father that you want to be?

STAR: I am learning to be the kind of person I want to be, and to stand on my own two feet.

GUIDE: And you are also learning to deal with your fear, with your sadness.

STAR: Yes, I am learning to deal with my fear and my sadness and my anger.

GUIDE: How do you feel about yourself? Can you tell your father?

STAR: I feel happy for myself, and I also feel sad that I can't help you. That I can't change you.

GUIDE: No, you can only change yourself. Anything you want to tell your mother? Can you accept her as a person? The way she is?

STAR: Somehow I don't know. I was mad at Father for so long about something that was so essential, that I realize that I was also mad at you, Mother, for a long time for not being able to help me when I thought you should be able to help me.

GUIDE: Can you help yourself now?

STAR: I realize you are the kind of person you are because of the circumstances you came out of, and I can accept you for the kind of person you are, and not expect anything more than you are able to give.

And I still love you, Mom. You are special. Looking back on my life, I don't know how much I hurt you.

But when I get with you, I feel really small; and I thought maybe because you knew, you would stand up to him better than I could. I just feel like a little mouse on the floor, and I would have done something more for myself, for you, and for B. [his brother]. Thanks.

GUIDE: You grew up in spite of it. Pretty hard. You did a great job. I think it's about time that you appreciate your own strengths. It wasn't easy to grow up. Can you appreciate yourself? This is yourself. [*The guide connects the Star with his stand-in, himself.*] Tell them.

STAR: I can appreciate my own strengths. I can appreciate that this is the way my father taught me. I love my own family. In spite of everything, I do love my family. I can appreciate that I would do anything for them, and appreciate that I have done everything I could for them. I will continue to do my best for them.

GUIDE: Can you love yourself?

STAR: Yes, I can. I can appreciate things I do well.

GUIDE: Do you love yourself?

STAR: I can love myself, and I do love myself.

GUIDE: How do you feel now, again?

STAR: I feel a lot better.

GUIDE: Is this a good time to stop? Is there anything you want to tell anybody? This is an ongoing process. I would like you to see it as a beginning. And when you look at the videotape, you will learn more. It's a beginning, and I really appreciate your doing that.

STAR: It is hard to concentrate. You forced me through it, but I am still elated at the point where I realize that was the point I was stuck at. The point I was stuck at was I firmly believed I heard my father say he wanted to kill me. And he never said it.

GUIDE: I remember that. You speculated. You didn't know when he said it, how he said it, but you heard it. And it was your own voice you heard. That is a big discovery. I told you you were going into this journey to discover what you didn't know.

Following this reconstruction, Mr. A. visited his psychiatrist once a month for three months, and then once six months later. He reported feeling good and building a warm relationship with his father. Soon after the reconstruction, his father became ill; Mr. A. spent significant time with him in the hospital.

After six months, Mr. A. asked for a copy of the videotape and decided to show it to his family (kids and wife) as a gift. At that time, he also gave permission to use it for teaching.

Mr. A. discharged himself from the group program (his anger group) a year later and was in contact sporadically with his psychiatrist for several months.

INTERNAL VISUALIZATION

A third variation of Satir's Family Reconstruction is the Internal Visualization format. The Star sits before the Guide and is led through the various scenes, family dynamics, coping patterns, unmet expectations, and feelings within the family of origin and beyond. Without external dramatization of the process, the Star is helped to become aware, accept, and change any aspects that still need attention. Through visualization, the Guide helps the Star face as many aspects and redecisions as time allows.

This format has the same goals and preparation work (family maps, chronology, and Wheel of Influence) as the classical Family Reconstruction. It uses the same process of identifying specific goals for change. It differs in that no role-players are needed, its focus is on a critical impact or on unmet expectations, and it can be done in a short time and at various intervals. Applying this variation and the Critical Impact format in psychotherapy settings is similar, in essence, to a Family Reconstruction.

This format is difficult, though, for newly trained Guides. It easily becomes only a fantasy trip, resulting in very little change. Guides benefit from experiencing and learning the classical format well before working with its variations. And working with the Critical Incident format before the Internal Visualization format is also recommended. This sequence helps Guides learn to tap people's yearnings and change their automatic coping patterns—and learning this is needed for success in all three formats. Once learned, this format is most easily used in individual therapy.

CONCLUSION

Instead of being preoccupied with pathology, illness, or pain, Satir focused on promoting wellness. Family Reconstruction helps the body and mind move beyond stress, survival, and coping to a more positive way of expressing and experiencing life. New eyes see old situations in a new framework, especially in relation to the Self.

The Guide works not only from family maps, but from a map of human wholeness. In life, the body registers what is going on and what effect it has on us. We each know this at some level. Becoming more fully human includes expressing and transforming the pain we felt, and still feel, from what happened in the past.

Family Reconstruction provides a spiritual, emotional, philosophical, physical, and cosmic experience. It is a way to regain and own our wholeness. As needed, it may also incorporate other vehicles for change, including those described in the next chapter.

10

Sculpting, Metaphors, and Mandala

This chapter discusses a number of approaches or vehicles that Satir used as part of her total model for change. The first two sections are interviews that Satir did specifically for this book. The approaches in this chapter include:

- Making contact
- Metaphors
- Sculpting
- The Self Mandala

These tools can be used in almost any therapeutic situation. Therapists can expand interventions by improving their ability to make deeper contact, use metaphors, and sculpt perceptions of what exists and what is desired. These tools can also be used in individual therapy sessions.

MAKING CONTACT

Satir had a powerful way of making contact with people, be they friends, strangers, or clients. We ("J/M/J") talked with her about this.

J/M/J: You make very special contact with everybody. Yet the contact seems to take many different forms. We'd like to know what goes on inside you, and what you perceive from the person.

VS: Let me see if I can answer it like this. Remember that I see the individual's internal essence. That's what I am connecting with. I reach out to touch them, and I can reach out with my eyes, my voice, my arms. I can tell you that there has to be a reaching out.

J/M/J: You reach out differently to different people. Does it mean that you have something different inside of you or you have processed their difference? [*We wanted to know how she perceived people differently and ask what she did with these differences.*]

VS: I don't always know how I know these things. If the center of my attention is a person, then everything about that person becomes connected with me. I look two ways. What is the person telling me about themselves, and what is my body getting in touch with in relation to their body?

There are about three sources of information. One is what I pick up from them. The second is what their bodies tell me, what I can see. Their body includes their voice. The third thing is what my body is telling me about what their body is doing. All this happens very fast.

J/M/J: Is that the sequence?

VS: Not always. I know when I work with my [American] Indian friends we hardly ever, upon first meeting, hug. On the second or third meeting, a lot of hugging might take place. Now, part of that comes from my having been with Indian people. It isn't that they object to or reject [hugging]. It is a foreign element to them. And there is a difference between my recognizing something being foreign as compared to something being scary. You look at the body or listen to a voice and right away you detect the difference.

J/M/J: The impact you have on individuals when first meeting them is very noticeable, much more so than other people meeting the same persons.

VS: I have some words for that. If the most important thing for me about a human being is their worth, then the second most important thing is respecting that. Therefore, I try giving that worth some validation from me in any way I can. That respecting and validating precedes any kind of acknowledgment of problems the person might have. That is paramount. I couldn't think about moving with anybody unless I had gone through that step of respecting and validating the person at his or her level of essence.

J/M/J: It doesn't seem that simple. Other leaders don't seem to stress this.

VS: One needs to manifest congruency and willingness to risk intimacy. I do not hear from any colleagues about any contextual messages, voice, touch, and space.

This is a dimension I stress above others. I think it is beyond words, beyond culture. The respecting and validating is universal. The specific, the unique, is the form I use to connect—be it a hug, a handshake, a surprised voice, or a reassuring tone.

You are in tune with the universal of that individual. I want to give the life force of the individual all the support I can give and all the connectedness

I can give. That will give the Self, the "I am," a chance of being seen, heard, and loved.

J/M/J: Now back to you. What happens inside you as part of the process?

VS: What I ask myself is, "Is this permissible for me? Am I contextually permitted to connect in any form or any particular form?" I might, for example, reach out differently on the street or at a party. Now if I reach out and the person were to veer off, I would want to note that, possibly articulate that, and do something about it if it all fits in his or her context and our context.

J/M/J: Anything you need to be careful about with yourself?

VS: Yes. My voice tone, my facial expression, my hands, my breathing, my eyes, my skin color all can give off messages to the other person. I need to be careful that I present an integrated, trusting whole to the other person.

In fact, the more chaos the individual is experiencing at the time, the more centered, more grounded I need to be. Otherwise the person misses the confidence and trust he or she needs to work through the chaos; if I do not, the person will use my lack of congruence and take it personally, internalizing it to define him- or herself.

J/M/J: Connecting with the universal seems clear. How do you differentiate your individual responses?

VS: I get from each person the mode in which he or she can be connected with. It is as if the being is giving me the conditions that are most acceptable to make a deep connection.

Sometimes I make a mistake, but not very often. Maybe three aspects need mentioning: (1) I have become a very thorough observer of nonverbal manifestations of self. (2) I might be in a slight trance and connect intuitively with the deeper nature of the person. With the basic belief expressed earlier, I hold that you can all learn this way of connecting and validating, too. While saying this, I am aware that I do always do this before I start any work with individuals or families. (3) I also look for feedback during the process of connecting. If, for instance, I take somebody's hand and I feel tightness there, I am going to respond and loosen my hold, and at the same time say, "Thank you," acknowledging the person's space and feeling.

J/M/J: Is there a completion or closure?

VS: I think when contact has been made, I can stop. Years ago I used to take a lot of time, almost holding on, to make contact. Now with a short contact, I feel I have connected at such a deep level of respect and validation that the person's self-esteem has been given a major boost.

J/M/J: Does the obvious body position have much validity?

VS: To me that is always a start. If the person stands with his arms folded, for instance, you only get a behavioral manifestation of what might be going on internally. To conclude from gross physical gestures the internal process often leads to serious guesswork. Use it as a start and go from there.

Then there is the double message. The discrepancy between affect and words, body and words. In earlier times, we used to say they were true and false manifestations. Now we know that both could be valid but only come from a different place. The discrepancy says more about their level of integration at any given moment. Double messages usually include the "should" part and the "want" part. Underneath the "should" part, one can often hear fear.

When I realize that there is nothing fearsome here, but the person is afraid anyway, I begin to look at something that is present but not showing to anybody yet, namely something the person learned and brought with him. And now, without any difficulty, I can surface that learning.

In a demonstration in a workshop, this often happens very early, at the beginning of my making contact with the whole group. Tapping the universal resources of a person, and using the universal process to do so, has a major impact on the learning of all present. The person who came on stage usually finds the experience enriching. What I feel I did was connect deeply with the person, validate him, and show the group how the process works. We can now teach all this much more clearly.

J/M/J: Back to discrepancy [in double messages]. How do you handle the difference?

VS: You take the voice, the physical, the auditory, the affect, the discrepancy. At a deeper level you come up with a gestalt. In that sense, each component says the same thing about the Self.

How many times have people observed a discrepancy and then accused someone of lying? This discrepancy is a comment on lack of integration.

J/M/J: What becomes background for you when you work with people?

VS: The background is the universal. It is like the alphabet, which I use to help me understand the specifics of each individual. So each one of us stands out as the foreground against the universal.

J/M/J: How would you summarize our discussion so far?

VS: I appreciate your questions. They give me a chance to reflect on what I do and remind me that I work from a basic belief of respecting and validating people in a way so that they can feel their own power and self-esteem. Even though I might connect with each on an individual, specific basis, the purpose and process is universal.

We have often heard people relate their experiences of meeting and being greeted by Satir for the first time. Regardless of the size of their groups, they would come away feeling validated, connected, important, acknowledged, heard, empowered, and energized by having Satir connect with them. Her making contact seemed to have the same positive effect with people regardless of their country or culture.

METAPHORS

Satir regarded metaphors as powerful tools for promoting change. The following interview provides an overview of how she perceived and used metaphors.

J/M/J: You seem to use a lot of metaphors in your therapeutic interventions. How do you relate the use of metaphor in therapy in general?

VS: There are so many things that have to do with meanings in terms of human beings, and often language is a limiting factor. So when I want to get some special meaning across, I will bring in a metaphor. By using a metaphor, I can make space between whatever is and what I am trying to get across. In that way a metaphor is an adjunct therapist.

For instance, let's suppose you are a client of mine and you are struggling with ways of trying to help some member of your family by taking care of him; but at the same time there is a strong dependency on you. So what I might say to you is, "You know, I am going to tell you a little story." And I'll tell you the story of two men who grew up together in a village, who were friends for a long time, since they were children. One of them grew up to be a rich fisherman, and the other man was and stayed poor.

They loved each other. So the rich man gave his friend a fish every day for twenty years. After years of the same help every day, the rich man said to himself, "I am not helping this man at all. I am really insulting him." So he pondered all night long about what he could do. He finally came up with a solution, so the next morning when his good friend came, he said to him, "Look, my friend, here is the fish for today. I also brought you a fishing rod, and instructions on how to catch your own fish."

As you can see, I moved the story between me and the person. The metaphor itself contains the message. In that way I can help people an awful lot.

J/M/J: So you get out of the person's system and look at it from outside, and you let the story act as the medium of therapy?

VS: Yes, I do that a lot. It creates a picture in a person's head that words do not seem to have the capacity to convey. That initiates a whole different process of change.

I also use a lot of metaphor in countries where the native language is not English. I have lots of experience with this because what I needed to do was to find ways to get the meaning across. Metaphors from the biological world of nature are the most effective ways of carrying meaning.

J/M/J: What happens when you work in different cultures?

VS: For instance, I love my work in the Oriental countries. It's as if I fit there. I have no problem with them, and they don't have any problem with me. I think it has to do with the fact that very soon people know that I am really connected with the person, and so they give me all the things I need to help that person give meaning.

J/M/J: How is the use of metaphor related to the use of the right and left hemispheres of the brain?

VS: Presently there is a lot of activity generated about the use of the brain and various parts of the brain. Also a lot of articles and books have recently been published, including the one John [Banmen] published.*

What I am most interested in is beyond the logical, to engage the intuitive to bring out the pictures, to bring out the sensing which gives juice to the form and possibly allows for deeper change. Metaphors give pictures, activate the sensing, the seeing, the hearing, and the touching that provide the brain with "an image," which in turn provides a process of perceptual changes.

J/M/J: Why is this so important in therapy?

VS: I think most therapy is conducted as an intellectual exercise. Even when some therapists ask their clients, "How do you feel?" and they get answers as to what the clients think, and they accept those answers, the whole activity is still only an intellectual exercise. I believe in and practice the use of sculpting, metaphors, and pictures to activate the whole brain and to engage the whole person.

J/M/J: Do you have a way of categorizing metaphors?

VS: Let me put it this way. Sometimes when I want to introduce something that seems very threatening, I'll look around for some kind of metaphor to use. Because part of the whole use of metaphors is

---

*Banmen, J. (1983). "Cerebral laterality and its implications for psychotherapy." *International Journal for the Advancement of Counseling*, vol. 6, pp. 99–113.

creating distance between the client and what I am saying, to reduce the threat.

When you talk about the de-enmeshment process, either between a parent and the client or a strong feeling and the client, the use of metaphor would be very helpful.

Some metaphors are related to preparing the client by tuning in to a general understanding of what they already have or know. For instance, somebody might be wondering about how they might go about doing something. Then I might say to them, "Have you ever had an experience of having something that you thought you did not know how to do and then discovered you had actually done it before?"

Then I might say something very simple, such as, "I remember one time I wanted to plant a garden and I wondered about what seeds I should use. I got all involved in thinking about the seeds, and I forgot to think about preparing the ground and when I would actually plant the seeds." Then I ask, "Have you ever had such an experience?"

I often use a metaphor like this to draw out all the steps, the choices, and awaken for the person the process that they already know but are not using in looking at their new possibilities for dealing with themselves and their situation.

I often use a metaphor to soften a perceived threat. I remember one time when I was with a man who was very scared about something he had with his mother. He thought about all sorts of different ways of dealing with it. To him I said, "I know a man who said he wanted to kill his mother because he didn't know of any other way to shut her up." So I sometimes go to an extreme with possibilities to decrease the perceived threat the client might carry about.

J/M/J: Any other uses you make of metaphor?

VS: Sometimes the metaphor is used to introduce a new level of thinking. One of the important things is that people start thinking in clusters of things. It's a way of introducing phenomenological thinking.

I try to use metaphors to make something unfamiliar familiar. When I work with the American Indian, I might use the Buffalo Woman as a positive value in the eyes of the client—something he is familiar with—and associate it with a desired but unfamiliar perception, pattern, or change.

Let me tell you something else and see if you classify this as a metaphor. I had a family in which the boy had stolen a car. As I worked with the family, it turned out he had actually stolen thirteen cars. I said, "My goodness, how did you get these cars going?" And he told me how he would fix this wire and fix that wire, and so on. He became involved. I was now connected. He seemed to feel more appreciated.

"You know what? You already have the makings of an engineer." I also knew his father was an engineer. "Now all you need to do is take your marvelous engineering skills and learn to apply them differently."

Without going into how this metaphor helped the father see his son differently, let me end the story by telling you that we made some great headway with that family in a very short time. This was certainly taking the familiar and making it strange.

J/M/J: How do you distinguish between the use of metaphor and the use of reframing?

VS: Sometimes I think one leads to the other. One difference is that part of reframing is to change the form and highlight the positive intent. The client might say, as I mentioned earlier, that he would like to kill his mother. I might reframe this by saying,

"What I am hearing you say is that you looked at some possibilities of dealing with your mother but you haven't yet found a way to deal well with how you would like to tell your mother that you don't like what she is doing."

In that way, reframing differentiates to some degree from what goes on in a metaphor.

J/M/J: Any other uses of metaphor?

VS: I also use metaphor to extend alternatives. My most frequent extension is to help people move from two alternatives to three alternatives.

J/M/J: We'd like to review some specific uses of metaphors you used in the Family Series videotapes (the Chico tapes).* We'll play the particular parts and hope you will comment on them. The following two quotes are part of the interview you had with the family. You are talking to the son, and he is responding to you.

The following is part of an interview Satir did with a father, mother, and 15-year-old son who is not attending school regularly. We quote part of the first session.

FATHER: If you don't go to school, I do worry about you, and I'm afraid you might get off with the wrong group of people. You might have problems. I've seen it happen to people before.

VS: Did it happen to you? Tell him about it.

FATHER: Yes, it happened to me. Association with the wrong type of people and getting off on the wrong road.

---

*In 1982 Satir did a three-day public workshop at California State University, Chico. This workshop was videotaped, and those tapes are now used widely for training purposes. They are available from the Avanta Network, 139 Forest Avenue, Palo Alto, CA 94301 (415-327-1424).

vs: [*To the son*] Are you feeling in any danger with people that you're aware of?

son: I don't feel in any danger at all. I feel pretty secure.

vs: I believe that you believe that, but sometimes there are other things that people see. [*To parents*] Is there anything in your minds that says your son is not seeing the whole picture?

father: If I act now, I might be able to prevent something.

vs: What kind of problem could he get into?

father: People related to the drug business, perhaps, and take money, and killings, and stuff like that.

vs: That's sharing the deep inside of you, that you are scared to death he is going to get involved.

father: Right.

vs: [*To son*] What do you do with your time when you're not in school?

son: Well, I read a lot. And I try to find someone to do something entertaining with, something entertaining to do.

vs: I'll tell you a picture that I have. Do you know what a toadstool looks like? I saw a great toadstool and you were sitting under it. You wanted to have excitement and new interests and so on. And you didn't notice that around the edges were interesting and funny things. Does that say something to you?

son: Maybe that I'm not looking out far enough. I'm not kind of expanding enough, not looking out far enough into the future to see what's going to happen. Maybe I should go out and look for more ideas and more to do.

J/M/J: That's part of the toadstool metaphor. Do you have any comments before we ask you some questions?

VS: Did you notice that these parents bring me this "awful kid" who isn't going to school? I find out by direct questioning that we are going to get into something pretty negative and that is not going to be useful to help me work with them.

The metaphor served at least two functions: it carried with it some possibilities for what might be happening, and it switched the context entirely. I switched the context from whether or not he is going to school to working at something that is really useful for him. I wanted, too, to switch the situation from a blaming position to something that is going to be exciting. We are, again, into new possibilities.

And then, you see, he comes right back and he tells me that there are all these things on the outside.

J/M/J: In retrospect, what do you think triggered the use of a metaphor at that particular time?

VS: Well, because I didn't want to go any more into the problem. I couldn't see that these people could have a way of getting into another context. In effect, they were stuck and only saw one solution: the son going regularly to school. But not going to school had started to mean getting into serious danger with drugs and violence. So I introduced something from left field, some pictures that go into the intuitive part of the person.

J/M/J: What do you think the effect of that metaphor was on the son?

VS: I saw that he immediately responded. He immediately shifted into the new context and agreed that he could change in the direction of reaching out and turning things to a more positive experience.

Now, suppose he didn't respond so quickly. I might have said, "Could you imagine yourself as a little boy under the toadstool?" I might have taken it a little further in that direction to get him out of the linear thinking, trying to resolve conflict.

J/M/J: It felt a little amazing how fast the son responded.

VS: That's right. That's why I encourage the use of metaphors. If you look at the rest of the interview, you will notice I was able to move him into action related to his future. Father later also became more focused on working toward more positive relationships, activities, and more acceptance of the son.

J/M/J: The use of the metaphor in this incident created a space between you and the story, and the son could find meaning from the story.

Would you have done anything differently, thinking about it now?

VS: I don't think so. I feel I achieved my goal, and the son made a dramatic move from the stuck place to new possibilities quickly.

Actually, as we talk, I must remind myself that metaphors often operate at several levels at the same time—all intended to move the person toward new possibilities.

J/M/J: We want to recall the next metaphor you used in the same interview, as you turned to the issue of attending school.

VS: [*To son*] What one thing could happen in your school to make you say in the morning: "Oh boy! I've got a real exciting thing to go to"?

SON: Maybe expecting to do something, like going on a field trip.

VS: So you go when school is going to be interesting. I thought you might. Now we have a real dilemma. Do you want a "plumber's license" (your diploma)?

SON: Yes.

VS: What could you do to make your life at school more interesting to get your plumber's license?

SON: Maybe go more often. Maybe find classes that are more interesting. Maybe think more about the future. Maybe study more.

VS: I think all these can work. How could you tell your parents that you are now ready to consider new possibilities for your future?

J/M/J: We noticed you stayed within the context of new possibilities.

VS: I tried to anchor his acceptance of new possibilities with going to school. Within the new context, he seems to be able to handle considering school much more easily. Now, part of going into the future is getting yourself prepared. Part of the [plumber] metaphor was humorous and something his parents would understand.

J/M/J: As you were using the metaphor of the plumber's license, what were you thinking about?

VS: I was trying to help the son think a little more clearly about the directions he wanted to go, to help him formulate something. There is a certain element of weaving that goes on in my work. The weaving of a piece of fact with a fantasy gives a metaphor with some new possibilities.

J/M/J: How about his parents?

VS: I know the rules of the family system are very important. My sense of it was that the parents were doing everything they knew how to help their son. But the ways they knew were very limited.

J/M/J: Do you think the son responded in a way that you had hoped for?

VS: Oh, yes. I was very pleased with him. It wasn't very long before he could talk to them directly.

J/M/J: The use of metaphors in the two incidents is intricately woven into the whole process of therapy.

VS: Absolutely. When people can do metaphorical thinking, they are already steps ahead in any problem solving. The linear method has nothing to offer compared to the metaphor in giving power to bring about change.

J/M/J: Any further comments or thoughts that come to you after having heard parts of your interview with this family?

VS: I have a metaphor coming to me. I start out on a walk and there is a road, and the road looks clear. Then I come to a place along the road where the road is not very clear, and there is a gate. Now, I cannot see the road on the other side. Still, I open the gate.

That gate is a metaphor. When I open it, there is usually something I never suspected/expected. Nevertheless, I go with it because I feel it is going in the right direction. Part of that trust is believing in the process. Metaphors are the tools to help people over the barriers. They are the bulbs or candles that illuminate new possibilities and provide for change. They are the links into the new.

J/M/J: Basically, you are helping the person experience himself in a different context and in a new light and provide a new meaning to the whole situation and person.

VS: Yes, exactly. Let me give you another picture that has come to me this moment. Imagine a room with a little old light which is about a fifteen-watt bulb. There are no pictures on the wall. We are sitting on hard chairs, and there is no rug on the floor. There is not a single plant. The room is dim, sterile, and barren.

What I do is bring in some plants, a rug, some furniture, and more light. I provide some warmth because that makes it possible for the organism to respond positively. Metaphors, meditations, humor, images are all part of making the juices flow.

J/M/J: It might help to state that the use of metaphors is process oriented, not content oriented.

VS: Yes. The content in the metaphor is always related to the process. Back to the toadstool: we were not looking at mushroom farming, but the process relevant to the picture was very significant.

J/M/J: What about feelings?

VS: Metaphor is another kind of way to talk about human feelings. The English words about feelings are very limited. Again, a metaphor makes it possible to get a new sound and a new sight, a new touch, a new feel, and a new thought about something. That is what creates the change.

J/M/J: Does the age of your client make much difference in your use of metaphor?

VS: Suppose I were working with a seventy-five-year-old person who is bored and who feels there is nothing left for him. Then I might say something like this: "You know, something just popped into my head. I saw an old father sitting on a bench at the foot of the mountain. He had in his hand a book that was all about what he had done thirty years ago, and there were lots of pages that were not written on."

I might use a metaphor like that to show the person that there were still a mountain to climb, pages to fill, life to live. In other words, the metaphor must not only be relevant to the change you are working on, it must be relevant to the person you are working with.

J/M/J: Metaphors are not static but versatile and relevant.

VS: One needs to be very versatile. I often use a book as a metaphor. In my book *Meditations and Inspirations*,* I have a meditation that goes something like this: "Go with me to a library, a library that you have never been to before. In the library everything is just the way you want it. And there is a book there. It attracts your attention. You go look at it. It has your name on it. You start reading the first chapter. It is called 'What Do I Want from My Life?'"

From there, I show the person his conscious responsibility and opportunity to write the next chapters.

J/M/J: When you do a guided imagery, what are you looking for?

VS: There is a lot of interest in imagery, guided fantasy, and visualization exercises these days. The biggest concern I have with this is that many people make these practices content based. They provide detailed static pictures instead of process-oriented

---

*Banmen, J. and Gerber, J. (Eds.) (1985). *Virginia Satir's Meditations and Inspirations*. (Millbrae, CA: Celestial Arts Publishers).

change that stresses positive expectations, perceptions, feelings, and possibilities.

J/M/J: How does humor fit into the use of metaphors?

VS: I'll give you an example. I remember somebody who was complaining and complaining about how crowded everything was. I said, "I want to take a moment to tell you a joke. The joke is about a man who lived in a rural area in the Middle East, a Jewish man. He was a very pious Jewish man. And he did everything he was supposed to do, especially within his religious teachings. Nevertheless, he complained a lot because of his crowded, small house. His mother-in-law, numerous children, and wife were all crowded into a very small space. Finally, the man went to the local rabbi and complained to him, hoping for some help.

"After listening intently to the pious man, the rabbi said he would give him the solution, but the man must do as he was told. The man eagerly agreed. Then the rabbi said, 'My son, go and buy yourself a goat and have it live with you in your house, and all will be well. Come back in six months and tell me how it has changed your life.'

"The pious man seemed puzzled, but he did as he was told. Six months later he returned to the rabbi saying how terrible it was having the goat with the family in the house. The rabbi again listened very intently and then said, 'You must go and buy another goat.'

"Even though the man felt unhappy, he did as he was told. In six months he returned and was again telling the rabbi how difficult it was to live with his mother-in-law, children, wife, and two goats in a very small, crowded house.

"Nevertheless, the rabbi instructed the man to buy a third goat. This he did. Six months later, the man returned, again complaining. During this visit the rabbi told the pious man to sell the three goats and return to him in six weeks.

"The man returned, beaming from ear to ear, and telling the rabbi how marvelous things were at home, how much room they now had, and how appreciative he and his family felt."

J/M/J: That metaphor stresses one's perception.

VS: You start with a belief, then perception, then ways of making meaning, then ways of feeling about all the components and one's self.

J/M/J: So the process is almost independent of cause and effect. The physical situation or problem might still be the same.

VS: I feel that looking at the situation in a different light first provides the client with a perception, a perspective, some hope, and a new picture. Other changes often follow quickly. Once you change your perception, it also reshapes your belief.

The metaphor is the most helpful intervention I know to begin to ask people to look differently at their beliefs and then have a new and different perception, a different picture. Change follows.

J/M/J: It seems to work similarly with people's expectations and feelings.

VS: That's right. Therapists need to know that we can go directly to people's expectations, perceptions, and feelings to help them change. In fact, changing these changes the person's self-esteem.

J/M/J: People cope better.

VS: When people change their perceptions, that really changes their coping. For example, I see a lot of people who tell me they did terrible things in the past. When I ask them how that affects them now, they tell me, "Terribly." They feel very guilty.

So I say, "You can keep carrying the guilt around for another ten years. You can give it to somebody else (blaming somebody else). Or you can have a new perception of what you did and of how you look at it now."

Sometimes I mention these three choices. At other times I move straight to the third choice and work on their perceptions, expectations, and feelings.

My sense is that I've said everything we had hoped to cover. I've enjoyed your questions and our discussion.

We feel that using metaphors in the therapeutic process is a powerful way to engage the right hemisphere, which brings about deep levels of change and transformation. We encourage their use. Actually, many of the Satir vehicles—such as coping stances, Parts Parties, and the use of ropes—are metaphoric processes. They externalize people's internal processes and demonstrate relationships.

The metaphor is probably the most fertile power possessed by man.

JOSÉ ORTEGA Y GASSET
1883–1955
IN *The Dehumanization of Art*

THE SELF MANDALA

The mandala of the Self describes Satir's holistic concept of the resources that are universal to all human beings. Variations are as many as people, but the basic resources are the same. For Satir, this implied that "I never have to ask myself when I go anywhere in the world, 'Am I going to find something generic I never found before?' Never.

But I am going to find all kinds of variations, and I will always know the core."*

   Satir's graphic picture of the mandala comprises eight concentric circles. In the center is the "I am." The "I" represents every human being—the person, the sacred and holy Self. The eight rings represent the following universal resources:

The Universal Human Resources

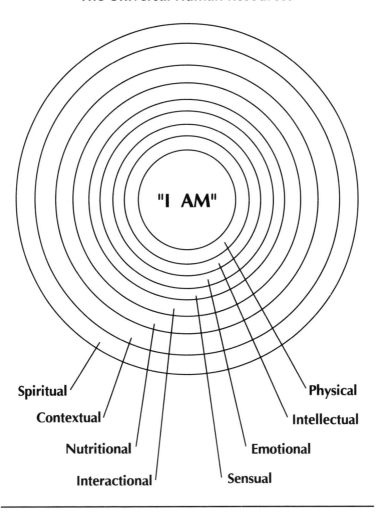

Spiritual

Contextual

Nutritional

Interactional

Physical

Intellectual

Emotional

Sensual

"I AM"

*Satir, 1984, Process Community, Crested Butte, Colorado.

1. Every "I," regardless of color, sex, religion, and culture, is housed in a temple, a place for the "I" to live: the body. All physical parts are included here.

2. The "I" is equipped with a brain, in its intellectual part. This circle refers to thinking, organizing, and using logic, as well as the brain's emotional, creative, and sensitive part.

3. Every "I" has feelings, emotions.

4. All human beings have senses. We may think of our eyes, ears, mouth, nose, nipples, navel, genitals, and the skin when we think of our senses. Our skin has millions of holes called pores, each of which is capable of putting something out and taking something in.

5. The next circle is the "I–thou" dimension, the interactional part. Human beings do not come into this world alone. We are always connected. The "me–you" was always there. For the egg in the female and the sperm in the male to unite and activate a new self, an interaction—an "I–thou" event—took place.

6. Then we come to the nutrition part: all the liquids and solids we put into our bodies.

7. The next ring is the contextual part. The context always has light and sound and space of some sort. It always has some time, movement, color, and temperature. It always has air. And it is always in the "now." That is the only unit in which we can experience the present directly. Everything else is a memory or a fantasy.

    Every context has these aspects, and every one of those aspects has vibrations, with their effects on us, because we are also acting and being acted on.

8. The eighth circle is the spiritual, the life force. This part is the universal energy that connects us with each other and with the energy of the universe.

We often treat these eight parts as though they were separate and apart from each other. Let's look at the professions, for instance. We usually put spiritual concerns exclusively in the hands of religion. Until recently, contextual matters were not acknowledged at all. Only in the last twenty years or so have we been aware of and concerned about our environment and the effects of modern technology on the planetary context. The idea that the air, color, and light are in the mainstream of our lives is a relatively new awareness.

We now know a relationship exists between a person's feelings of comfort and the color of paint on the walls. As a result, color is now increasingly taken into consideration in hospitals, office buildings, and architectural planning. We also know a relationship exists between people's productivity and their work environment.

For a long time nobody paid attention to the nutritional part, except when one was sick. Nutritionists worked for hospitals. Only in the last few decades have we become aware of the connection between nutrition and health in a major way.

Attention to the interactional part was given mainly in relation to "bad behavior." When it came to the sensual part, the only people who acceptedly made use of it were those in the performing arts. The emotional part was virtually relegated to moralists. The physical was in the hands of physicians; the intellectual, teachers. Most of the time those people didn't speak to each other because each part was considered the whole.

Around 1946 came the first idea that these parts were interdependent and that people are integrated. In the form of psychosomatic manifestation, the awareness grew that a relationship existed between how somebody thought and felt and what his or her body did (the functional operation of the organs).

Psychosomatic symptoms often were looked at as "crazy." The psychosomatic basis simply meant, however, that a relationship existed among thought, spirit, emotions, and the physical. This was the beginning of the integration of the idea that we have parts that interact. In the mainstream we have not yet integrated all these parts. We are moving toward a concept of holistic. We are trying to discover, for instance, how it happens that a thought can raise goosebumps.

Satir consistently found ways in which we can see how these parts affect each other. She developed demonstrations and exercises to illuminate this concept of wholeness. Consequently, a linear diagnosis never fits in her system. Instead she developed a picture of a *systemic diagnosis*, which describes how a series of related variables develop in a certain order and sequence to accomplish a common goal.

This means that a person's body, for instance, operates under effects of his or her feelings, thoughts, context, and so on. The person's emotional and spiritual life are equally important. Satir stressed a balanced, harmonious approach in which each part is of equal value, connected and interdependent. Any outcome (symptom) needs to be analyzed, understood, and accepted as the composite of the mandala's eight parts, which are linked in a constant process of transformation. The need for wholeness underlies the interplay of these universal parts.

Satir suggested looking at any behavior or physical symptom in terms of these eight parts. Questions include: How is the person in terms of:

- how he or she is living? (Are there twenty-five people in one dark room with no color or air?)
- what he or she eats?
- the people with whom he or she has connections?

- what he or she allows him–or herself to see, to spur imagination and dreams?

- feelings about him–or herself?

- his or her body? (What kinds of opportunities does the person give his or her body? How is the person related to his or her body? Is he or she full of taboos? Does the person treat his or her body as a sacred temple that needs to be cared for, related to, learned about, loved, and valued?)

- thoughts? (Is the person looking only for "the right way," or does the person give him- or herself permission to use creativity?)

We have no simple cause-and-effect answers, only a process for discovery. When we know and accept all our parts, we have a spiral of all these interacting. Sometimes one part is up front, sometimes another. We benefit by remembering that they are all connected.

So when something happens, we can ask ourselves questions about our eight parts. Where am I in my feelings of love for my life force and myself? Where am I in terms of what I've been eating, thinking, feeling, and what my body is doing? What have my interactions been with people?

We can take a self-administered inventory to find out where we are. If we perceive any of our eight parts negatively by discounting, denying, or rejecting it, we may experience stress. The challenge is to understand the relationship of all these parts, to look at new possibilities in viewing the Self and its internal connections. Let's take a simple physical symptom: having a cold. That condition affects our thinking and performing, our feelings about socializing, our need for food, our awareness about ourselves, our beliefs, the environment we choose to be in, and our general sense of being.

We need to give attention to our awareness. First, we can inventory how we are treating ourselves. We do this to notice not only what is wrong but also to pay attention to those parts that are puzzled or joyful, and to the new choices they offer us.

Satir's Demonstration of the Mandala

One of Satir's powerful tools for demonstrating a concept was the use of ropes. The rope is a metaphor for connections—and in the context of the Self mandala, a lifeline. It represents a metaphor for Satir's picture of the universe, in which every individual is connected to a source and to other people. In this demonstration, the rope as a lifeline always ends up having a mind of its own, and it always fits what is going on with the person and his or her parts.

For this demonstration, Satir would ask for a volunteer to represent the "universal person"—the "I." She would put the rope around the waist of this person, symbolizing the umbilical cord. The "I" person invites people from the group to enact his or her different parts. As various parts come up, they are connected to each other with a continuous rope tied around their waists; the rope is long enough to leave about three feet of space between people.

As this evolved, the "I" person stood in the middle, holding the end of these ropes in his or her hand and being surrounded by and connected to all the parts. Satir then instructed each "part" person to imagine eight tracks radiating from "I." She then told them to move forward and walk along their own track, being separate from and paying no attention to each other. "I" would stand absolutely still in the center.

This represents a picture of all our resources having the ability and the potential to move in harmony. They have equal place and power to be recognized and accepted. It can also represent our universal resources at birth.

In the next step, Satir told four parts to walk clockwise and the other four to walk counterclockwise. As they did, their ropes got snarled, and they became cramped and unable to move. The "I" person, their owner, became stressed, felt tight, and suffered the pulls and pushes of the eight parts. (Since this is a systems picture, one person's movement affects others, as represented by the rope that connects the whole system.)

Satir would then tell everyone to freeze. She asked "I" to look and describe what he or she saw. This person gradually became aware of where the parts were in space, how they felt, and which were close or distant. (Some were visible or invisible to "I" at this point.) Satir asked "I" which part was sending a message of pain around "I's" waist, and she encouraged "I" to question the parts to discover what was going on and who was tangled with whom.

This empowered and reminded "I" that he or she was in charge of these parts. Satir then told "I" to instruct the parts, step by step, to get into a comfortable and free position. As the process evolved, Satir asked the parts to talk with their owner and make a sound when they felt pain. So "I" needed to converse, direct, acknowledge, rearrange, and pay attention to each part as that person was affected by other people's movements.

This is a potent demonstration of the connectedness of all our parts. How little we sometimes know where our pain comes from! Untangling the rope while the parts are all still connected to "I" also symbolizes a holistic approach to treatment. The concept of "I" being in charge, rather than the therapist, is important. The therapist provides safety, direction, encouragement, hope, and support during this time of chaos, empowering "I" to be in charge of the struggle among his or her parts.

Sometimes it takes one to two hours for all the parts and "I" to get back to their original positions, free to move in harmony while being connected by the rope. New awarenesses, familiar sounds and responses from the parts, and the process of becoming free and painless lead to new learnings for the Self. They also lead "I" to integrate his or her parts.

Self-Acceptance Demonstration

In a different demonstration, Satir asked the "I" person to identify the parts that he or she was intimately familiar with and proud of. Then, because of the rules that "I" grew up with, there was another set of resources that he or she might not have acknowledged, would rather have hidden, was ashamed of, or was not utilizing.

For example, if "I" believed that his or her body was not attractive, and grew up with rules that feelings should not be shown or expressed (and that he or she consequently should not acknowledge senses), these resources would be neglected, hidden, or denied.

Satir directed these parts (body, feelings, and senses, in this case) to sit together closely with their heads down. She then covered them with a blanket. Having hidden them, she then told their owner to sit on them. The other resources walked around "I" and the hidden parts, symbolizing that these were the parts "I" used to communicate with the external world.

The hidden parts, who could not move, nonetheless had their own needs and lives. They wanted to have a place, they wanted to move, and they couldn't. Satir told them to do anything in their power to act out: to pinch "I," who sat on them; to try to get hold of the parts walking around them; and to use their power to change this situation.

When no one could move any farther and "I" was usually tangled and in pain, Satir asked everyone to freeze. (The "I" person's pain symbolizes symptoms: the parts he or she is sitting on poke him or her, and the other parts are affected as well.) Satir then asked "I" to converse with all the parts about how they felt, what they wanted, and how they could get to where they wanted to be. She would tell "I" to take charge and direct each part into a position in which it was comfortable, free, connected, and in harmony with the others and with "I."

During this process, collisions would occur that could each be translated into person-specific significance. For example, if the freeze found the intellectual part and the emotional part standing widely separated, Satir might ask the "I" person if that experience felt familiar or had any significance. Usually the person recognized and acknowledged that in real life these two parts were often at odds and that "I" had to take sides instead of using both harmoniously.

"I" and his or her parts can then make new connections in awareness. This is like taking time to breathe, be quiet, look around, see where we are, and take charge. Whenever we feel tightness, we can stop and handle it as a message that something is out of harmony.

This process also brings into awareness that, while we have parts we know well, we are only just getting acquainted with and beginning to appreciate others. We can be in charge and at the same time get information from all our parts.

We can use this demonstration in many creative ways as well as in other cultures. It serves well for demonstrating various concepts; you can also use it for diagnosis and intervention.

SCULPTING

Satir's use of sculpting came out of her continuing innovativeness in helping people learn to take responsibility for themselves relative to other people or situations in a given context. She called this *congruence*, which she recognized could be achieved verbally *and* affectively (nonverbally). People could express their inner landscapes and, from their growing awarenesses, could organize, define, and explain these pictures. In doing so, they could also take the risk of adding new dimensions to them.

They could then find new meanings in their lives and be more authentically themselves.

Satir would demonstrate her picture of the family through a sculpting. For instance, members' coping would be demonstrated by the stances; power, by variations in their vertical positions; and intimacy, through their horizontal distance from each other. Families who learn the coping stances find them a useful shorthand way to identify what is going on among themselves. They are usually pleased with their ability to recognize that "Oh, I'm blaming now" or "You're being super-reasonable." This is the first step in awareness, and it helps people realize how others perceive them.

A picture of a four-member family might look as follows. Father could be super-reasonable and stand on a chair (expressing his power). Mother could be kneeling on the floor (expressing her coping through placating). One child could be closer to Father, blaming another person. The other child could be irrelevant and stand most distant from the rest.

After each family member shares his or her feelings about this sculpting, each then takes a turn sculpting his or her perception of the family relationships. After some sharing and discussing, the Guide invites each family member to show his or her desired picture of these relationships. The therapeutic process is to move the family from their earlier dysfunctional pictures to a more desired, supportive set of relationships.

Given her years of working with thousands of families, Satir knew that just as we learn our ways of relating, coping with our feelings, and behaving within our families of origin, we can reshape these patterns. If they do not serve us well in the present, we can add to them and transform them. In our infancy, it was appropriate to wear diapers. As adults, this is no longer appropriate for most of us. We have learned new behaviors and transformed our old patterns.

Sculpting promotes this kind of change in a largely wordless process. While Satir valued words and their meanings as one form of communication, she perceived that couples, family members, individual clients, and therapists often use words as a means of avoiding others or distancing themselves. Words are often a behavioral defense.

So she used sculpting as one way around becoming mired in words. She conceptualized it as a (usually) non-verbal use of oneself in space. It offers another set of awarenesses that get beneath the defenses of denying, ignoring, and distorting. Instead, it taps into our kines-thetic responses, which can be very powerful.

There is a quality of drama or theater about sculpt-ing—and about many of Satir's other exercises, interventions, and vehicles for change, as we have already seen. The ancient Greeks certainly knew the effects of good drama: they made potent use of masks, choruses, and catharsis. J. L. Moreno, the father of psychodrama, also made extensive use of posturing.

Satir first recognized the power of perception of self and others when sculpting in 1951, with her "Golden Boy" family therapy session (see chapter 1). Many other therapists have used this kind of intervention. As part of her focus on the use of self, Satir knew how therapeutic it was to be able to show ourselves, to delight in or be astonished by realizing how others perceive us, and to share our meanings with others. For many, these might be parts we do not yet know or have not yet expressed.

Sculpting is a way of informing ourselves and others about our internal process in relation to others and our-selves. Satir set up pictures in which we could manifest our relationships and feelings rather than talk about them. With a family system, sculpting is a way to become more aware of the family's context and the context of each individual player. We gain a richer panorama of the variables that have shaped a particular family, its mean-ings, and the individual members' lives—their values, beliefs, and rules. Arranging bodies in space, each member expresses his or her perceptions, rules, expectations, feelings, longings, yearnings, and who he or she is.

Sculpting's kinesthetic use of the physics of space may, for example, help one family member demonstrate to another how distant (or smothered) he or she feels. It is also a relatively quick way to portray family roles and rules, and individual likes and dislikes. For example, when a family has a rule that anger must not be expressed, a sculptor can have the members pose their bodies to show anger and then ask them to smile at each other.

Beyond showing the way things are, sculpting also highlights choice points for further exploration and areas that may raise questions for various family members. Having emerged, feelings and bodily responses that may have been out of awareness can never again be not known. In the hands of a competent therapist, these discoveries can be awarenesses rather than judgments or criticism. Sculpting is a safe way to externalize what we know, perceive, feel, and think. It is a metaphoric process of expressing our internal pictures of interaction (or its absence).

A therapist might say to a couple, "Let's use nonverbal sculpting to take a look at each of your perceptions of your relationship. What space do you want between you to feel safe, comfortable, and familiar?" This gives the partners an opportunity, perhaps for the first time, to depict—and to perceive—how much space or closeness they each need, and what this means to the other person as well as themselves.

A five-foot woman communicating with her six-foot man, for example, may feel a fuller sense of equivalency when she stands on a step or stool and can communicate eye to eye. Without this elevation, she might tap into some old fears of submission and domination and feel threatened or overpowered. Looking up at him may give her a sense of strain in her eyes and neck.

For a small child, similarly, standing adults can be like fearsome giants. Talking to a child from such a position is not the optimal way to connect. As you visualize this for yourself, see if any old pictures emerge. How different this experience can be for both people when they are on eye level.

Personal boundaries are another important awareness that can emerge through sculpting. We each have an energy field surrounding us, usually extending about eighteen inches from our bodies. At times we are open to having this boundary penetrated; at other times, we want people to respect this boundary. This is a felt sense, and close friends or therapists can be sensitive to it (as well as to their own boundaries). Clients may need education about boundaries, and you can encourage them to experiment to learn about their own and each other's boundaries.

Sculpting externalizes the ways a family communicates, the individual and the family life cycles with their various developmental stages, intergenerational patterns, and perceptions of inclusion or exclusion, enmeshment or estrangement, and dominance or submission. Each family member may have quite a different picture of the family in space, and you can use this to point out our uniquenesses and differences. Again, this discovery can be a rich resource rather than a barrier. For instance, when each member of a family has a different perception of the youngest son's behavior at home, sculpting these differences may lead to greater understanding, acceptance, and openness among family members. It may provide them all with new choices.

How to Use Sculpting

No formula exists for using sculpting. Like any effective intervention, it thrives best in a climate of connectedness, trust, and safety. As a guide, the therapist needs to be fully present and in touch with the family system's dynamics and with each individual.

The therapist strives to enlist the family's cooperation and achieve a dynamic balance with a sensitive sense of timing and creativity. Family members can then be supported and can support themselves in being open to new possibilities. These initial sculptings are not a panacea, but they begin a process that clears the way for new awarenesses, questions, and further exploration.

It is important to process these perceptions: any "ah hah!"s, changes in perception, feelings, thoughts, or reactions people may have experienced as they watched or were being watched. Bringing out this information is a delicate matter. It is important for the therapist to be creative in guiding feedback and perhaps beginning to move family members away from their familiar stances and patterns.

Asking each member to sculpt the family (including the sculptor) in the way he or she most wants it brings out the person's hopes, expectations, yearnings, and sense of self-worth. It can also expose what is often unspoken (or deemed "unspeakable"), denied, ignored, or distorted within the person or the family.

After you help people process this stage, take them back to their original sculptings of the current stress and ask them to take whatever literal steps they need to achieve their own physical comfort. In the ensuing processing, this can be explored literally or metaphorically to discover how each family member keeps him- or herself from having more of what he or she needs. The task is to make a bridge between what each person would like to have and what each actually has.

The more the therapist has integrated his or her own life experiences, the more creative that person can be in guiding sculpting. The use of self comes from our own experiences in our families of origin. Therapists' creativity and effectiveness are heightened when they have awareness and have worked with their own blocks.

Sculpting is also useful for working with systems outside the family. It can stand on its own as a vehicle of change for systems of any kind: educational, religious, professional, and so on. Power structures, conflicts of interest, boundaries, connections—these are universal among human systems and can be made evident through sculpting.

To summarize, then, sculpting is an in-motion interaction that uses bodies in space to make overt the family's (or other system's) patterns of interrelating. It also externalizes people's inner processes.

As with this chapter's other vehicles for change—making contact, using metaphors, and working with each level in the Self mandala—sculpting can help deepen the therapeutic process. The next chapter explores additional tools to promote this deepening.

11

Other Vehicles of Change

This chapter covers some of Satir's other vehicles or approaches, which she used and developed over the years:

Meditations

Family rules transformed into guidelines

Temperature Reading

Humor

We also look at the Satir model as it applies to individual therapy.

MEDITATIONS

Satir utilized numerous ways of helping people enter and make use of their brains' right hemispheres. Meditation is one of these ways. It was her practice to begin her teachings and workshops with a meditation, and she often closed the day's sessions with another. These helped participants to:

- Focus their energy
- Preview the work ahead
- Open their brain's affective, intuitive right hemisphere
- Quiet their inner dialogue
- Be more fully present in the "now"
- Open new choices and new possibilities
- Integrate their parts and resources

Satir once said, "What we read in meditations is the affirming of the fact that we are divine beings, we are capable of learning, we are loved and lovable and that we can love, that we are manifestations of life, and that we are shepherds of our own lives."

Satir grew up on a Wisconsin farm with a belief in a positive, non-punishing God. Her mother, a devout Christian Scientist, profoundly influenced this aspect of her life. Throughout her 73 years, Satir believed that we are all layered with endless possibilities.

While her spirituality underpinned her belief system, it was not until her later years that she articulated it more clearly—and nowhere more beautifully than in her meditations. Satir recognized that, in many forms, all life is meditation. It is a way to spiritual consciousness. She also accepted meditation as a form of ritual, one that can be a strong influence in healing.

Her earlier meditations often focused on breathing, feelings, and concentration. She used these as a path to the intuitive part of ourselves. Later her meditations grew in depth and importance. Believing we can live more fully in the immediacy of the moment, she said, "What I am hoping for as I do meditations, for both you and myself, is to heighten the awareness of what is going on right now." Her later meditations center on affirmations, positive perceptions, choices that fit, new possibilities, and acceptance of the self.

Meditating is not an intellectual process, even though thoughts occur. Satir addressed the right hemisphere, the intuitive side, where change and growth are possible. She used meditations to bring together what is scattered and give us a sense of power, positive thoughts of ourselves, and the chance to be aware of loving ourselves. She also helped people integrate their many internal processes as they worked toward a higher sense of self-worth. She did a considerable amount of reframing of parts that no longer fit or were needed.

In her later years, Satir also saw her meditations as a form of connecting with one another in the awareness that each of us is not alone.

After Satir had asked workshop participants to sit comfortably, close their eyes, and breathe deeply, she would lead them in a meditation. The following example demonstrates the various aspects described earlier.

Developing Your Self-Esteem Maintenance Kit*

Now, at this point I would like to give you your self-esteem maintenance kit, which I hope you will receive, accept, and become familiar with using.

The first thing in this kit is a detective hat, which you put on immediately when there is a puzzle or a question or an effort to understand: How do the pieces fit together? How do you explore for the gaps and find the things that fit? This is in contrast to judging. Many people judge before they explore, but I would like to recommend to you that you keep your detective hat handy for any time a question, puzzle, or gap appears, so you can go on a journey of exploration.

---

*Unless otherwise noted, the meditations in this chapter were transcribed from various Satir workshops attended by the authors. For other meditations, see *Meditations of Virginia Satir*, edited by Anne and John Banmen (Palo Alto, CA: Science and Behavior Books, 1991).

The second thing in your kit is a medallion that you can hang around your neck. On one side in beautiful jeweled letters, it says, "Yes." Underneath that "Yes," it says, "Thank you for noticing me. What you ask of me at this time fits just fine. The answer is yes."

And on the other side in equally beautiful jeweled letters is the word "No." Underneath that it says, "Thank you for noticing me. What you ask of me at this time doesn't fit at all. The answer is no."

This is the key to your integrity. Yes and no are both loving words. When you say yes and you feel no, or when you say no and you feel yes, you have eroded your integrity and weakened yourself. So keep your medallion fresh within your awareness, and always say the real yes and the real no, keeping your integrity intact and keeping your strength strong.

The next thing in the kit is an empowering wand, a courage stick, a wishing wand—all three. All three names can stand for the same thing. And when you feel a wish or a desire to move in a direction, you can take this empowering wand in your hand and move, dragging your fears behind you if they're there. If you wait until all your fears are taken care of, you probably will never move ahead. As you take that empowering wand, wishing wand, courage stick in your hand and move forward, many times your fear will have been dissolved by the time you reach where you want to go.

And to take this wand and use it to empower yourself means you use yourself as a reference: Does it fit? Where do I want to go? You are the one who sees the vision. No one else can see the vision, and many people—not knowing your vision, not under-

standing it—will try to dissuade you because they think you will be hurt.

Many people do not trust going into the unknown, but with your vision to guide you and your hope to guide you, you can move there—and most of us have to go alone. Or, if not alone, you cannot be dissuaded by the people around, who out of their fear try to dissuade you. The growth in all of us is strong and wants to have continuing new expressions. And so your giving yourself permission to move in the direction of your visions—of your dreams, your hopes, and wishes—is what brings you to new growth levels.

The next thing in the kit is a golden key. The golden key enables you to open any door, to ask any question, to make speakable what is unspeakable, and to attempt the undoable—to make it doable— opening up the possibilities, looking in all the cracks, noticing even the smallest kind of movement. That's your golden key.

The next thing in the kit is a wisdom box. The wisdom box is part of your heritage. It's part of what you came into the world with. And for me, I have located it by going into my navel two inches and going up toward my heart. Halfway between, I find the wisdom box.

This wisdom box is in contact with all the wisdom of the universe—all the wisdom of the past and all of that which resides within you. It is that part which you sense sometimes giving direction; sometimes it's called the still, small voice. It is that part deep inside that knows and that tries to give directions.

Like a thought or a feeling, you will not find it on a surgery table. You won't find the wisdom box there, but I don't question the presence of a wisdom box. It is that part of us, when we are cleared of all

*our defenses and all our fears, in which we can hear
the stirring of our growth and our wisdom. Perhaps
our greatest job in life is to remove all that stands
between ourselves and our wisdom, and then to recognize that all human beings have a wisdom box. It
needs only to be tapped.*

*Look again at your self-esteem maintenance
kit: your detective hat for exploring, your medallion
for your integrity, your empowerment to go straight
to your vision, your golden key to look at anything,
and your wisdom box to be in touch with the wisdom of the universe. Your body is the manifestation of the universe, with all it contains.*

*Let yourself now be in touch again with your
breathing, and if those tools are not already within
your grasp, or you have not already used them,
could you give yourself permission to try them on for
size and let them become yours?*

*As you make more use of your wisdom box,
and all of your tools, you can go into your psychological closet to examine what is there for you—
what you need right now. And you may find that
there are things there that came about as a result of
your saying yes when you felt no—which might
include anger, rage, or resentment. Or you may find
things there that have said to you in the past, "You
don't deserve to go farther, you have done bad
things." But you will recognize this for what it is: a
misunderstanding of you and yourself. And as you
clear your closet of these things by sorting them, by
noticing them, and by letting them go, you can
make room for new things that come as a result of
new ways of viewing yourself.*

*Opportunity for new visions and ways to get
there is enhanced by your connection with the center of the Earth, which brings energy upward to your
feet and legs and gives groundedness—the ability*

to think, to know, collect knowledge, and to be rea-sonable. You also are a recipient of energy from the heavens, which moves downward through your face and neck into your arms and torso, bringing with it the energy of imagination, of intuition, of sensing—the kind of thing that gives color and song and tex-ture to your life.

And as the two come together, they create a third energy—that which allows you to move from the inside of yourself to the outside, where you can connect with those eyes and ears and arms and skin and ideas that are ready and open. For those that are still in bud form, not yet ready, allow yourself to notice, love, and pass by.

So this morning, as you come into this day, give yourself permission to know that your under-pinnings are solid; that you are a wonderful, mag-nificent being of this universe, and you have only to learn about that magnificence.

And now if there is anyone in this world, including yourself, who would need energy from you, anyone you want to send it to—world leaders, fam-ily members, friends—take this moment to send energy from yourself. Send it with a love message that says, "Use this as you can." And very gently let your attention come fully here and gradually open your beautiful eyes, looking comfortably around. And if any movements or sounds want to come out, just let that happen.

The self-esteem maintenance kit is a ritualistic, symbolic metaphor Satir used to increase people's sense of inner resources and self-esteem. The idea is to take greater responsibility and be connected to our deeper source of wisdom. From the symbolic right-hemisphere experience of the detective hat, medallion, wishing stick, golden key, and wisdom box, Satir moves our focus back to our bodies, our breathing, and our connectedness with others in the present.

The next example shows that Satir's meditations include poignant affirmations of self-worth.

To Be More Fully Me*

I need to remember

I am me

and in all the world there is no one like me.

I give myself permission

to discover me and use me

lovingly.

I look at myself and see

a beautiful instrument

in which that can happen.

I love me

I appreciate me

I value me.

Interested in framing each day in positive energy terms, Satir viewed the world as a place that holds endless opportunities for us to choose and to act on. In this next meditation, she underlines that we can use our uniqueness to empower ourselves to make these choices, and

---

*From *Making Contact* by Virginia Satir (Millbrae, CA: Celestial Arts, 1976).

that we can let go lovingly and with appreciation what-ever no longer serves us well.

The Unfolding of a New Day

Open a new day

A day which may bring many things

you did not expect.

Neither positive nor negative

the day has not yet unfolded.

Allow yourself to

fully take in what this day will bring.

Give yourself permission to

take in only that which fits.

Feel good about your

ability to sort what fits.

No need to feel bad about leaving

that which does not.

You can see that knowledge is

a way of loving ourselves.

Finally, we quote one more meditation to show her emphasis on increased choices and increased connected-ness.

Connectedness with Self and Others

Allow yourself to become

Intimately connected

With all your parts.

So free, to have options

And to use those options

Freely and creatively.

To know that whatever

Was in the past,

Was the best that we could do,

Because it represented the best we knew.

It represented the best in our consciousness.

As we move toward knowing more,

Being more conscious,

We also then become

More connected with ourselves.

And in connecting with ourselves,

We can form connections with others.

Satir's meditations lift up the spirit of each of us: that inner, precious "I am." She connects our intellect—our mysterious abilities to think and know—to the intuitive, affective part. This helps create a wholeness and an integrated Self.

In another way, her meditations address the various parts of the Self mandala described in the previous chapter. Throughout the meditations, she highlights our capacity for relatedness within and without—the "I–Thou"-ness of each of us.

Satir's meditations are poetic *haikus* of her total paradigm, her conviction that we are manifestations of a universal life force. Each meditation is like a deep well in which we can search and explore. Ultimately we realize that beneath each well is an underground stream in which we are all joined.

FAMILY RULES TRANSFORMED INTO GUIDELINES

We touched on family rules in Chapters 3, 5, and 8. This is a more thorough discussion of rules and their transformation.

How Rules Arise

As human beings we all have to learn how to deal with ourselves, the people around us, and our conditions. When we first come into the world, we find ourselves in a physical situation of light and sound. Then come the learnings about how we are supposed to deal with this miracle, our selves: our bodies, minds, and feelings. Which feelings are okay, which are not? What kinds of thoughts may we have? What may we not look at? Should we think only the thoughts that Mother or Father want us to think? What if they don't agree, or in some cases don't even talk to each other?

How do I treat my body? Can I look at it? Do I get my hands slapped if I look at the wrong places? Every person gets an education dealing with these questions. The answers become our rules for surviving, and we learn them so early that we do not always remember. Family rules can be explicit (verbalized) or implicit (not verbalized but strongly integrated).

Satir concluded that, in a very general way, most of us live inhuman lives because we obey inhuman rules about ourselves. Here are some common examples from workshop participants.

- Don't show your feelings.

- Don't show off.

- Don't talk back.

- Always be nice.

- Sex is bad.

- Mothers worry, so be good.

- Fathers punish, so obey.

- Always be on time.

- Don't boast—pride goeth before a fall.

- Mistakes can kill, so never make one.

Rules in the family are an extremely dynamic, vital force in our growing-up experiences and learnings. Rules intend to socialize: they provide guidance, motivation, and limits. However, many rules regulate the freedom to comment and to whom we may comment, as in: "Children should never talk back to an adult, or to a teacher, or to people in power." This implies children should behave as if grown-ups were perfect or superior and knew everything.

Other rules are about feelings. Can I express fear, helplessness, loneliness, comfort, tenderness? And to whom? Family rules often suggest people are not supposed to feel what they feel, but what they "should" feel: "If I feel a little weak, I should act strong. If I feel fearful, I should act brave." These rules say which feelings I should not have, which ones I can share, and which I should pretend or believe do not exist. Some families say angry feelings should not be expressed, or that people should never talk about feelings.

Another set of rules relates to gender and to roles. Who may do what and talk about what and with whom? In some families, women are not supposed to be powerful and men are not supposed to be tender. Especially in Western society, men are never supposed to have fear, nor are they supposed to admit not knowing what to do. If a man has fears or tender feelings, he keeps them to himself.

It is easy to mix up our personality with our rules for how to live and then ascribe our ways to genetics. Once we cut off our feelings or say only certain feelings are okay, we rechannel our energy away from our own experiences of the world, suppress or fight our feelings, and follow our rules as best we can. In this case, the energy gets rechanneled into physical, psychological, or social difficulties.

Two other common rules are, "Do not ask for what you want, but wait until somebody gives it to you," and "It is not nice to ask for things." Some families show love on the basis of, "Do not ask for love. Wait until I give it to you, and that will mean that you are loved." Many of us, for instance, receive Christmas presents we cannot use from people who love us, and yet we thank them profusely and keep the gifts. Again, the rules are that we can neither ask for what we want nor say what we do not like.

Once we relinquish our freedom to ask for what we want, we create a situation of dependency. We have to use another person to be our pipeline. Often love is conditional: it comes with strings attached. Examples include "If you love me, you will know what I mean," or "If you love me, you will do as I say." In other words, we expect others to read our minds.

This attitude often extends beyond people who love us. We sit in car A and expect the driver in car B to do our driving. Expecting people to read our minds can be dangerous to our health or even to our life.

By now we have the rules "I cannot say what I feel; I have to say what I am supposed to feel," and "I cannot ask for what I want; I must ask for what you want me to want or what I should want." To keep a kind of consistency, a third rule evolves naturally: "Do not see or hear what is.

See and hear what should be." In other words, become blind and deaf to your own reality.

For example, let's take a rule about swearing. Father swears—can I hear it? May I comment? How do I learn about disagreeing? How do I ask when I don't understand? Think back to how your family handled these issues. Were there many things you could not talk about? Was the rule to talk only about the "good, right, appropriate, and relevant" things? Did you hear, "No matter what, you should look happy"?

Having developed these restrictions, it now becomes very easy to add the next rule: "Try to keep the status quo by not rocking the boat. Do not take any risks, because if you do, some terrible thing will happen. There will be chaos, or something bad will happen to you. Everybody knows that chaos is terrible."

This attitude limits our freedom to change. It labels change as abnormal. In some families, these rules do not change as the children grow up. The same rules apply to a twelve-year-old as to a six-year-old. People translate consistency into sameness: "The same rule is good for everybody." They resist normal developmental changes in each other and in themselves.

Another rule is to deny in words what we have actually done. For example, we are supposed to say, "I do not want to rock the boat" (when we already have), or "I do not want to ask for what I want," or "I do not want to see what I see."

"Civilized" people cannot say what they feel. They have to say, "I am fine," regardless of how they feel. Or they say, "You make me angry," projecting their feelings onto others.

In other words, the idea is to lie about the Self or to blame others. Most people live in a way of not asking for much, not taking risks, and never talking about their feelings. Often they blame their condition on the outside world.

We would like you to take a moment to think of what you "shouldn't" have looked at when you were a child, what you "shouldn't" have listened to, said, or touched. Then let yourself be in touch with the fact that we tend to generalize all those rules. The effect is as though we literally were blind, couldn't hear, and were paralyzed from moving in many ways. Naturally the world becomes a scary place. Our prohibitions do not allow us to examine our situation or change anything.

Think too about these rules as ways in which your parents wanted you to be good and to be protected from hurt. In the process, though, you also received tools that crippled you. They didn't mean it, they just did the best they knew and had learned. For example, let's look at rules about anger. Anger is a signal that something is not in harmony, like the red light in cars that indicates something important is out of order. In a family whose rule is that anger should not be shown, this most important emergency piece cannot be manifested. Yet the anger still exists. When a child gets angry, the parents punish him or her. Because of dependency on these adults, the child develops fear and catastrophic expectations about expressing anger. The rule also becomes survival related: "If I show anger, Mom won't love me, and I will die."

"Shoulds," "musts," "nevers," and "always" lead to threats, as in "You had better . . . , or else . . . will happen." The most fearful threats for a child are the loss of being loved or of being sent away. Anything that defeats our current existence has life-and-death significance. In this context the rule becomes law, becomes compulsory. We are *compelled* to live up to it to survive successfully, i.e., to be loved. If we don't, we know we will be punished. And we may die.

Parents follow what they learned and what is familiar. Some rules continue through generations. Family secrets, "don'ts," and "shouldn'ts" are transmitted verbally and nonverbally to the child as a "no choice" message. Again, they therefore become compelling. As in the following example, rules can also become destructive delusions. Nancy, age three, asks her mother something. Her mother gets angry and scared and tells Nancy to keep quiet. Nancy learns, "I must never ask questions." For her, this then turns into a law. Afraid to be rejected, she won't ask anyone questions. As a child, she has no experience against which she can measure this false belief. Consequently, she might validate it as a survival rule in her adult life as well.

When we are children, our punishment is external. Later we judge and punish ourselves internally for obeying or disobeying our rules. Today the context in which most of us live reinforces our inhuman rules, and we thus continue our inhuman behavior toward ourselves and others. Satir said,*

> *The context in which we live needs to be changed so it is fit for people to live in. For me, the simplest and most direct way is to develop individually the Five Freedoms: the ability to see and to hear, to own what we see is going on, to take the risk toward change, to move, and to ask for what we want. I do not think we have achieved those freedoms yet, by any means. I am hoping that we are going to be able to do so since there are so many evidences of growth emerging in so many different parts of the planet.*

Transforming Rules

At least one rule always underlies a behavior. Rules have survival value, and we need to respect our rules for helping us survive as we grew up. When our parents did not know how to handle differentness, they may have used survival rules to keep the family "safe." Examples include "Never let anybody know [about the differentness]" or "You should never talk about it."

---

*In a speech at the World Federal Association for Mental Health Congress, Vancouver, Canada, 1978.

Deeply embedded even in our adult lives, these rules may no longer fit our situation. They defeat us and become barriers in our lives. Satir therefore developed a process of transforming rules into guidelines. When inhuman rules can be changed into human ones, the family and the individual can operate within the Five Freedoms. The transformation process adds new choices and possibilities, as with the transformation of our parts. Transformation does not mean giving away anything. Instead, we add and thereby change.

Satir followed three steps to change any rule into a guideline. A basic principle is not to throw out the basic wisdom and purpose of the rule. Rather, the point is to change the compulsion into choices.

In Nancy's case ("I should never ask questions"), the first step in moving from compulsion to choices is to change "should" to "can":

> "I can never ask questions."

This allows us to use a choice word, a "can possibly" instead of a "must."

The second step is to expand the choice, changing "never" to "sometimes":

> "I can sometimes ask questions."

The third step is to expand the "I can" with three or more possibilities:

> "I can ask questions when I am in a
> school-related situation,
> when I don't understand, and
> when I want to explore things."

Through this process, we expand our choices rather than being compelled by one predetermined outcome.

Satir often had her workshop participants make a family-rule inventory, very much as we do in a Family Reconstruction. The assignment had five steps:

1. Make an inventory of your family rules. See if you can list at least a dozen early-childhood family rules.

2. What are these rules accomplishing for you now? Look at the survival aspects of each rule. Look at the kernel of wisdom in each.

3. What would the rules look like if you made them into guidelines? [Follow the preceding section's three steps.]

4. Which of your current or old family rules still fit? Is there a high cost attached to keeping them?

5. Which family rules that you received in child-hood have you passed on to others? Can you now change the compelling part of these rules and help make them into guidelines for others?

We need to give ourselves permission to pay attention to how we legitimize our old rules. Learned rules become universals and get dressed up in many ways. When we are two years old and feel angry, we have a temper tantrum. When we get to be forty, we call it getting into a fight, and then we may legitimize it into our context. When we are little, we can say, "I can't ask for what I want." When we are grown up, we still can't ask, but we say we are being polite.

We find ways to dress up stuff and rationalize it for ourselves so we do not have to deal with it. It is almost like working out reasons to keep ourselves helpless. If we believe, for instance, that "I must control everyone and everything," our internal dialogue might go like this: "If I don't, things fall apart, and if they fall apart it will be my fault and I will get so enraged that I'll kill someone. I'll have to pay for that, of course, and I'll be killed." (Taken to their ultimate conclusion, rules usually end with ". . . or else I'll die or someone else will die.")

Changing rules into guidelines facilitates congruent communication, increases self-esteem, and helps people become more relaxed, free, and in touch with their own values and truths. It is a process in which the physiological link is very clear and clean between the words and the body. As people proceed through the steps of adding choices to their rules, their breathing deepens, muscles relax, and a whole physiological change becomes visible. Their entire being demonstrates a new freedom and harmony in mind, body, and feelings.

Transforming family rules into guidelines is appropriate for use in Family Reconstructions, individual therapy, family therapy, and in our own personal growth.

TEMPERATURE READING

Having people experience improvements directly was a major part of Satir's effort to help groups improve their communication and self-esteem. One approach she developed is the Temperature Reading. This is a way for group members to experience their human environment, internally and externally, and to change the "temperature" within them, between them, and among them. This exercise focuses directly on the process while containing the content within five categories:

1. Appreciation and excitements
2. Worries, concerns, and puzzles
3. Complaints and possible solutions
4. New information
5. Hopes and wishes

Temperature Reading is an effective vehicle for being responsible with self and others. This technique grew out of a need to clarify and detoxify potentially troublesome situations by finding out how group members felt when they arrived for their time together. Within families, for instance, the potential exists for sharing many appreciations, complaints, puzzles, new information, and hopes. Temperature Reading gives everyone an opportunity to voice both their satisfaction and dissatisfaction in a mutual context. It provides a safe and trusting context for straight communication, validation, and giving and receiving information in a congruent way.

The process of a Temperature Reading is simple, and it can be useful with any group. We recommend approximately half an hour each day for this exercise. That is usually enough time for key issues to emerge once everyone has become accustomed to the process. Initially, the Temperature Readings may take longer than half an hour as people work out the best ways to function together. As they overcome old rules about commenting and sharing, they get used to communicating in the best possible ways.

Readings are especially useful when a therapist teaches a family to practice daily readings during the time the family is in therapy. Often this then can become a regular activity or part of a weekly family meeting. Setting the same time period aside every day (after dinner, for example, or at breakfast) helps family members plan their time accordingly. Focusing on the five categories at a particular, predetermined time also frees everyone to continue their work in the meantime. They know they will have an opportunity to speak about their needs and interests during the next Temperature Reading.

To begin, one person directs the reading. After the process is familiar, everyone can take turns conducting or facilitating. Children often like to begin the Temperature Reading. They may want and need to know a lot more about what their parents are feeling and thinking. The main point to remember throughout the process is that people are of value and what they say is also of value.

Appreciations

The first category, appreciations and excitements, is directed toward other people. It is an effort to be inclusive and to encourage group or family members to begin with the positive aspects of life together. This is very much in keeping with Satir's total approach: to find, acknowledge, and share the positive. It also increases the trust and intimacy among people and allows for more productive handling of their worries and problems. Appreciations help set the stage for cooperation.

People frequently do things for one another, but somehow we do not often talk about it. We are usually much more able to point out all the things that are wrong. Many of us were brought up with the belief that if nothing went wrong, no one needed to say anything. At work and at home, we often take each other for granted and do not verbalize our appreciation.

In Temperature Reading, we share our appreciation for others, being as specific and present-based as possible. The first step involves one person using first-person "I" statements to communicate appreciation for another person in the group. The idea is to stay away from generalities such as "I like your cooking." A more specific message is: "I liked the dinner you cooked yesterday, especially the way you prepared that chicken dish." We speak directly to the person, situating ourselves nearby and keeping eye contact.

Sharing appreciations alleviates those instances when we lie in bed at night thinking, "Is it worth it? I don't think anybody really notices how much I do for everybody." Instead, we give voice to the good things that others have done. Our appreciations focus on positive feelings and are shared openly.

People can take turns sharing appreciations or just share them at random. Not everybody is expected to have an appreciation for everybody else at each Temperature Reading. More natural, spontaneous sharing is recommended.

Worries

The next category is called worries. It includes concerns and puzzles. (Sometimes we actually call this category "puzzles.") Adults often do not express worries for fear of appearing inadequate or stupid. To cover up their worries, parents often raise their children to believe that adults know everything.

When people fail to address worries and concerns about other family members, they create the possibility of rumors and assumptions. By expressing worries, they can clarify these rumors, remedy their uncertainties, and come to a greater understanding of themselves, others, and the world.

To feel comfortable about what every family member is doing, people express their concerns or puzzles and ask appropriate, nonblaming questions. Questions that clear away puzzles begin with *what, how, when, where* and, possibly, *why*. Through such questions and their answers, we develop the freedom to clarify without activating other people's defenses.

Cultivating a nonthreatening atmosphere in which to communicate is essential to the well-being and learnings of the whole family. Avoid questions that are really statements, as in, "Who didn't do the dishes last night?" Instead, encourage people to make "I" statements about their feelings of dissatisfaction and to use questions for expressing concern or confusion.

People also need to be clear about how much information they want. Satir often told the story of the new mother who knew that some day her little boy would ask her about sex. To prepare, she took courses in sex education and studied numerous books. One day her son said, "Mom, where did I come from?" Here was her opportunity to tell him everything she had learned. When she finally slowed down and took a long breath, her son said, "No, I didn't mean that. I mean, where did we come from? Tommy came from Chicago."

Unanswered puzzles or concerns often feed feelings of insecurity and perpetuate low self-esteem. Temperature Readings provide a structured means of precluding such consequences. Otherwise we can make trouble for ourselves by focusing on our worries without sharing and reframing them.

Complaints and Recommendations

The third category is sharing problems. The person who identifies a problem also offers possible solutions. One reason for this is that whoever finds a problem or complaint is often also the most knowledgeable about possible solutions. Before people complain that something is wrong, they usually compare the situation with a past experience, or they have an unmet expectation or ideal.

Children have fun with complaints, especially when they can develop their own recommendation as a possible solution.

Voicing complaints may also uncover potent angry feelings. It is important when we feel this anger that we acknowledge it. We do not have to act out our feeling of anger. Taking ownership for our anger by acknowledging it to others may help us deal with it. We may still need to acknowledge our hurt, fear, and our underlying expectation, but we do not need to take out our anger on others.

An example is, "Dad, I feel angry when you give privileges to Bob [a younger brother] that I never got when I was his age. I want you to know how I feel, because sometimes I take it out on Bob. And sometimes I feel that you love him more."

Satir's intention was to help people take greater responsibility for their own internal worries and concerns by sharing them and subsequently getting some straight, honest, supportive feedback from others. She encouraged people to respond to each other and to communicate in a congruent manner. The purpose of the Temperature

Reading is not for participants to argue about or solve each concern, but to hear each other, learn to negotiate, and perhaps agree to disagree.

New Information

Sharing information is the fourth category. New information takes many forms. It might be announcing a concert for the coming week or drawing attention to a current sale. We often assume that if we know about events, appointments, and preferences, everyone else knows about them too, without our needing to say a word. These assumptions frequently make communication difficult.

Temperature Readings also emphasize more personal information: new decisions, achievements, and activities. Sharing this information is an important aspect of building a family team. It helps ensure that everyone has the same news and can operate with the same understandings. No one feels excluded or passed over. Being heard leads to feeling validated and to having higher self-esteem.

Hopes and Wishes

In the fifth category, the focus moves into the immediate future when people share their hopes and wishes—"sending our wishes into the universe," as Satir frequently said. A hope that is not verbalized has little chance of being fulfilled, whereas an articulated hope has many opportunities of being actualized. There is no guarantee of getting what we wish, of course, but when we verbalize our hopes, we and others can marshal energies and resources more directly toward realizing these hopes.

Many of us have learned not to talk about our hopes and wishes. We may have censored them since childhood, fearing our mothers or fathers would be upset to hear them. Permitting ourselves to talk about our hopes and wishes is sometimes enough to free us from the uncomfortableness of this censoring.

Once we are open to opportunities, finding resources is one of the ways we can make our wishes become realities. Others are often interested in our wishes and can help us realize them. Family life becomes richer through support of people's hopes and wishes.

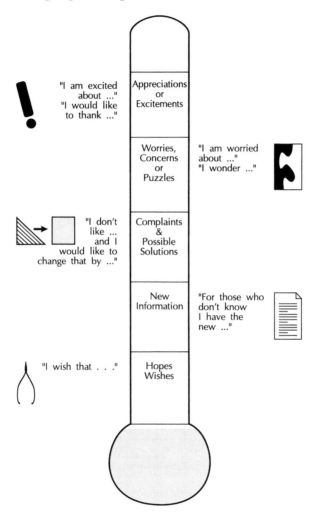

Outside the family, one of the most frequent uses of Satir's Temperature Reading is in the classroom. Numerous teachers have a daily reading with their students. Satir herself used daily Temperature Readings in her workshops. It often became the means by which participants raised their self-esteem, built closer relationships, and helped run a smoother workshop.

We have also had excellent reports from people using Temperature Readings at staff meetings. These people tell us of the healthier work climates this practice has helped develop. Organizational development consultants are using Temperature Readings in situations that stress excellence through human endeavor.

Of course, people can also use the five steps by themselves, working from "What do I appreciate about myself?" to "How do I achieve my hopes and wishes?" We encourage you to practice Temperature Readings in your workplace, your family, and with your clients.

SATIR'S MODEL FOR INDIVIDUAL THERAPY

People often asked Satir what part of her contributions have value or use for therapists doing individual therapy. After nearly thirty years of developing and promoting family therapy, could she offer individual psychotherapy anything significant? This section provides a partial answer; a more detailed description of applying the Satir model to individual psychotherapy is beyond the scope of this book.

One of Satir's most significant concepts relevant to individual psychotherapy involves the primary triad. The premise is that many dysfunctional learnings for any client came from the primary triad—Pa, Ma, and Kid— and that these learnings need to be identified, accepted, and transformed to help the client regain his or her birthright of high self-esteem.

To Satir, the primary triad is the unit of identity. As such, it provides us with the setting for low or high self-esteem. In this context, we also learn communication and coping patterns. Satir evoked these patterns through her classical stances by sculpting relationships and coping behaviors.

The primary-triad experiences also provide us with models for how to cope under stress, how to deal with feelings, how to experience uniqueness and sameness, and how to deal with intimacy. We learn about enmeshment or the lack of boundaries, and about distance or lack of intimacy. Family rules often become so ingrained that the familiar becomes more powerful than that which provides us health or comfort.

The client's representation of his or her primary triad becomes a map of areas for the therapist to diagnose and assess. This map also helps design an agenda for necessary changes and transformations. The primary triad becomes the historical context within which to help the client change. The process does not require the presence of the parents, nor do the parents need to change for the client to make therapeutic changes. In fact, even if the parents are dead by the time therapy starts, the process still benefits the client in his or her developmental issues.

The primary triad provides the opportunity to help a child feel validated, accepted, and capable. It is a set of relationships in which individuals begin forming healthy personhood and high self-esteem. It is where the child learns about trust, intimacy, and taking risks. The primary triad holds the potential of being a great source of strength and nurturance. It is the source of major learnings, the most important being a sense of identity. It can also represent a time of learning dysfunctional behaviors and experiencing pain and rejection.

During early developmental experiences with parents, children develop their own coping mechanisms. If the triad is a dysfunctional system, the child usually develops dysfunctional coping patterns. The modeling impact of the parents on the child is strong and needs special attention during therapy.

Satir felt strongly that therapy can be viewed as the act of healing the primary triad. As the issues that took place in that triad are raised in individual therapy and become understood in their original context, they illuminate rather than contaminate the present. For instance, a person who acts extremely demanding, critical, dependent, and needy with the therapist may be repeating an old pattern that relates to his or her parents. Exploring these old ways of coping and finding new choices provides the opportunity for change. Clients can thus free themselves of their primary triad's negative impact by reconstructing old learnings into new and healthier learnings. They develop their inner resources into positive, responsible patterns of self-management.

The Client Ralph

Ralph's case demonstrates how the Satir process applies to individual therapy. The accompanying figure shows his family-of-origin map.

Ralph came for therapy because he felt depressed. He had been married two years to a very successful, confident, and sometimes domineering woman. Ralph had not shown any sign of depression during his first year of marriage. Now, at the end of their second year, he had become moody and withdrawn again, as he had five years earlier. Finally he became depressed.

During his initial therapy sessions, Ralph looked at his family of origin. He saw his father as domineering, opinionated, and critical. In times of stress, he blamed others for what went wrong. And Ralph saw his mother as pleasant, hard-working, and accommodating. In times of stress, he saw her placating others, especially his father.

Ralph soon realized his internal conflict was related more to his primary triad than to his wife. He would need to be careful not to copy his father's dynamics and become domineering and blaming. Could he learn to appreciate his wife for herself rather than reacting to her as he reacted to his father?

The early sessions also uncovered some strong anger Ralph had toward his father, which he had ignored or denied.

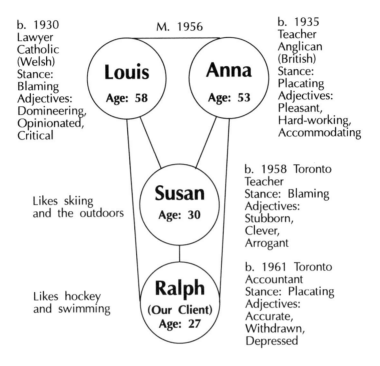

b. 1930
Lawyer
Catholic
(Welsh)
Stance:
Blaming
Adjectives:
Domineering,
Opinionated,
Critical

M. 1956

Louis

Age: 58

Anna

Age: 53

b. 1935
Teacher
Anglican
(British)
Stance:
Placating
Adjectives:
Pleasant,
Hard-working,
Accommodating

Likes skiing
and the outdoors

Susan

Age: 30

b. 1958 Toronto
Teacher
Stance: Blaming
Adjectives:
Stubborn,
Clever,
Arrogant

Likes hockey
and swimming

Ralph

(Our Client)

Age: 27

b. 1961 Toronto
Accountant
Stance: Placating
Adjectives:
Accurate,
Withdrawn,
Depressed

The family-of-origin map is an assessment/diagnostic tool. In the Satir model, clients describe their families and therapists draw maps to identify coping patterns and dysfunctional coping experiences, and to see what changes are needed for the clients to become more congruent and have higher self-esteem.

From the map, the therapist asks some important questions. For example, when Ralph's father was under stress and blaming others, wanting to control his environment by controlling them, what effect did this have on Ralph? What did Ralph learn from his father in terms of dealing with stress? How did Ralph cope or react to his father's blaming? Was Ralph the target?

When the therapist and Ralph looked at the coping patterns of his father, it became clear that Ralph was not dealing well with stress either. Both men in this family felt powerless. Ralph felt powerless by abdicating responsibility, and his father felt powerless by blaming others. The consequences were the same: not dealing with stress successfully, feeling inadequate, and having low self-esteem.

When Father blamed him, Ralph felt it was his fault. Father had successfully conditioned Ralph to feel responsible for Father's reaction, but Father did not know how to manage his own reaction. Ralph had been the target of a lot of his father's criticism. Now Ralph allowed himself to feel his anger and resentment more fully. Once he made the connection between his father's behavior and his own reactions, he felt more focused, hopeful, and in charge.

In the same way, the therapist asked about what he had learned from his mother about dealing with stress. How did he deal with her placating? How did he feel knowing that he had copied her placating stance instead of his father's blaming?

Neither Father nor Mother seemed to have taken responsibility for their feelings. Father projected his feelings, and Mother held hers inside. How did Ralph deal with his feelings? What meaning did he make of his parents' dealing with their feelings so differently? How did his way of dealing with feelings affect his life?

Ralph remembered seeing his mother dealing with his father in a very placating way, seeking peace at all costs. He recognized he was following the same pattern in attempting to achieve peace with his wife. When he realized he had copied his mother's coping stance, he felt his anger and resentment even more strongly.

The therapist and Ralph dealt with the anger, resentment, pain, and disappointment that had emerged through Ralph's flashbacks and reconnections. He realized for the first time, he said, that he let his feelings influence him in ways similar to his parents' ways. Instead of expressing and dealing with them, that is, he had kept his feelings inside, became emotionally lifeless, consequently withdrew more and more, and finally became depressed.

Through his awareness, acceptance, and understanding, Ralph began to come to terms with his own emotional confusion and depression. He needed help to separate himself from his parents' dominance, establish his own sense of values, and learn new ways of dealing with his unmet expectations.

Next the therapist looked at how Ralph experienced intimacy, how he experienced trust, and how he was validated. The therapist then assessed Ralph's level of self-esteem. Together they evaluated how enmeshed Ralph was with his mother and how reactive he was in relation to his father.

Subsequently, they looked at Ralph's perceptions that still provided emotional baggage. They explored how the same vistas could be seen with different eyes and in a different framework. This meant accepting his parents the way they were and acknowledging that they did not live up to his expectations. It also meant perceiving them in a broader context as people who were not perfect but who had lots to offer him in his growing up. In this process of discovery the client's perceptions change from being stuck at an early childhood level to a broader, more accepting level. Satir's type of reframing transforms perceptions by adding new perspectives, thereby opening new choices. The next step is for the person to validate him- or herself as a separate person.

Following this, the therapist and Ralph looked at Ralph's feelings. Feelings, according to Satir, belong to us. We can handle them, manage them, and, of course, use them to add joy, pleasure, and excitement to our lives. (For a fuller discussion, refer back to Chapter 7 on transformation.)

Ralph had difficulties being intimate and close. This probably reflected his holding his feelings inside and not sharing them, and maybe not even owning them. He had become so enmeshed with his feelings that he and his feelings became one. His feelings now overpowered him and controlled his life emotionally.

Having gotten a good grasp on how he had developed his coping and what he still needed to do to free himself from his past influences, Ralph wanted to find a better way to handle his feelings in the present. He wanted to stop depending on his early childhood patterns of avoidance. To establish congruent intimacy in the present, he had to learn to let go of his childhood expectations about how people around him "should have" expressed closeness and acceptance. However, he could instead establish closeness and acceptance based on his expectations in the here and now.

Individual Therapy and Family Rules

Family rules, in the Satir model, are perceptions, behaviors, and beliefs that we learned in our primary triad and that now have an (often negative) effect on our self-esteem. Our rules had a life-and-death significance in childhood and therefore are often considered "friends" in later life—albeit restrictive and limiting friends that can cause a lot of pain.

Usually hidden from conscious awareness, they require detective skills to be uncovered. Sometimes indirect evidence lets us know they exist: family rules are often the energy behind negative feelings, repetitive negative behavior, defense mechanisms, and low self-esteem.

From Satir's primary triad perspective—and as in her whole system of transformation—therapeutic interventions need to be made at these levels of experience:

- Expectations
- Perceptions

- Feelings, and feelings about those feelings
- Behavior

For example, Ralph still wished his father had played more with him when he was young. Ralph needed help identifying this expectation, letting go of it, and then finding a present-day close relationship with somebody he admired to fulfill that yearning.

Looking again at Ralph's map, the therapist asked him what family rules had been implied in his primary-triad experiences. He said he had internalized these rules:

1. Fathers have the power and are always right.

2. To survive, you discount your own feelings. You placate.

3. Mothers and wives are pleasant, helpful, and unselfish.

4. Work is more important than self.

5. Intimacy is not important in family life.

6. Values about self come from outside.

Satir believed that fear, hurt, and anger are the three main feelings that need therapeutic attention. We develop these feelings over the years as a result of our expectations and perceptions. These feelings often manifest themselves as the result of the same life experiences: they are different sides of the same coin. When we consider our negative feelings as reactions to our expectations and perceptions, we can then deal with them more successfully. This can be done within the family context or in a one-to-one relationship with a therapist.

Many people find it difficult to let go of the enmeshment of self and feelings. To help with this letting go, Satir would first use a number of well-known techniques to build the client's self-esteem:

- Make physical contact with the client.

- Use therapeutic humor to encourage the client to take the situation in question less seriously.

- Make personal contact through unconditional acceptance.

- Help validate the client's resources and choices.

- Build hope.

With the help of these and similar techniques, Satir helped clients feel more empowered and able to face and accept hidden or painful feelings. Once they make that de-enmeshment step, clients usually have a new sense of empowerment and some new hope of being back in charge of their lives.

Exploring the primary triad provides clients and therapists with the dysfunctional material that needs changing. The negative impact of the primary triad, if not resolved, is brought into the present as clients perpetuate its dysfunctional coping patterns. Present feelings and coping mechanisms often can be changed only by changing the client's reaction to the primary triad, the context in which these patterns were established.

With the therapeutic process now under way, Ralph quickly began taking better charge of his own feelings, perceptions, and expectations. The therapist and Ralph also looked at the expectations his parents still had of Ralph. He discovered he had internalized their expectations and was still trying to fulfill them. Once he realized his ability to separate himself from their expectations and listen more closely to what he wanted, he felt a great sense of relief.

Satir's primary triad concept provides an opportunity for the therapist to help create the context in which clients in individual therapy can relate their experiences into a process of change and transformation. In Ralph's case, this was achieved by using the family-of-origin map, working through unmet expectations and dysfunctional coping mechanisms, as well as working through his unexpressed negative feelings.

Satir's focus on process instead of content makes individual therapy especially effective. Instead of dealing with the experiences themselves, she focused on the impact of those experiences. With her view that the problem is not the "problem" (the identified issue, or content) but how we cope with the problem (our process), Satir's approach in individual therapy identifies the antecedents for our dysfunctional coping and offers us methods to free ourselves from their effects.

12
Conclusion

Originally this chapter expanded Satir's vision of the future: her plans, her commitments, and her focus. After her untimely death, we three remaining coauthors rewrote this chapter to discuss the networks Satir had developed, her activities during her last few months, and some of what is being planned to continue her mission.

During 1988, Satir and a few colleagues spent most of May in the Soviet Union. It was a dream come true. She had wanted to make an impact in the USSR for a long time, and she did. In a four-city tour, she introduced and demonstrated her approach to working with families. Professionals, professors, graduate students, and the public received her warmly and enthusiastically.

On her return, she did not feel well. Thinking food had caused her stomach pain, she expected to recover quickly, though. In June she attended the Avanta Network's annual meeting in Ontario. July saw her in Mount Crested Butte, Colorado, for her eighth annual International Satir Summer Institute. The four of us came three days early to do last-minute planning and preparation for the advanced program (Module II), which was in its fifth year. Satir felt very tired, had very little energy, and looked exhausted.

During the first day of the advanced training program, she became jaundiced. On the advice of a participant physician, she agreed to be driven to Grand Junction for some diagnostic tests. These tests revealed a growth on her pancreas.

Within a few days, Satir left for Palo Alto, California, and entered Stanford Medical Center for further diagnosis and treatment. Tests determined that she had cancer of the pancreas and liver. Her options included chemotherapy and radiation treatment, but these were considered merely palliative. She chose instead to undertake a nutritional approach to healing at home.

During this time we witnessed a tremendous spiritual strength and energy to fight her cancer. However, after a few weeks, her body did not tolerate the heavy regimen.

In her last few days, she spent much of her time being with colleagues and preparing for her departure. She felt and acted very much in charge of all the preparations and last-minute decisions. She had often talked about living 125 years to accomplish all the tasks she felt were necessary. Within the context, she made a very conscious, difficult choice to give up treatment and accept her death.

She revised her will, gave presents to people who were close to her, and accepted her death with grace and dignity. She said to one of us during her last few days that we were not to glorify her, the person, but to preserve her beliefs and her paradigm and to continue teaching in her spirit and with full commitment. She also asked us not to model her lifestyle of not taking care of herself. She said, "I took care of everybody out there, but not of Virginia."

Shortly before she died, she wrote:

Sunday, September 5, 1988

To all my friends, colleagues, and family:

I send you love. Please support me in my passage to a new life.

I have no other way to thank you than this. You have played a significant part in my development of loving.

As a result, my life has been rich and full, so I leave feeling very grateful.

—Virginia

Five days later, at 4:50 PM, she died comfortably and serenely in her own home, surrounded by her family and some of her friends.

The world acknowledged her life and her death through numerous memorial services and obituaries in the United States, Canada, Israel, Germany, England, Hong Kong, and elsewhere. Periodicals and professional associations such as the American Association for Marriage and Family Therapy paid tribute to her and her contributions to the helping professions, especially family therapy.

Focusing on process to bring about change in a systemic approach is often considered Satir's major therapeutic contribution. Not only did she believe that change is possible, she also provided potent vehicles to facilitate change. In the course of writing this book, we reviewed the literature and found that very few therapeutic systems are clear about how change takes place.

Although she actually became best known for her vehicles, her tools for change, these were only a means to an end. They helped people move toward congruence, high self-esteem, wholeness, and personal responsibility.

Over and over again, Satir found that people are resilient, have tremendous ability to change, and can transform major dysfunctional patterns of coping into wholesome, congruent ways of being and interacting.

In parallel with other innovators such as Carl Rogers and Abraham Maslow, Satir developed and deepened a way of seeing human beings as having great potential to maximize their inner resources, their self-esteem, and their choices of doing and being. From her early days until her last, she was on the forefront of human development.

Satir's focus expanded from the individual to the nuclear family and its system, and then to the systems of the extended family and the community. Ultimately, she turned her attention to world peace. Expanded in a meaningful context, her work toward congruence between people would result in global peace. Her last poster, "Peace Within, Peace Between, and Peace Among,"* is an expansion of her vital, basic concept of congruence in the world at large. As we complete this chapter without her, we see Satir's model of human communication and growth as a major alternative for the present stage of history, in which greater openness, individual dignity and respect, and a democratic point of view are sweeping the globe.

While she developed and taught her model throughout the world, Satir also formed two organizations, which now continue her work.

INTERNATIONAL HUMAN LEARNING RESOURCES NETWORK

In 1969 Satir formed her "Beautiful People" organization. This was a group of people who had studied with her at her many month-long experiential training seminars.

---

*Available from Celestial Arts Publishing, Millbrae, CA.

Drawn together because of their strong commitment to Satir and what she stood for, they registered as the International Human Learning Resources Network (IHLRN), a nonprofit organization, and began meeting annually in various parts of the world.

They met to experience Satir, each other, and themselves on a deep level of humanity and to share their skills. They also developed a strong focus on connectedness. The week-long annual meetings currently involve just over a hundred people from around the world. More people apply to attend than can be accommodated.

The program is very flexible and develops throughout the week. Participants have many opportunities to share their expertise and their views. They can present talks, attend various presentations, and enjoy social activities. The meeting encourages creativity and play in a stimulating and caring environment.

In 1989 IHLRN held its twentieth anniversary in Hacienda Vista Hermosa, Mexico, where it had started twenty years earlier. In the wake of Satir's death, the group decided to continue its annual meetings, newsletter, and activities. Membership is open by invitation from a member or by participation in any Satir workshop. (For information, write to the International Human Learning Resources Network, c/o Dr. Michele Baldwin, 1550 N. Lakeshore Drive, Chicago, IL 60610.)

The 1990s look bright and active for IHLRN. With the enthusiasm of its members, the group plans to expand its activities by helping potential students with scholarships to attend Satir training programs.

For years, the main working forces of IHLRN were Robert Shapiro, a close friend of Satir, and Michele Baldwin, co-author of *Satir Step by Step*. After Satir's death, Baldwin was elected as the group's first president.

THE AVANTA NETWORK

After her book *Peoplemaking* appeared in 1972, Satir received hundreds of requests annually to lead workshops and participate at conferences. She dedicated most of her working time to meeting as many of these requests as possible.

In 1976 Satir invited about fifty people from the United States and Canada to meet in Forest Knolls, California, for several weeks of training and to explore the idea of forming an educational training organization. The idea would be to prepare a cadre who would teach her approach to change and growth, and possibly fill some of those workshop requests she could not meet herself.

Forty-two people responded to her invitation. Some of their preparation involved hands-on training and consultation with local community agencies, under Satir's supervision. They also participated in programs developed by Satir that focused on teaching family therapy, doing family therapy, and giving communication workshops.

All the work took place in triads, and this began the practice of working in triads that continues to this day in Satir seminars. Virginia had planned it, of course, to help people experientially resolve difficulties that stemmed from their primary triads and to experience a nurturing triad in the process. This was a major step in implementing her model of working within the primary triad and the three-generational context.

In 1978 a formal organization was constituted in Aspen, Colorado. It was called the Humana Network until the following year, when Satir learned that Humana was a protected name of a health care delivery system and therefore not available. Satir renamed the group the Avanta Network.

In March 1979 the group made its first public appearance in San Francisco's Grace Cathedral. In the morning, Satir made an experiential presentation to about a hundred people from the helping professions. In the afternoon, Avanta members led small groups in discussions and demonstrations.

By 1980 the Avanta Network had its federal tax-exempt status and consisted of close to one hundred members from the United States, Canada, France, West Germany, Venezuela, Israel, Holland, Czechoslovakia,.and Hong Kong. Satir had attracted a lot of enthusiastic people who were committed to her vision as part of their own. To wit, the purpose of Avanta is the development and transmission of ways to:

Enhance self-esteem

Increase interpersonal communication skills

Provide a process model for personal and professional growth

Avanta is dedicated to helping people learn new ways to use themselves creatively in any setting in which they assist in the process of change. Its mission statement is:

> *To support the empowerment of individuals as we connect and work with organizations and peoples through the Satir growth model, to respect differences, transform conflicts, develop possibilities, and take responsibility for their own lives, health, work, and relationships toward the goal of human connectedness and healing in the world.*

In 1981 Avanta offered its first International Summer Institute training program (commonly called the "Process Community"). Satir became Avanta's director of training and held that position until her death, rather than being its chairman or president. This, she said, gave her more flexibility and created a less hierarchical organization.

At the first Process Community, she selected nine members to assist her to train the more than ninety participants. For three weeks in Park City, Utah, the trainers operated in triads to lead three groups of thirty-odd people in experiential learnings such as Parts Parties, Family

Reconstruction, and other family-of-origin work. The focus was on process and personal growth, with the idea of helping individuals to apply the Satir model first to themselves and then to their professional work.

We three coauthors found that first Process Community a moving, significant experience. To have such a large number of professionals attend and respond positively encouraged us to plan similar programs. It was the first time that members of Avanta took a major teaching role in training others in the Satir model, while we got training and experience ourselves.

After its first successful Process Community, Avanta moved the training program to Mount Crested Butte, Colorado, and increased it to four weeks each summer. By 1985 participants had encouraged Satir to offer a second level of training (Module II), similar to the first but with more focus on skill development. (In 1981 we three had become a training triad. In 1985 we became the Module II trainers, which we are to date.)

The objectives of the International Summer Institute are to develop people's personal and professional understanding of family and work systems. Training centers on the key aims of:

- Increasing self-esteem and personal competence
- Practicing self-care
- Managing conflict
- Increasing team effectiveness
- Creating climates for developing trust
- Enhancing effective communication
- Understanding how our family of origin is reflected in our present lives, understanding what to do about it, and using our resources for giving ourselves new choices.

While the International Summer Institute became Avanta's major annual event, Satir filled the rest of her

334

calendar with training programs around the world. During this time she squeezed in as many one-day, two-day, and week-long programs as possible. During her last few years, she also did some intensive work for educational purposes (by having it videotaped and made available for distribution).

From the year the Avanta Network was founded, Satir always provided new training experiences for members at the annual meeting. These five- to seven-day conferences were usually attended enthusiastically by over a hundred people, and Satir took the opportunity to reconnect with them, update their training, and help build a community of support and cooperation.

Following the 1985 "Evolution of Psychotherapy" conference, sponsored by the Ericksonian Foundation in Phoenix, Arizona, Satir spent a larger amount of her time working toward world peace. Her 1988 trip to the USSR was one result of the spontaneous peace session she and Mary Goulding organized at that conference. Over eight hundred had attended that session, and thousands of conference-goers signed a telegram to U.S. President Ronald Reagan and USSR President Mikhail Gorbachev encouraging world peace.

Avanta is directed by a Governing Council (nine members elected for a three-year term each). The council oversees the organization, raises funds, and conducts long-term planning. Members had been selected by Satir, based on intensive training with her. Now new members are recommended by three Avanta members and approved by the Governing Council. Leadership qualities and intensive training in the Satir model are still required.

Avanta's offices are headed by an executive director and staff at:

AVANTA: THE VIRGINIA SATIR NETWORK
2104 S. W. 152 nd Street
Suite # 2
Burien, Wa. 98166
206-241-7566
e-mail: Avantan@aol. com

FUTURE PLANS

Avanta members developed their own training programs even before Satir's death, and these represent some of the past, present, and future developments in Satir-derived work. Family Reconstruction workshops offered by individual members were followed by several "Peoplemaking" organizations. These nonprofit volunteer groups teach Satir material to the general public. Peoplemaking Colorado and Peoplemaking Midwest were the first two such groups. Individual Avanta members also offer various Satir programs around the world. We three coauthors started an annual training program in Hong Kong in 1985 and in Taiwan in 1987.

Next came the Satir institutes, in which Avanta members and other interested individuals established regional centers for teaching and learning the Satir model of change and growth. The Northwest Satir Institute (for Washington state and British Columbia) was formally registered in 1987 and spearheaded much of this development. During the first two years, it trained its own eighteen-member faculty; now it offers professional and public workshops and training programs. Similar centers include the Midwest Satir Institute in Chicago, the Southeast Satir Institute in North Carolina, and the Hong Kong Satir Center in Asia. The Avanta Network office has further information about how to contact various institutes.

The Avanta Network plans to extend its training into shorter (say, seven-day) workshops focusing on special areas of interest. These include:

- Using the Satir Model in Treating Substance Abuse
- Men's Groups Within the Satir Model
- The Satir Approach to Education
- Satir Family Therapy
- Women's Groups Within the Satir Model
- The Satir Model for University/College Faculty

Avanta members plan to offer these programs in various locations in the United States and Canada, in addition to other programs offered by the Satir institutes.

Satir had plans of her own, of course. Less than a month before she died, she designated the major portion of her estate to establish a Satir Learning Center. Her will appointed a seven-member committee to do this, and these people have been meeting quarterly since 1989 to deal with the many issues associated with Satir's mandate.

Strong objections existed to a center housed in a building where a staff would teach courses and hold workshops, so the committee explored alternatives. In Satir's philosophical sense, the Learning Center is within each of us who has been trained by her and is teaching and using her model. Some Avanta members would become the faculty of the Satir Learning Center—wherever they lived and worked. The "center" would be like a nucleus, or a pulse that would energize and coordinate the work of these faculty members.

They would provide programs, courses, and workshops and use the Satir model in their own professional practices, be it in education, therapy, medicine, religion, business, or the arts. In parallel with or through organizing such training activities, the Learning Center will also continue developing Satir videotapes, teaching manuals, and books.

At times when we watch some of Satir's videos, we still feel a mystery and magic as she helps people become more wholesome, more congruent, and as they leave behind deeply ingrained dysfunctional coping patterns. And while we may have given you, the reader, a sense of the Satir model and its myriad aspects, we encourage you to attend as many Avanta training programs as you can if you choose to apply her system in your personal and professional lives. Reading about it is not enough; the magic comes in experiencing your own growth, change, and inner healing energy.

If you tap your inner resources and nurture them, you and those you help will find what you need to facilitate more healthy functioning. You can learn how to make better connections with yourself and others, and you can add to your own tools to help people. When we relate to people and validate them, they begin validating themselves. We can thus empower each other to be more ourselves.

Another aspect we hope you have integrated into your psychological map is that the past can contaminate the present in many ways. Separating any negative effects of the past can help free people's spirits in the present.

Most important, we hope you now see more hope and happiness for yourself, your family, your colleagues, and the whole world: the family and beyond.

Appendix A

With Whom Am I Having the Pleasure?

Much of life's meaning and satisfaction are based on relationships with other people. Since congruent and genuine relationships are an expression of self-esteem, they are some of the indicators in the Satir model of becoming more fully realized.

A long time ago, when Satir discovered that we seem to relate differently to some people than to others, she sought out factors that contribute to this difference. She found that at least 90 percent of any difficulty between two people had to do with their relating to their pictures and assumptions of each other rather than connecting to each other.

Thus we first meet our representation of a person. Our initial transactions are with this picture of him or her. For therapists who have been taught to diagnose and categorize, this can be a trap. The therapist may be treating a picture ("I've seen paranoids before," or "I've treated other schizophrenics") instead of meeting a person. Any time we start off on a transaction, a helpful question is: "Am I meeting my picture of the person, or am I meeting the person?"

Satir believed that this awareness is a basic part of congruence. Meeting someone congruently involves a full acceptance that we first meet with our picture of that person. What else is there to meet? Pictures of comparable experiences are all we have until we have new experiences.

Satir said that whenever she was with a group of twelve people or more, she found everybody she had ever known. What that said to her is that all of us, as human beings, are more alike than different. So the chances of picking up something familiar in every person are close to 100 percent.

Thus we do not "meet" any person right away. The issue is whether we have ways, over time, to get to know people as they are. All of us have spoken and will speak with masks, and we have as much to do with keeping the mask on as anybody else. Any communication that is not congruent is going to foster the continuation of the mask.

Satir's experience was that families and people with coping difficulties have not discovered either the persons they are or the persons they live with. Instead, they may have some words for their pictures: "You're my mother/supervisor/doctor/contractor." These are all roles. They are like different hats people wear. Labeling people according to their roles does not say anything except that you hang on to the roles as a way of relating.

All we have to bring to our first meeting is our past experience. Our first experience of someone new is going to be an inner one, an experience with ourselves. What changes this and takes us beyond this point? We share. Taking our courage, we express something we are experiencing inside. We check out something with the other person.

Before we can check out anything, we need to put it out. Some of us do not express our experiences. We just assume that what we experience is accurate of the other person, as in: "You know, you're just marvelous," or "I know exactly what you're thinking." Checking out such experiences is a matter of following up with a question such as, "Is that so?"

What follows is a transcript of Virginia Satir doing a "With Whom Am I Having the Pleasure?" exercise in a workshop. We then give you the exercise methodology, the "how to."

I'd like to do a little piece of a laboratory which requires that we be in pairs, and go further with how we meet one another. Would you like to do that? All right. What I'd like you to do is pick a person who on the outside for you is as different from you as you can be. If you are a man, pick a woman, different skin color if you can, different eye color if you can, different age if you can. Pick something that's different. So, go find somebody, and then the whole group will be in pairs. Go find somebody like that. You can't show your navels. Please don't show anybody your navels, I'll save that for later. [Group assembles into pairs.]

When you find somebody for a pair, sit down. All right, would you now separate as pairs, to be sure that you are not stuck with any other pairs, so you have plenty of space between pairs. Now, I'd like you, if you all can, to put your belly button toward your partner, turn to him and look at it, and if you can't, imagine his belly button. Now, in your mind, in your mind now, what I ask you to do is close your eyes, and I want you to say to yourself, "I have a belly button and my partner has a belly button." Just with your eyes closed. "And that belly button means that we all came via the same route, and it also means we are all born little." Then let yourself know that, what it means.

And then let yourself know that you know fully that this is the way it is. And then let yourself know that this is a universal symbol of equality. It's the universal literal reminder where we came from.

And I'd like you in your mind also to think and see that the belly button is the center, the vital center of your well-being. And then, while your eyes are closed, and you are looking at your belly button as your center, will you look up in the direction of your heart, and see that the point of your heart is right into the center, if you were to make a dial of thirteen inches (or eighteen) from the center of your navel and your heart would be fully within this radius. So, when you think belly button, you also think heart.

Now let yourself, with your eyes closed, be in touch with your own breathing and feel it as the breath coming in, moving, filling your whole body. And when it goes out, it takes tensions out on an outgoing breath. Just let the tension come out. And while the breathing is going on, give yourself a message of appreciation for you, of your own uniqueness. And then give yourself a message that for you to discover yourself in relation to the other person, that person in relation to you, you in relation to yourself, and the other person in relation to him- or herself is a matter of discovery and not judging.

When you can, let your eyes gently open. And now I am going to ask you to stand. I want you to look at each other in all the ways. Now I want you to just do exactly what I said before we wouldn't do. To look at all the ways that you are different from each other. Every way you can think of: height, weight, age—every way you can think of—by how you look.

Afterward, devise questions til you find all the ways you can think of that you are different from one another. If you have to, look at an eyelid and say, "Gee whiz, my eyelids go up a quarter of an inch more than yours." Everything that you can see and discover about how you are different from each other. First in looks, and then explore how else you are different by questions and as far as you can go about how you are different from the other.

So, you have to examine each other. You already know about the belly button, so you won't need to worry about that any more. Just to examine, look, and then share with each other how I am different from you. "My ear goes up this way half an inch more," or down half an inch. "You have one, I don't," or "I've got bigger feet."

Are you with what we are doing? Really look into all of this, and to see. So you do that with each other now. And I'll come back to you in exactly fifteen minutes, and I'll see what happens.

This was all to see the ways in which you are different from each other. What was that like for you? Some of us are always so busy trying to do and be the same that we don't put that much on how we are different. And this time with your eyes closed ask yourself, do you feel any different at this point about your partner than you did when you sat down? Do you feel any more connected or do you feel more distant? Or what do you feel as a result of sharing your differences? As you look back on your experiences when sharing, were there some times when you came to a little tender spot where there were some differentnesses that were discussed? Were there some places when you came to differentness when you felt really a great feeling, a good feeling? Were there any things like that?

Now, let yourself be in touch with your breathing, whatever this experience was for you. So just now let yourself settle back into yourself, and breathe normally and rhythmically and comfortably. In a moment I am going to ask you to open your eyes and just look tenderly at your partner.

Now, just let your eyes open, and just gently look at your partner, and your partner is going to be looking at you. Just for a moment. And with your eyes open looking at each other, again just be in touch with how you were feeling about yourself and about them, and then let your eyes close again.

This time, when your eyes are closed, could you let yourself remember back when you first saw your partner, sat down with your partner for the first time here. Does your partner really look any different to you? Do you feel you might look different to them? Well, whatever it is, it's an experience.

So let yourself again be in touch with your breathing, normally, comfortably, rhythmically, and give yourself a message of appreciation for you. You and all of your beauty and all of your dimensions. Mentally, perhaps, give yourself a message that you are a treasure: the only one exactly like you, a treasure. And then maybe you can also allow yourself to call yourself a miracle.

And as you say, "I am a miracle, I am a treasure," what kind of feeling do you have as you allow those words to come to you? Even if they are new, or your use of them is new, just be in touch with what it feels like to consider yourself a treasure and a miracle.

And breathing normally and comfortably and rhythmically, feeling your body, your feet giving you support from the floor, know you have the ability to move, and to think and to feel. And again, breathing comfortably and normally, feeling yourself expand in your own treasurehood, in your loveliness . . . and as you are doing this, again let your eyes open, looking at your partner, beholding them, as well, as a treasure and miracle.

And then again let your eyes gently close with the feeling of your being in the presence of a treasure and miracle, and you also being a treasure and a miracle. And see what that feels like for you. And very gently let your eyes open.

I'd like now to do something else. Now, it fits into this. I call it, "With whom am I having the pleasure, you or my picture of you?" And what I'm going to ask you is to look at certain things and to be in touch with certain things.

So the first place for you is to have your chairs directly facing one another so that your eyes and your ears are in touch. [People move their chairs.]

All right, now there will be several things I'll like you to focus on. And you will be doing a lot with your eyes closed and your eyes open. So, what I'd like you to do now is to just get yourself comfortable. You are sitting directly across from your partner, but now let yourself be centered. Just be centered.

All right. Now as you are centered and breathing, also give yourself a message of appreciation for you. That message will eventually go in to that place in yourself which is perception and give that some support.

And now, with your eyes closed, I'd like you to think about yourself as a camera, and your eyes are lenses. So, at this moment, I would like you to open your eyes, look at your partner. You're taking a picture. And close your eyes.

All right. It takes only a second for a camera to click the shutter. And now, with your eyes closed, I'd like you to look at the picture that you took of the person in front of you. This is not the person, this is your picture of that person. Think about it, and if you can in your mind's eye, also see it, whichever way you can do it. Just let yourself respond to that picture now.

What do you feel about that picture, and the person in that picture? How clear is the picture to you? Many

345

*times the click of this camera is what a whole lifetime of
perception is built on.*

*All right, you had a picture now that you took of
your partner. And I'd like you to put it in a mental filing
cabinet in your mind, somewhere close by, because we
are going to bring it out again.*

*Now, as you open your eyes again, look at the per-
son in front of you for any ways that they remind you of
anyone you've ever seen before, or heard about in the
funny papers, in the movies, in your family, the family
you grew up in, your community, historical figures, whatever. Any way in which this person in front of you
reminds you of anyone you've known before. So let your
eyes gently open and look at that person for any ways in
which they remind you of anyone you've known before.*

*And then, let your eyes close. And if that person
reminded you of anyone, let yourself know how you feel
about that person. [Pause.] And then let the picture of the
person this one reminds you of come to your mind's eye.
And now, haul out the one you took before and put the
two together, and see how much they look alike.*

*While you are doing this, just keep track of any
body responses that you might be getting: tightnesses or
loosenesses, or floods of old movies that come back.
Anything like that, just keep track of it.*

*Now this time, as you gently let your eyes open, let
yourself notice what you notice first on this person. You
noticed the person's hair or teeth or eyes or now the person's hands are folded or whatever. What do you notice
first? And after you've seen that, close your eyes. And
then, let yourself remember what you've noticed. Was it
their pair of glasses?*

Well, what else do you put with that? Someone who wears glasses for you is what? Smart? Nearsighted? Showing off? What? What else do you put with that? What else do you expect from somebody who wears glasses? Just figure that out for yourself.

And while you are doing that, if your body is giving yourself any kind of responses, just let yourself know it. [Pause.] *And again, just be in touch with your breathing, as you remember to do it. You will be breathing, but you can breathe in awareness.*

Now this time, as you gently let your eyes open, tell yourself what you think your partner is seeing and hearing in relation to you, and what your partner is thinking about you, inside. What you think your partner sees and hears about you and thinks about you or feels about you inside. Your idea about that person's fantasy about you, "what I think you think about me." And then let your eyes close, and let yourself be aware of what you told yourself about that. No matter how good or tough or whatever it was, let yourself know what it was that you thought your partner was thinking and feeling about you.

And then let yourself know how you are feeling about what you tell yourself. Are you scaring yourself with that? Are you making yourself feel juicy? What are you doing with your picture of what your partner is thinking and feeling about you? [Pause.]

Now this time, with your eyes still closed, let yourself remember if you have ever heard anything from any other source about this person. Have you had any gossip? Have you read anything in the paper about this person? Have you got any information from anybody else or any other source about this person? Let yourself remember it if you have.

And then ask yourself what you are feeling as you gather together all that past information, or information from another source. What are you feeling as you pull that together?

And again, what are you feeling and thinking in your body as you pull this together? Examples: "My son's girlfriend's mother's second husband's grandmother told me that you . . ." Or, "I read in the paper that you got a thousand dollars for a contest," or whatever. All information that is third-party.

And now, with your eyes still closed, let yourself remember whether you have had any previous contact with this person. The first time you met was when you came to this seminar. You probably had some previous contact. If you met your partner when you were in kinder-garten, maybe you had some previous contact with this person. And let yourself know what at this moment that contact was, and how you feel about it now. Now with your eyes still closed, I'd like to remind you that you are now stuffed with information, all of it of your own mak-ing.

Now, if at this time I were to say to you, "All right, we are finished with this now and you just go on your way," your picture of the person in front of you would be what you carry in your head right now. And that's the way I find most people do it. But I'm going to ask you to do something different. I'm going to ask you to say pri-vately to yourself, "This is my information that I have at this moment, and I'm going to check it out."

Now, when I say that to you, do you say to yourself, "Ohhh, I couldn't say that! That's too personal"? Just be in touch with any kind of barriers you have, or excite-ment. Now share with each other.

348

And now, let yourself know what it meant for you to share this mine of information with your partner. How did it feel to put words to things that maybe you've felt in the past and didn't put words to, and now you did?

And what do you feel about your partner at this moment? About yourself?

Now, if at this moment you were to take another picture at this point and the picture is different, let yourself know how could it have happened, that the picture would be different? Not that much time has gone by. People didn't have a chance to get older—too much older.

Well, let's check. Get your camera out again. Just let your eyes open. Take another picture of your partner now and see what it looks like this time. And then close your eyes again. And let yourself remember that first picture you took, and see if this picture looks different in any way: fuller, or more clear, or different in any way.

And then prepare yourself for opening your eyes, and I'm going to ask you a few questions.

For how many of you was the second picture different from the first? Let me see. Isn't that interesting? My goodness gracious! Look—almost all the hands went up. Now, if you think how did that happen, because as I said, nobody grew that much older. They didn't even have a chance to take a walk.

All right. Now let me check a couple of other things. How many of you found that your partner did remind you of somebody else? Let's see. Look around at the hands.

Okay, how many of you were quite aware that you did see something in somebody over other things? Their hair, or their nose, or their clothes, or something. How many noticed that?

Okay, now, how many of you were quite aware that, of course, you had a fantasy about what the other one was thinking and feeling about you? How many of you noticed that?

Okay, now, how many of you had third-party information about your partner? Something that somebody else told you? Let's see. Third-party information. A few of you. Okay.

All right, how many of you have had previous contact with your partner? Before you got to do this exercise? All right. Our brain always makes something out of everything. Can't avoid it, because that is the nature of it. So you see a tail over here and a head over there and they are fifty miles apart, but all you can see is those two. That must be a long animal. That's all you can see. We do those funny things to ourselves. So we make something out of everything. And then, if we have to behave as though we know what we are talking about, we can't let anybody change our minds.

All right, now we get into third-party information. As children, as students, as any group that is in a learning level or in some ways got themselves into a lower power level, third-party information is rampant. Rampant. When I go to schools, for instance, I shudder when I see those awful cumulative folders. Now here you are, you were in sixth grade last year, and the teacher wrote a whole lot of things about you, and the next teacher that comes in reads the cumulative folder and then treats you in terms of that cumulative folder. What was the picture of the teacher who had you? In doctors' offices, in therapists' offices, what do you suppose goes on record? The therapist's picture, that's all.

If you can count bones, that's the only thing I accept, that this person had five bones when he came in. I accept that. But not how that person thought about those bones, because that's that person. I find out about that myself.

Third-party information. Your grandfather, you know, or your great-grandfather, or the lady next door, or so on—for many people, adults have got more of the truth than you do as children. Did you ever get into that bind? That the lady next door told your mother what you were doing? And you said, "No," and your mother said, "Wait a minute, she is a grown-up, she knows." Anybody know about that one?

Now, we come into the previous contact. Most all of us had previous contact. And it's very easy to think of the previous contact, and people haven't changed any. So, we do a new thing every day.

Now we come to the next part, which is the inhibitions; how I can't share with you what I think and feel. I am going to treat you in terms of what I think and feel. And if I am loving toward you and want to be honest, I'll let you know what that is so you can help me check it out.

Now, we get to the sharing, the literal sharing, with each other. That you did. And those were the steps to get to new closeness that you have, and the new possible excitement that you can have with each other as people.

All right. Take any group of people and ask them to go through this kind of exercise and you will heighten

*the ability of the people to feel loving, more confident
and more able. And you could see how it happened.*

*All right, what I'd like you to do at this time is to
all turn towards your partners. And as you do, I'd like
you to close your eyes, starting with yourself, be in touch
with your breathing, and see what it sounds like now as
you give yourself a message of appreciation and leave
that partner in a way that fits for you.*

The following is another version of this process, a
guideline for this direct experience of meeting someone.
We encourage readers to either tape-record this exercise
and do it with one other person or find a third person to
be the Guide. This exercise is useful with people with
whom you would like to increase your intimacy or with
whom you have difficulty staying connected. It can create
a clearing between you and another person.

To start this exercise requires two things: a centered
body and a comfortable position in which you can see
the other person face to face, eye to eye, and at arm's
length. Whenever you want to create a learning atmosphere you want to start from a centered place and pay
attention to your breathing.

Close your eyes and just be in touch with your
breathing. Feel it come in. Recognize that it is your life
breath. Feel the magnificence of it and then allow it to go
out. Then, somewhere deep inside, give yourself permission to be open, with the recognition that you can digest
and keep from this experience what fits for you.

Now, open your eyes and look at your partner as
someone with whom you are interested in spending the
next half hour or so to do some self-exploration, learn
new ways of relating, and learn about the process of connecting. Now reflect on what you are about to do. Notice
any response going on in your body. Give yourself permission to take the risk of acting with your awareness.
Breathe. You can be sure that you and your partner have

a lot in common and many differences as well. What neither one of you knows is what is internal in the other.

CAMERA

Close your eyes. Think of those eyes as a camera with the ability to work quickly. They can open like a camera shutter and close in a split second. You can take a picture and immediately develop it in your mind's eye.

Now open your eyes, take the picture of your partner, and close your eyes. Look at the picture you just took. What are you thinking? What are you feeling? What is happening in your body?

Allow yourself to notice your breathing and any tension that may have developed in your body.

Allow yourself to relax.

PROJECTION ("HANGING HATS")

Now, in your centered space, open your eyes, look at the person opposite you, and with your camera, take a picture and gently close your eyes. Ask yourself, "Of whom does this person remind me?" What is familiar to you? Think about all your relatives, your family, your current family, characters in movies, history, the funny papers, fairy tales.

Then ask yourself, "How do I feel about the people my partner reminds me of?" And then look and see what is happening in your body as you now think of the people your partner reminds you of, in little or big ways. What are you thinking? What are you feeling? What is happening in your body?

STEREOTYPES

Now open your eyes, look at your partner for what stands out for you. It could be the person's gender, glasses, hair style, skin color, teeth arrangement, or hair color—whatever stands out most for you.

Then close your eyes and let the picture of what stands out for you come clearly to mind. Whatever stands out for you, be aware of any prejudices that are activated in you, whether positive or negative.

With closed eyes, again ask yourself what you are thinking now. What are you feeling? What are your body reactions? Does the information you have at this point lengthen or shorten the bridge between you and your partner? What do you know now that you did not know when you first sat down?

EXPECTATIONS

With your eyes closed, imagine what your partner is thinking and feeling about you. What is your fantasy about what that person is thinking and feeling about you as he or she has seen and experienced you?

No matter how torrid or florid, how flowery or scary, or shades in between, allow yourself to know what that fantasy is for you. Then very gently open your eyes, look at your partner, and give yourself that message of what he or she is thinking and feeling about you.

Again, close your eyes and let yourself know crystal-clearly what your fantasy was. Then ask yourself, how do you feel about that? How does the fantasy you have make you feel and what does your body do as a result?

Breathe and give yourself a loving message. Relax, and alertness will increase.

THIRD-PARTY INFORMATION (GOSSIP AND RUMOR)

Now, with your eyes still closed, review for yourself, silently, all the third-party information you have about your partner. That is, all the gossip, all the things you have read anywhere about this person, and anything you have heard from anyone.

See clearly what this third-party information is, and then ask yourself, how do you feel as you are allowing yourself to come in touch with this sort of information? How is your body responding as a result of what you are thinking and feeling about the gossip in your head?

With your eyes still closed, let yourself remember any direct past contacts that you had with the person in front of you. Let yourself know what meaning you are making of that past contact now. Again, let yourself be in touch with what you are feeling and thinking as you become aware of the meaning you are making of that past contact.

RULES ABOUT COMMENTING

With your eyes still closed, let yourself become aware that your head is stuffed with all kinds of data. For the last fifteen minutes or so you have been generating new information at accelerated, skillful speeds.

Also be aware that thousands—millions, perhaps—of people have gone this far with other people and that's been the end of it. So what you have in your mind right now, if you never do anything more with it, is that the other person is who you have made him or her up to be. You have created this picture all yourself.

Does this help you to become aware of how we do not check out, how we distort, how easy it is to feel misunderstood, disconnected, and so on?

With your eyes still closed, you can now consider doing what most people do not do. First, become aware that all the information you have is the best you have, given who you are. Your experience is yours, the best you have, and it really has very little to do with the other person. It has to do with you. Therefore, your experiences can be used as resources for discovery. They are not conclusions for basing your behavior on.

So now allow yourself to give yourself the freedom to share with the other person your picture of what happened to you. Be very clear that the other person is listening to your picture.

Center yourself, and if there are any little things running through your mind saying, "Oh, I couldn't say that," pay attention to the taboos or the barriers that come between what you are feeling and thinking at this time.

Now give yourself permission to share fully:

What you saw—your camera picture

Of whom or what that person reminded you—your projection

What stood out for you—your stereotype

What thoughts and feelings you fantasized your partner thought and felt about you

What third-party information you have heard about your partner—your gossip

What occurs to you now about your past experience (if any) with your partner

RULES ABOUT
SELF-DISCLOSURE

Let your eyes gently open, and begin by telling your partner how you feel about sharing. Then go ahead and share
as much as you want or care to.

DISCUSSION

Allow your eyes to close, relax, and be comfortable. Just
let whatever came to you in the quietness of your own
insides bathe you in what you found as you shared. Let
yourself be in touch with that. And now let yourself see if
you now have any different ways of viewing yourself and
the other or both. If you were to take a picture now, how
would it differ from the first? If you notice no difference,
ask yourself how come? Just be in touch with that.

Then look back and see if you had any kinds of barriers to commenting. What happened when you let yourself go beyond them, if you did?

Now, again allow yourself to be very comfortable,
your body relaxed, and your mind alert. Let your eyes
open and look at your partner and just be aware now of
what you see now as you look at him or her. What does it
feel like to you? What does your partner feel like to you as
you look at him or her now?

Let your eyes close again and ask yourself whether
you see differently, or see more of your partner and feel
differently, or see more about yourself? Then, when you
are comfortable, let your eyes open and share with your
partner.

Ask yourself the following questions with a pause in
between for time to answer:

- When you looked back at this last time did you
  see your partner's many parts?

- Did you find that your partner reminded you of
  someone else?

- Did you notice something that stood out for you about your partner that you hadn't noticed before?

- Did you have any third-party information or gossip?

- Did you have any thoughts or feelings in your mind, or deep inside, born out of past experiences?

- How did you deal with your inside information differently than in past experiences?

Discuss these questions with each other.

CONCLUSION

Close your eyes and go back into yourself. Be aware of what happens as you do this.

Do you feel you could go farther, be more congruent and intimate with this partner, and deepen the connection? Make a note of this. Open your eyes and look at your partner, and in some way express what you feel about yourself and what you feel about the other person. Then make a closure.

The first step is to accept that everybody we meet has the capacity for activating all our projections, our hat-hanging, and our old stereotypes, and that we are not always aware of it. Then we can begin to appreciate how it is there are so many difficulties in making congruent contact.

It helps to know and feel that there are some things having to do with our past that we project onto others. It helps us get in touch with our barriers, such as, "Oh, I'd better be careful," or "I feel humiliated [or immobilized]." We discover the pure gold that is there for our growth when we take the risk of recognizing our projections, stereotypes, and the old rules we can let go or transform into guidelines.

As our awareness grows, as the hat-hanging decreases and the stereotypes fade, we become more connected with ourselves and other people. We empower ourselves. We learn more about taking care of ourselves, not just taking care of others.

It is natural to approach people in terms of our own images. The way most of us have been brought up, it is also natural not to see ourselves from the outside, from a relatively objective perspective. Hanging hats, for instance, is closely related to what we learned about survival with the significant people who had more power over us early in our lives than we did over ourselves. When we hang hats on people and interact according to roles, we tend not to acknowledge fully our own power and human equality within that context.

We need a way to be clear when we get into trouble with people. We get into trouble, usually, out of our defenses and rules. Then we stop seeing and hearing and trusting our inner wisdom. If we come only from my picture of "Sam"—which is full of assumptions, unchecked-out ideas, and images that are not shared—then we keep escalating any misunderstanding with Sam.

Contrast this with the great joy of really connecting with another person, when there is a flow between us and we move together with that person in a dance of light.

Congratulate yourself when you become aware of hanging a hat and projecting, stereotyping, fantasizing, operating from gossip and the past. Give yourself permission, if you choose, to check out your pictures, your fantasies, your information. Then make the changes to bring yourself and the other person closer together.

We all have certain kinds of ways of paying attention. At present we may fill in what we learn with extra information from our own past. We see something, we think, "That means . . . ," and we fill in the rest of the story with our own ideas and images. This is like having a "dream book." We see things in the outer world the way we have a dream: something happens, we assume it means X, and X means Y. We end up having a dream about—rather than checking out and responding to— what is actually happening.

For instance, suppose you have dark eyes. And "everybody knows" that dark eyes mean thus and so and such. So, now we relate to you according "so and such."

The more two people are together, the longer is their past experience. Past experience has a way of being translated into expectations. "Last week Friday when I saw you, your tongue was hanging out. And three weeks ago I saw your tongue hanging out. So I have come to think of you as somebody whose tongue hangs out." This is just a glimpse of how our images and expectations can arise, and it is how we interact until we find something more.

We need to honor our past and also remember that our perception of it can change. For example, if we have known two people with orange eyes, and they both have been honest, orange eyes therefore mean honesty. Everybody knows that! So after this, we know that everybody with orange eyes has to be honest, because that was the conclusion of our individual research.

"Research" like this goes on all the time. We create abstractions from experience that comes from a very small universe. Reputable research of any sort, on the other hand, takes care to work with data collected under conditions that accurately represent the world. No legitimate conclusions can be based on two experiences that pretend to show us our way around the world.

Think of how many experiences you had growing up. We all had one biological father and mother. Some of us had substitutes along the way, but very few had more than two or three. Out of our experiences with these people, some of us weave a whole universe: "That's how men are," and "That's how women are." We can make generalizations out of remarkably little evidence, and then we can continue into adulthood finding confirmation for our childhood conclusions.

This kind of thinking is a kind of natural thinking, and it comes up again and again. People often say, "That's how it was." Satir used to respond, "Sure, that's how it was," and then help people become the type of researchers who change their conclusions when they find new information. Someone might say, "I know, I once saw a man forty-five years ago, and he wore red pants. And you're wearing red pants now, so . . ." and would find a way to put all the new material into the old conclusion. It sounds ridiculous, and it happens every day.

Another human tendency is to imagine what other people think to themselves about us. That brain of ours makes something out of everything. Unfortunately, a lot of us give ourselves terrible fantasies, such as, "Oh, they must be thinking awful things about me. They're seeing my extra ten pounds [or my this or that]!!!" Sadder still, many of us never find out what a failure we are at mind-reading.

Nor do we live very much in this world without getting third-party information. This is called gossip, rumor, or testimonials, to be nice. Families often run on rumors or third-party information. For example, Pa finds out how the kids are through Ma. Ma finds out about the oldest daughter through the neighbor. Pa and Ma find out how the kid is through the teacher. Likewise, therapists may talk together to find out from each other about the three members of one family whom they see separately.

So what does it take in therapy to enable people to let themselves take new information and replace an old image with a new one? How is it going to be possible for a therapist to help somebody shift, especially on past experiences? Gestalt is a word that covers things that belong together, and things that belong together have an order and a sequence. Satir talked about what she considered to be the human gestalt. The aim is for us to know that at any time we look at someone, we see only what we see. That image is owned by us, and we can describe it, but it does not signify anything about the other person. Not a thing.

Sadly, a lot of people do not recognize this approach, especially many therapists and other people in authority. They see what they see and then conclude that is all there is to see. Some presume to write fantastically long descriptions of faces and inner dynamics after first seeing people for a brief time. The trap is that they mistake the piece for the whole. And then they get stuck with it. This misuse of the human gestalt and this lack of awareness leads to inhuman treatment of others.

Think what would happen in our personal relationships if we said to ourselves, "I see what I see and that's all I see. I saw you move," or "I heard you whistle." That we did not see anything else does not mean nothing more exists. It means we did not see anything more. If we interview with somebody, for instance, at least 19,742 things may go on every second with each of us. We are not going to see everything. So we see what we see. Think what would happen if we understood and made it clear with people that all the feedback we give at any moment is our picture of that moment, in that situation, with that particular person.

The bridge is that every time we look, we see something. Someone says something to us. Our brain naturally makes meaning out of it. We cannot avoid this, because our brains are built that way. Out of the meaning we make, we have a feeling. This feeling relates to what our brain has told us, not to what the other person is saying.

Assume you look at a woman wearing a pair of red pants, and you like red pants. So you say, "I like her." Many things are there to see, and you see what you see. It does not say anything about all there is to see. It does not say anything about what you see tomorrow, and it does not say anything about what you saw yesterday. It says only a little piece right now, and that is all any of us can say.

After we take the first look, we can take a second, a third, a fourth, and so on. Each time, we learn something. When Satir worked with couples, people often told her, "I know my partner. We've lived together for twenty years." Satir would say, "Oh, everything? It must be boring now. Nothing more to find out?" The point is that each observation is a beginning, whether it is our first observation or our experience many years into a relationship. It is a beginning by us, with much to follow.

The following transcript of Satir during a workshop demonstration shows how each individual sees only a piece of a whole picture.

> *"I'll give you a little illustration. Mickey, you stand up. Gerard, you stay where you are, and look at Mickey. Bill, you look at her* [Mickey]. *Gary, you look at her. David, you stand on that and look at her.*
>
> *Now each of you, would you please say what Mickey looks like. You tell me what she looks like.*
>
> *She has brown hair and a white blouse? How do you know? You only saw her from the back. She may have only half a red pantsuit. You're making an assumption.*
>
> *All right, Gary, will you tell me what she looks like?* [Pause.] *Did you draw a picture? Put it on the board so we can see.* [Watches him draw.] *That's her mouth.*
>
> *All right, Bill, tell me what you saw.* [He responds.] *So, you would agree with Gary about what her lips looked like. Good.*

What do you see, David? [He responds.] *Very good.*

Who else did I ask to look? Sandra, what did you see? An ear that came through her hair. Her eyes look blue. Half a smile. A full set of half teeth. One strong arm. A lot of decoration down her blouse. Veins full of blood. You looked at the veins and thought they were full of blood. You made an assumption. A pretty good assumption, but nevertheless . . .

One of the other things to work on is observation. What is really observation, and what is interpretation and assumption? That's another whole big trip, you know.

What did you want to say, Bob? [He makes a flattering comment about Mickey.] *Now, for him to say that, he absolutely is not looking at her. That's not to say she's not the world's most beautiful woman. That's not it. You see, he's giving a conclusion. It sounds good, and he may feel it, all right, but what I'm trying to differentiate here is that everybody told the truth as far as they knew it. And look at all the opportunities for arguing.*

What an individual says about someone at that moment in time really has no relationship to the total effect. They never do. It's just like when you're growing up. One day, you heard your mother say, "Oh, my goodness gracious! That arm of yours is very strong." Then, you thought, "Oh my God! The other one must be weak." Or, "You're getting just as tall as your brother. I wonder what I'm going to do with you?" Your brother was already six feet tall, and you had terrible ideas. All your mother was saying was you were getting taller, and then she added almost as tall as your brother. You saw how much taller he was and had all kinds of fantasies. We get all kinds of funny things like that.

So, the focus, all that it is, describes where it comes from. That's all. It's yours. It has nothing to do with the total picture. In fantasies, it's always like this.

At each point in the exercise, the trap lies in making an interpretation and an assumption that we carry over into something else. It is easy to add our assumptions into a whole lot of other things. Instead, we can say, "This is what I'm seeing at this moment in time." Then we can add, "This is what I made of it, and this is what I made myself feel as a result." Satir tried to help people gain this awareness so they could be less and less trapped by automatic patterns, and spend less time trapping other people.

We all love to hear good things, but most of the time we do not know where they came from. When we were growing up, for example, our mothers may have said, "You're a nice girl," or "You're a nice boy," or smiled when we did something. We often had no idea what this referred to. Or somebody came along and said, "Don't!" and we had no idea as to "Don't what?"

We often overlook the connection between an observation and the ownership of that observation—as it is, at that moment in time—by ourselves or the other person. For instance, just seeing a nose can sometimes bring up all kinds of olfactory odors, smells that we have or know or remember. You may remember your father's smells, or your mother's smells, and you have a whole experience with yourself just by seeing someone's nose. The bridge of all this is that awareness is a beginning.

When we have an immediate negative or positive reaction to somebody we really do not know, it comes from our old movies. We meet each other with our old pictures. Although these may form the base of our reaction, they have nothing to do with the other person's here-and-now existence. Sometimes our reaction involves pain, a stabbing kind of pain or a feeling of wanting to push away. This indicates we are also using ways of interpreting and coping that we used as children. Noticing this can be of great value when it comes to clearing up assumptions, interpretations, and misunderstandings that usually arise when people interact in such a situation.

Let's look more carefully at the business of meeting someone and perceiving something that reminds us of somebody else. It is the sensory stimuli, whether in sight or sound or touch, that trigger something to happen in us. This is the beginning of how we make a connection. If we look at somebody and get strong impressions, we can do two things. We can sort out whether we are receiving those impressions or responding with material of our own. Suppose we see a woman who is lovely and white-skinned. When we see the white skin, it can trigger something like: "white skin, beautiful woman, softness." If we perceive only that, and we are then able to see through our own interpretations, we distinguish between responding to what we see and seeing what is there.

In a treatment intervention, if Satir thought a client was feeling badly, the way she would put it was: "I noticed right now your shoulders are kind of dropping and your voice sounds like it's way back in your throat, and your eyelids look kind of droopy. From that, I'm getting the impression that you are maybe feeling bad." In other words, she reported her description and then her interpretation. Then she checked it out to see whether it fit for the client.

Turning to the imagination, we find more opportunities for awareness. We use our imaginations often—where else could we first get any idea about what other people are thinking? Unfortunately, most of our imaginings trap us because we do not check them out. Earlier parts of this book discussed how we give ourselves negative messages. When we combine these with imagination and attribute to others what we think are their feelings, we attribute to them what is in our own heads. And we are limited to what we can attribute to others by what we feel and think about ourselves.

The way to grow in our ability to add to this is to hear the other person. "This is what I imagine you're thinking. Tell me whether or not it fits." The other person has at least two possibilities: to answer yes or no. If our imagination matches what they are thinking, that is fine. If not, what can we add?

If Toni serves David spinach, for instance, what does it mean when David does not eat it? Toni may wonder about all sorts of meanings, including not being loved. Without distinguishing between the actual events and what they triggered, Toni would not necessarily proceed to ask David about David's meanings and intentions. Asking may reveal that David simply does not like spinach. It does not have anything to do with his not loving it, let alone his feelings about Toni. It is just that spinach makes him gag—nothing more. This is not a comment on anything or anyone else.

Using situations like this as an exercise leads into all the ways we can begin to use ourselves to enrich, nurture, grow, and expand our relationships and our ways of dealing with each other. The trap lies in keeping our imagination to ourselves and attributing our ideas and feelings to the other person. The bridge is that we can start out with this, because it is the best we have. Then we can create a situation in which the other person confirms or denies that it fits.

What one person confirms at one time might not be true for the next person, or for the same person at another time. So it is not enough to assume, "I asked once, and that's enough. Back in 1972 I checked this out." With each time period and each person, we face a new experience. Each person brings something with him or her at each moment. How do we know where we are sitting? How do we know where the other person is looking? How do we know where he or she is coming from? Each of us can be looked at in a variety of ways, and each person's imagination differs. When we bring up our imaginings and check them out with other people, we move a long way toward congruence.

All these parts have to do with what we observe, whose hats we hang on to (whom the other person reminds us of), and the stereotyping we do ("That's how you are and therefore . . ."). In addition, it involves our imaginations. Satir sometimes responded to people's questions about each other, "I don't know their imaginations. You go ask them."

Our heads are good for lots of things. Input from the outer world comes through our heads to the rest of us. To be able to see something with fresh eyes is important. None of us is invulnerable to being with our imaginations rather than with our here-and-now realities. We have all had much practice in this. It includes incidents such as, "Oh, my gosh. I've been talking to my husband [my brother/my boss] and I called him Bill!"

Recognizing that we can be trapped by our imaginings makes it possible to view ourselves in a totally different light as we redevelop our process with someone. The exercise—"With whom am I having the pleasure, you or my picture of you?"—helps us keep in our consciousness that we carry around cookie cutters to look at people. We have our own lenses, and we have already filtered out so many things that we sometimes do not really see who is there.

One of the beliefs in the Satir model is that people can connect when they first meet. When we have a problem and are not meeting the person, we know at least one of these things—our old pictures, interpretations, imaginings, stereotypes, or role labels—does not match the here-and-now person with whom we are trying to connect.

In therapy sessions, workshops, and trainings, the material and exercises in this appendix can help people move from a dysfunctional status quo—including unexpressed anger, hostility, and fear—to a higher level of consciousness, more intimate connections, and greater respect and acceptance of self and others.

Appendix B

Family Reconstruction Tools

Once the date of a Family Reconstruction is set and the client (the "Star") is selected, the therapist ("Guide") and client meet to establish contact, examine what the Star wants to change, and explore certain facts about the Star's family of origin. The first tool in this exploration is the family map.

THE FAMILY MAP

The universal map, or most basic family plan, consists of three people: an adult male, an adult female, and a child. The Satir way of presenting this is represented in the acompanying figure.

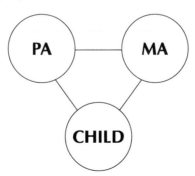

As Satir's concept of family spanned three generations, we expand this map to include the Star's maternal and paternal grandparents.

The analogy of a map is useful for outlining the territory of Family Reconstruction and making its route easier to travel. It helps to remember, though, that the map is not the territory. The family map simply helps us learn about our internal and external reality by illustrating who was involved in the Star's early existence, even though these relatives may no longer be present. The family map symbolizes most of the "cast of characters" that will appear in the Family Reconstruction.

Preparing family maps takes place in four stages. The first asks for details of the Star's parents:

- Date of marriage
- Names of each parent
- Birthdates and birthplaces
- Current ages or ages at death
- Religious affiliations (optional)
- Occupations (optional)
- Ethnic backgrounds (optional)
- Education (optional)
- Hobbies (optional)

For the purposes of illustration, we use a biologically intact nuclear family. Adaptations can be made for single-parent families, stepfamilies, and other families made up of members other than the original biological parents and child(ren).

In the second stage, the Guide asks the Star to add these elements for each parent:

- Three descriptive adjectives
- His or her primary coping stance under stress
- His or her secondary coping stance under stress (optional)

As discussed in Chapter 9, the Star's construct of reality is what operates in Family Reconstruction, so objective accuracy is not critical. If the Star does not have certain information, the Guide encourages him or her to "make it up." Stage 3 is illustrated below.

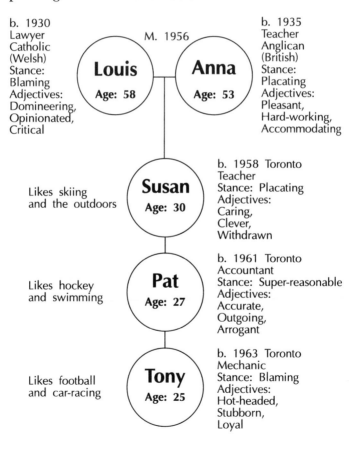

b. 1930
Lawyer
Catholic
(Welsh)
Stance: Blaming
Adjectives: Domineering, Opinionated, Critical

M. 1956

Louis
Age: 58

Anna
Age: 53

b. 1935
Teacher
Anglican
(British)
Stance: Placating
Adjectives: Pleasant, Hard-working, Accommodating

Susan
Age: 30

Likes skiing and the outdoors

b. 1958 Toronto
Teacher
Stance: Placating
Adjectives: Caring, Clever, Withdrawn

Pat
Age: 27

Likes hockey and swimming

b. 1961 Toronto
Accountant
Stance: Super-reasonable
Adjectives: Accurate, Outgoing, Arrogant

Tony
Age: 25

Likes football and car-racing

b. 1963 Toronto
Mechanic
Stance: Blaming
Adjectives: Hot-headed, Stubborn, Loyal

The Star adds:

- All the children, from eldest down
- First-stage information for each child *(listed above)*
- Second-stage information for each child *(listed above)*

In Stage 4, the Star creates three separate third-stage maps: for his or her maternal grandparents, paternal grandparents, and current family. In addition to third-stage data, the Star indicates (from his or her perspective):

- Family rules of parents and grandparents
- Any family patterns (e.g., occupations, illnesses, coping stances, causes of death, etc.)
- Family values and beliefs (e.g., value of education, money, etc.)
- Family myths and secrets
- Family themes

For presentation to the group, the Star usually puts all these maps on large flip-chart paper, to be displayed or hung during the actual Family Reconstruction.

Compiling the family maps smooths the way for constructing the next tool, a chronology of the family's life.

FAMILY LIFE CHRONOLOGY

The family life chronology is the second step necessary before the actual Family Reconstruction begins. It covers three generations, beginning at the birth of the Star's oldest grandparent and ending when the Star comes of age (eighteen, nineteen, or twenty-one, in most jurisdictions).

For example, the Star's oldest grandparent may have been born in 1901, and the Star may have come of age in 1975.

This chart integrates the following information in chronological order:

- Birthdates of each family member

- Dates of important family events (e.g., moves, marriages, divorces, deaths, reunions, tragedies) and achievements (e.g., graduations, promotions)

- Dates of important historical events (e.g., wars, natural disasters, economic upheavals)

The family life chronology usually takes four or five sheets of flip-chart paper.

1917 Grandpa Castello born
1918 Grandpa Jones born
1920 Grandma Jones born
1923 Grandma Castello born
1931 Grandpa Castello drops out of school
1934 Grandma Jones family moves to West Coast
1936 Grandpa Jones graduates high school

Births of the next generation, major life & historic events, etc. listed

1958 Dad graduates high school
1963 Mom graduates high school
1963 JFK shot
1965 Mom & Dad marry and move to Pennsylvania
1970 John born

More moves, history, deaths, retirements, etc.

1988 John turns 18

WHEEL OF INFLUENCE

The wheel of influence chart shows every person who supported the Star emotionally or physically during childhood and adolescence. These people gave the Star something, and the Star responded or reacted to it in some way. The Star also responded or reacted to these people's interactions with each other.

The more people the Star names in his or her wheel, the more influences and resources that person had to draw on in his or her development. People to include are: family members of three generations, others who lived in the Star's home (or in whose homes the Star lived), special teachers, friends, imaginary playmates, pets, and treasured toys.

The Star writes his or her name in the center, surrounded by circles representing the other people—like a wheel with spokes. The spokes can vary in width, with thicker lines indicating greater closeness.

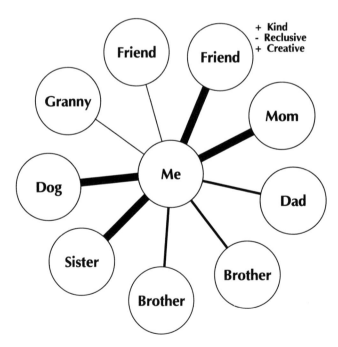

Beside each name, the Star lists three adjectives that describe that person. (With family members, it is enough to use the same adjectives as in the family maps.) Then the Star labels each adjective as positive or negative, as shown in the illustration.

During Family Reconstruction, the maps and diagrams described in this appendix are displayed to help orient and focus the Guide, the Star, and the participants. The Star is free to keep these after the reconstruction.

Books and Tapes by Virginia Satir

Books

Banmen, Anne; and John Banmen (Ed.). *Meditations of Virginia Satir: Peace Within, Peace Between, and Peace Among.* Palo Alto, CA: Science and Behavior Books, 1991.

Banmen, John; and Jane Gerber (Ed.). *Meditations and Inspirations of Virginia Satir.* Millbrae, CA: Celestial Arts, 1985.

Englander-Golden, Paula; and Virginia Satir. *Say It Straight.* Palo Alto, CA: Science and Behavior Books, 1991.

Grinder, John; Richard Bandler; and Virginia Satir. *Changing with Families.* Palo Alto, CA: Science and Behavior Books, 1976.

Satir, Virginia. *Conjoint Family Therapy,* Third Edition. Palo Alto, CA: Science and Behavior Books, 1987.

——. *Making Contact.* Millbrae, CA: Celestial Arts, 1976.

——. *The New Peoplemaking.* Palo Alto, CA: Science and Behavior Books, 1988.

——. *Old Sayings I Just Made Up*. Palo Alto, CA: Avanta Network, 1989.

——. *Self-Esteem*. Millbrae, CA: Celestial Arts, 1975.

——. *Thoughts and Feelings*. Palo Alto, CA: Avanta Network, 1989.

——. *Your Many Faces*. Millbrae, CA: Celestial Arts, 1978.

——; and Michele Baldwin. *Satir Step by Step: A Guide to Creating Change in Families*. Palo Alto, CA: Science and Behavior Books, 1983.

——; James Stachowiak; and Harvey A. Taschman. *Helping Families to Change*. New York: Jacob Aronson, 1977.

Schwab, Johanna; Michele Baldwin; Jane Gerber; Maria Gomori; and Virginia Satir. *The Satir Approach to Communication: A Workshop Manual*. Palo Alto, CA: Science and Behavior Books, 1989.

Audiotapes

Satir, Virginia. *The Memorial Series: Teachings of Virginia Satir*. Palo Alto, CA: Avanta Network, 1989.

Videotapes

Satir, Virginia. *Blended Family with a Troubled Boy*. Kansas City, MO: Golden Triad Films.

——. *The Essence of Change*. Kansas City, MO: Golden Triad Films.

——. *A Family at the Point of Growth*. Kansas City, MO: Golden Triad Films.

——. *Family Series I* [including a family interview, various Parts Parties, and Family Reconstructions]. Available through Dr. John Banmen, 11213 Canyon Crescent, N. Delta, BC V4E 2R6, Canada.

——. *Family Series III* [including Family Reconstruction]. Available through Dr. John Banmen, 11213 Canyon Crescent, N. Delta, BC V4E 2R6, Canada.

——. *Of Rocks and Flowers: Dealing with the Abuse of Children*. Kansas City, MO: Golden Triad Films.

——. *A Step Along the Way: A Family with a Drug Problem*. Kansas City, MO: Golden Triad Films.

——. *Virginia Satir on Communication, Parts I and II*. Palo Alto, CA: Science and Behavior Books.

Index

Abandonment issues 34, 305
Abuse 93-94, 164, 179
Acceptance and acknowledg-
ment
    and change 74, 79, 114, 158
    and congruence 65-66, 77,
    143
    and integration 143, 180,
    200-201, 202
    in primary triad 317
    by self and others 114, 255,
    292
    and survival stances 35, 76
    by therapist 94-95, 104, 113,
    157-58, 324
    vs. vicious dogs 184
    See also Parts Party, Self-
    acceptance
Addictions
    as dysfunctional coping 62,
    100
    and family systems 100-101
    and Satir model/workshops
    164-65, 336
Add-on theory *see* Change
Adolescents 43, 63, 94, 263
Affect
    congruent 32-33, 73
    defined 69-70
    incongruent 32-33
    as reflecting the present 71
    use in therapy 129, 162,
    256, 257, 283
    See also Survival Stances
Affirmations 21, 145, 292, 297

Aging 183, 221, 270-71
Alcoholism *see* Additions
Altered states *see* Awareness,
    Trances
Anger
    as accumulating 166
    and blaming 43, 167
    changing in therapy 78,
    165, 166, 235, 323
    and conflict 179, 313
    and congruence 165, 171,
    179, 184-85, 305
    and expectations 152, 313
    expressing 184-85, 313
    and fear 166, 305, 313, 323
    and hurt 152, 166, 179, 313,
    323
    and incongruence 39, 43,
    126, 155, 166, 167, 171,
    179, 305
    as protection 106-107
    rules about 34, 111, 305
    and self-esteem 166-67, 179
    and sculpting 286
Anxiety
    and change 57, 108-109
    in childhood 57-58
    dynamics of 39, 108-109,
    114, 180
Assagioli, Roberto 177
Atmosphere *see* Context
Avanta Network 327, 332-36
Awareness
    adding to 81, 97, 114, 163-
    64, 286

and central nervous system
55-56
and expectations 151-52
and family systems 100,
222, 225-26
and fear 323
vs. harmony with Self 171,
179-80, 225
and incongruence 126-27,
171
and inner parts 281
as opportunity 228
past vs. present 228
and primary triad 317
as reactive 155, 222
and revenge 63
and therapy 93, 323
See also Symptoms
Panic 166, 180
Paradox 187, 202
Parents *see* Child-rearing,
Family Systems, and
Primary Triad
Parts of the self
acceptable vs. unacceptable
34, 176, 182, 199, 203, 281-
82
accepting 181, 183-84, 195,
203, 278-79, 281-83
awareness of 203, 279, 283
conflict among 178, 181-82,
187
connectedness of 178, 183,
187, 278, 281
demonstration of (ropes)
279-81
denial of 179-80, 183, 279,
282
dynamics of 181-82, 185,
191, 280
and early development 177,
187
electing 181
and growth 179, 182, 184
integrating 181, 233, 279-
83, 292, 293
are like carousels 193
are like dogs 184
and parents' values 182, 187
as resources 177, 183, 277,
280
transformation of 176, 191,
199, 278
universal 181, 191, 277
value of each 176, 177, 182,
186-87

Parts Party
characters in 191-93
classical form of 121, 176,
204
context for 194
drama in 176, 190
goals of 178, 183, 184, 185,
186, 202
Guide's role 190
Host's role 190
and linear thinking 193
meditations for 195, 203-
204
as metaphoric 274
processes/steps in 176, 187,
188
as spiritual 203-204
theoretical background
of 177
transformation in 186, 190,
199
variations on 204
Patterns
affected by parents 164,
217, 227
automatic 164
changing 29, 62, 106, 136,
144, 156-57, 163, 234, 284
recognizing 134, 164
repeating 133, 179
value of 106
See also Survival Patterns
Peace 8, 81
"Peoplemaking" organizations
336
Perception(s)
adding to, in therapy 27, 79,
87-90, 158
basis for 133, 154-55, 223-
24
and behavior 8, 131
as camera 345
changing in therapy 28, 75,
79, 91, 114, 128, 154-55,
158, 232, 261-63, 272-73,
361, 368
as choices 228
as construct of reality 211
affected by context 229
denial of 55, 303
distortions in 133, 224, 303,
362
and early development 22,
55, 154, 223-24, 227, 232
vs. interpretations 124-26,
144, 155, 362